HOW LATIN AMERICA SAVED *the* SOUL *of the* CATHOLIC CHURCH

Edward L. Cleary

Paulist Press
New York/Mahwah, NJ

The cover photographs are by Gregory A. Shemitz http://3vphoto.com and are used with kind permission of the photographer and of *The Long Island Catholic*.

The interior photographs are by Deacon Gregory LaFreniere and are used with kind permission of the photographer.

Every effort has been made to contact those whose faces appear in the photographs in this book. If we have been unable to contact you, we apologize for publishing the photographs without your explicit permission. Please contact us so that we may thank you and send you a copy of the book.

Cover design by Joy Taylor
Book design by Lynn Else

Library of Congress Cataloging-in-Publication Data

Cleary, Edward L.
    How Latin America saved the soul of the Catholic Church / Edward L. Cleary.
        p. cm.
    Includes bibliographical references and index.
    ISBN 978-0-8091-4629-1 (alk. paper)
    1. Catholic Church—Latin America. I. Title.
    BX1426.3.C54 2009
    282′.809045—dc22

                                                                                        2009022550

Published by Paulist Press
997 Macarthur Boulevard
Mahwah, New Jersey 07430

www.paulistpress.com

Printed and bound in the
United States of America

Contents

For Ginevra Cesarini Strasser
and Paola and Richard

INTRODUCTION

The Transformation of Latin American Christianity

When Pope Benedict XVI flew to Latin America in 2007 for his first papal visit he was seeing for himself the region in which more than half of the world's Catholics live. The church there faced a drastic challenge in the large number of Catholics who became Protestants and especially Pentecostals. Nearly 40 percent of the world's Pentecostals are estimated to live in Latin America. The vast majority of them had been Catholic.

In *The Next Christendom: The Coming of Global Christianity*, Philip Jenkins has shown how the center of global religion has moved south.[1] Religion in Latin America stands on the center of the stage. With that spotlight upon it and with Hispanics, mainly with roots in Latin America, forming nearly half of the membership of the Catholic Church in the United States, the condition of the Latin American Church is of profound importance.

In a word, the Latin American Church is central to Catholicism. The region represents a large share of the world's Catholic population—a population that is growing in numbers. Faced with greatly lessened religious participation and with fewer priestly and religious vocations, the churches in Europe, the United States, Canada, and Australia face uncertain futures and diminished influence, often due to clergy scandal and perhaps an unwise choice of priorities. To an extent only being recognized now, the future of the Catholic Church lies south of the border.

This is also true for Protestants, whose mainline denominations have precipitously declined in the north while Pentecostalism grows luxuriously in Latin America and other southern regions. So strong is the impression of growth of Pentecostalism in Latin America—their churches seem to be everywhere one looks—that few journalists have taken time to look directly at the Catholic Church. The central assumption has been that as the number of Pentecostals has increased, the number of Catholics has declined.

How well is the Latin American Church doing? The people of God there are doing many things well. The church in Latin America has many problems and failings, but it shares in a religious revival that bears the marks of strength and fulfillment, matching institutional and people's needs. Based on evidence presented here, this book argues that Latin America is saving the soul of the Catholic Church. First, this chapter presents fundamental evidence of growth and other positive achievements. Then succeeding chapters show the important workings of how this has been accomplished.

Two sets of evidence are presented: statistics on growth and frequent national polls on confidence. First, then, we will look at the workforce of the church where it is thriving. While we cannot deny the losses to other religions, most journalists' reports ignore the strong religious revival that has taken place in Latin American Catholicism. The result of this revival can be seen in overall growth in important sectors. In the forty-year period between 1964 and 2004, the number of priests in the region increased by 40 percent.[2] This stands in marked contrast to the well-publicized decline in clergy in the United States and Europe. In Mexico alone, the number of priests more than doubled from 5,834 to 13,173 during this period. There, as in most of Latin America, the increases to the priesthood have consisted mainly of Latin Americans and not foreign missionaries. At the same time, the number of seminarians in colleges and theological schools has increased 599 percent between 1972 and 2004. The number of religious sisters has increased modestly, providing some 128,000 pastoral workers and contemplative prayer sources in the region.

Thus the replacement rate for priests by seminarians within Latin America has been the most favorable it has been in decades. Foreign missionary presence is noticeably declining. While figures on foreign origins are seldom kept in Latin America, church statisticians have been able to track the trend in Chile. In 1965 slightly more than half (51 percent) of the priests in Chile were foreigners.[3] By 1996 the percentage of foreigners dropped to 29 percent. While a few foreign missionaries became Chilean citizens, the great majority of replacements came from young Chileans entering the priesthood. In contrast to the United States, priests under the age of forty form a very large sector in Chile.[4] Every indicator shows a similar trend elsewhere.

John Allen has called attention to what has happened in two countries in which the priesthood was moribund.[5] Bolivia had the most remarkable increase. In 1972, the entire country had 49 seminarians; in 2004, the number was 650. In Honduras, the national seminary had an enrollment of 170 in 2007, an all-time high for a country where the total number of priests is slightly more than 400.

But the most impressive numbers are the millions of dedicated laypeople that evidence lay participation in and commitment to the church. More than 1,200,000 serve as lay catechists, a key office in the church. The majority of these are mature Christians, and they function as more than volunteer religious educators: many serve as parish and community leaders. Some are vernacular intellectuals, persons who interpret the religious messages of Christianity in local cultural terms. This has especially occurred among the several hundred thousand catechists among the indigenous people. Remarkably, 118,784 Catholics became lay missionaries, mostly within Latin America, as reported in 2000.[6]

Thus, in general terms, the church has gained the workforce that it has hoped for almost two centuries since it was devastated by the loss of Spanish clergy and religious after the Latin American Wars of Independence (1810–1825). There are still not enough clergy to serve the full range of spiritual needs of members but the contemporary increase represents new and important strength in clergy and laity. Further, faced with increased competition from a diverse set of religious actors, the Catholic Church has responded with its own institutional resources and with lay participation, which has led to its own internal movement of religious revitalization and diversification.

Then there is the issue of confidence. For the eleven years in which polls have been available (1996–2007), the church has received the highest level of confidence of any institution in Latin America, in the 70 percent range. This has been true across countries and over time. Latinobarómetro, the major polling entity for Latin America whose results are carried each year by the *Economist* and are cited in *Foreign Affairs*, covers eighteen countries in the region (see Table 1). Its results for 2007 also show main trend points for eleven years. Very little change in this high level of confidence has surfaced over time.

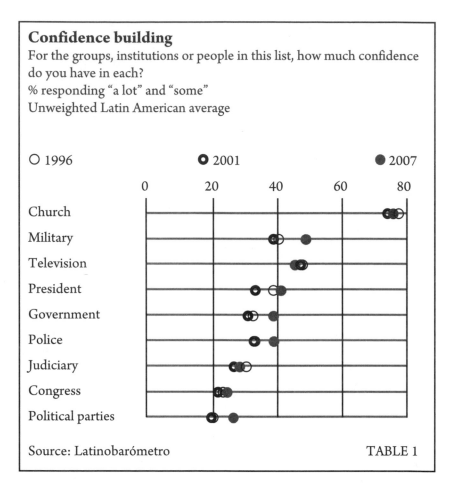

Confidence building
For the groups, institutions or people in this list, how much confidence do you have in each?
% responding "a lot" and "some"
Unweighted Latin American average

○ 1996   ◉ 2001   ● 2007

	0	20	40	60	80

Source: Latinobarómetro   TABLE 1

Why this confidence in the church that contrasts so strongly with what is believed to be its declining influence in the United States and Europe? One could argue that the church in Latin America gained this confidence by emphasizing the issues that matter to people at the grassroots. But a much wider range of reasons of how the church gained and maintained the confidence of the people became evident in investigation required for this book. These reasons form the rich motif of the succeeding chapters. Thus, even anyone reluctant to believe the evidence about confidence would still have to argue against all the other signs of growth and strength. This book then is fundamentally a description and analysis of vitality.

Christianity at Mid-Twentieth Century

In 1950 Christianity in Latin America was about to undergo momentous changes. On the surface, though, few indications of change showed themselves to observers. Rather, historians and social scientists tended to depict a Latin America dominated by the presence of the Catholic Church throughout the region. The church had few challengers; Protestants were few in numbers, relatively in the same percentage range as Catholics in Scandinavia and England. African and indigenous religions were practiced mostly on the margins of Latin American society. The small numbers of Marxists, even in Cuba, did not appear to pose the same threat to Christianity that communists did in China and Eastern Europe.

The Catholic Church was in a privileged and only marginally threatened position. Internal weaknesses and external threats would soon become apparent, however. In the following sections, we will examine three developments: First, how did awareness of institutional weakness become clear to sectors of the church? Second, how did region-wide social change facilitate new religious choices and changes? Lastly, Pentecostalism, the challenger to Catholicism, will be discussed.

Institutional Weakness and Response

Great disparities existed in the practice of Catholicism in Latin America. In Mexico and Colombia, very high percentages attended church weekly, whereas in Cuba, by contrast, only handfuls attended Mass on Sundays. In many countries, the Catholic Church appeared weak, even moribund. Throughout the region, the church could be described as otherworldly in emphasis, without much regard for social justice.

A small revitalizing sector existed among the laity—militant Christians who saw themselves as different from other Catholics. At a landmark Latin American conference, a key group, Catholic Actionists, gathered in 1953 at Chimbote, Peru. They described Latin American Catholics as only nominally Catholic, with an appalling minimum of religious instruction. Furthermore, Latin American Catholicism consisted of a traditional set of pious customs, a superficial substitute for the demands of the spirit and dictates of the gospel. The Catholic Church in Latin America, they concluded, needed a profound revitalization.

The Vatican had reached the same conclusion earlier. In the late 1940s, Rome selected priests who were young, progressive, and closely tied to the laity to become bishops. Some had studied in Europe or were deeply influenced by Christian Democracy and the European Catholic Revival, exemplified by Jacques Maritain. Helder Câmara illustrated the change marked by these prelates. A bishop by his thirties, Câmara proved a great success in pulling bishops together to form the Brazilian Bishops Conference (CNBB, Conferência Nacional dos Bispos do Brasil) in 1952.

Throughout the 1950s and 1960s, the Vatican created new dioceses at a great rate and appointed young bishops with modern ideas to head them. Rome also encouraged the sending of hundreds of missionaries from Europe, Canada, and the United States. These missionaries contributed significantly to a religious revitalization. The church, transnational by nature, expanded its national and international connections, structures, and activities within Latin America and the larger world. These organizational structures would prove to be crucial for the communication of theological and pastoral innovations that would follow.

The Vatican, through Italian Archbishop Antonio Samoré, encouraged Latin American bishops to create a Latin American Bishops Conference (CELAM). This proved to be a key organizational innovation. The bishops established a general secretariat at Bogotá, Colombia, in September 1955. Contrary to the previous Latin American tendency to emphasize traditional piety and individual charity, CELAM leadership began to stress concern for the political and social issues that affected the lower classes and a much broader participation by lay Catholics in the church and in public life.

In the late 1950s, the church became acutely aware of threats to its religious and ideological dominant position in society. In January 1959, Cuba fell to communist rule and the majority of priests and sisters were expelled or left the island when the Cuban government nationalized their institutions. Similar threats were made in Guatemala and the Dominican Republic, where alleged Marxist threats gave rise to civil wars and U.S. interventions. Protestants began to fill in where priests were sparse. To meet the challenges of Protestantism and Marxism, the Holy See requested that 10 percent of the abundant number of priests and religious women then available in Europe, Canada, and the United States be sent to Latin America. Consequently, thousands made their way to Latin America. Church offices and religious congregations in Europe, Canada, and the United States sent hundreds of millions in aid money to bolster the Latin American Church from the 1960s to the present.

The foundation was laid for the Latin American Church to absorb the great transforming event of the Second Vatican Council (1962–1965). Some 600 Latin American bishops attended Vatican II. They largely went as learners, known as a bloc to European and U.S. observers as "the church of silence." At the Council a number of Latin American bishops employed as their advisers their more recently educated clergy or active laity who were in touch with progressive European theology and movements that dominated the council discussions.

During the Vatican Council, Latin American bishops in Rome met among themselves and agreed that a special conference should take place back on their own soil to continue the renewal efforts spearheaded by Vatican II. Most important for the process of applying the ideas of Vatican II to Latin America were the young theologians, many of them European trained. These Latin Americans, at first a handful and then fifty or more, formed the core group who were charged with writing the basic documents of the all-important Medellín Conference (1968).

Political and Social Environments Affecting Religion

Beginning in the 1950s, processes that increasingly affected the lives of communities and individuals reshaped Latin American society. Technologies that facilitated industrialization; rail, air, and highway systems; telephone and digital communication; transistor radios and television—all of these deeply affected Latin America, changing virtually all spaces in which men and women lived. Within a few decades, Latin America shifted from being primarily agricultural and rural to being urban and industrial, and even more, oriented to the service sector.

While these changes were visible and increasingly taken for granted, other changes affecting individuals and institutions within Latin America were not as perceptible. On the personal level, what sociologist Max Weber foresaw came true. Many were forced to migrate because of the lack of opportunity to farm at home or the attraction of a putative better life in towns and cities. Many Latin Americans became free of the ties to their families and local institutions that held them in a particular social space with generally traditional arrangements. By moving, they became, in Weber's terms, masterless slaves. Whereas they had lived as indigenous or peasant persons, practicing Catholic or indigenous religion without consciously choosing their religious identity, they were now free. Their religious status would now be acquired rather than inherited.

In the 1950s and 1960s, people left farms or villages and went to cities, breaking loose from social control of family and neighbors and exercising freedom of choice. Most migrants to cities continued to believe in God, but some chose what appeared to them to be more attractive religions than Catholicism. To remain Catholic, as the majority did, often meant a conscious choice, implying a conversion to deeper commitment to faith and religion. Competition was forcing choices. From the 1970s on, the same social forces that changed city living increasingly affected persons living in villages and open country. Popular media—millions of ten-dollar transistor radios, mimeographed newsletters and other common media, often in indigenous languages—appeared in rural populations with messages that differed from those communicated by traditional cultures. Thus messages from religions competing with Catholicism and with one another reached the peoples who lived in remote areas. A massive change within religion and culture began under these influences.

These social changes also resulted in failed economic policies, new grassroots political demands, and increasing unrest. Especially during the1960s and 1970s, but continuing later in places like Chile, the military took over the government and imposed authoritarian rule.

The freedom from family ties and from traditional organizations facilitated new religious choices. From perhaps 6 million members in the 1960s, Pentecostal groups grew at an accelerated rate to about 40 million members in 2007. Since this is about 10 percent of the population of Latin America, one cannot claim that the region has yet turned Protestant. In terms of church attendance, however, it appears that there are more practicing Protestants than Catholics. Two issues are of special concern here: First, who are the Catholics that convert? Second, do Pentecostals continue to practice, or do many drop out?

Catholics Who Convert to Pentecostalism

If it seems as if the whole continent is converting, a sizeable percentage is. One in four persons in São Paulo, Brazil, is a convert to another religion. Many converted within a three-year period.[7] Guillermo Cook, a recognized Protestant authority on base Christian communities, and other observers began giving alarmed reports of persons who had belonged to Catholic grassroots groups in Brazil who then converted to Pentecostalism.[8] No numbers have been verified. Given the dispersed nature and lack of communication at the grassroots level, one had to trust those "in the know." These conversions were regarded by some as proof of the failure of the progressive church's strategy of empowering laypeople and promoting liberation theology at the grassroots.

If true, this would be the first time in world history that a large-scale conversion occurred among strongly committed believers. Andrew Walls, perhaps the greatest living scholar on world Christianity, believes that conversion is largely done by persons without strong ideology. Cases do exist of committed persons converting to from one ideology to another, say from Marxism to Christianity. However, these amount to less than 10 percent of conversions.[9]

What kinds of Latin American Catholics become Pentecostals? No one knows with certainty. No survey data exists on either the regional or national level. Fifteen years of study of Pentecostalism and other Latin American religions, and interviews with Pentecostal and other Protestant leaders lead me to believe that the vast majority of Catholics who became Pentecostal were indifferent, intermittently practicing Catholics. If true, would their becoming practicing, ardent Pentecostals be a "loss"? The church considers Pentecostalism a valid form of Christianity.[10]

Studies in the last ten years allow for more profound comments about conversion than numbers estimates.[11] First, large numbers of Latin Americans are converts. In populous São Paulo and perhaps much of Brazil, about one-fourth of the population are converts, mostly from (probably nominal) Catholicism or from no religious affiliation to Pentecostalism, Kardecian Spiritism, and Afro-Brazilian churches and temples. Many conversions (46 percent for Pentecostals and 30 percent for Afro-Brazilian religionists) took place in the last three years of the São Paulo study (1993–95).[12]

Second, many Latin Americans are trying on a new religious identity, and the result has been a revolving-door period in their religious history. As in Brazil, there are accounts of numerous conversions in Guatemala City. This is not surprising since Guatemala probably has the highest percentage of Pentecostals, thousands of ardent Mayan practitioners, and a Catholic religious revival.

Third, many Latin Americans practice more than one religion in the same year, or even on the same day. The walls between some religions are built very high by their pastors. Pentecostal pastors keep records of attendance, and Pentecostal members watch their Pentecostal neighbors. They report deviant behavior (including attendance at Catholic churches, Afro-Brazilian *terreiros*, or Mayan ceremonies). In contrast, *Veja*, a Brazilian weekly, reported that many Brazilians feel compelled to try "what works." A Brazilian senator, a self-described good Catholic, employed spiritist healers when his daughter, who was injured in a car accident, did not respond to modern medical practices in a hospital.[13] Countless interviews with urban professional Brazilians showed a similar propensity to try Afro, Kardecian spiritism, Pentecostalism, or New Age practices as needed.[14]

Is this whirlwind taking place only now? Probably not, but Latin American social scientists lack time-sequential surveys of the phenomenon. Many religious adherents spin in with enthusiasm, but leave after they learn the demands of the new religion. Older Pentecostal religions are perfectionist, demanding external changes (no drinking, womanizing, dancing, etc.) and expecting internal changes of heart.

Stereotype of Pentecostals as Fervent Churchgoers

In 1980 social scientists began commenting that for every Catholic who attends church a Pentecostal or other non-Catholic is practicing his or her religion.[15] Since 10 to 12 percent of Latin Americans are Protestant (especially Pentecostal), so the argument goes, they can be contrasted to the 15 or so percent of Catholics who practice their religion regularly.

In a widely circulated paper, Renato Poblete wrote: "Evangelical Protestants, particularly of the Pentecostal type now number in their ranks about twelve per cent" of the Latin American population. "The hard facts show us, then, that twelve per cent of the population are devoted and zealous evangelicals."[16] Editors at the U.S. Catholic Conference gave these observations prominent attention in the conference's documentary service, *Origins*.[17]

More recent studies show the hollowness of this presumption. Large percentages of Pentecostals do not go to church regularly, at least not in Poblete's Chile and probably elsewhere. A survey of Chilean Evangelicals, most of them Pentecostals, found the majority of them nonobservant, to say nothing of their being militant Christians. Fifty-two percent did not attend church weekly. Almost 38 percent very seldom or never attended. They neither went to church every Sunday nor followed the Pentecostal pastors' admonitions in many of their attitudes.[18] Kenneth Scott Latourette, the great church historian, provides evidence of this erosion from as early as 1956.[19]

Most of the older commentators on Pentecostalism, such as Poblete, have been social scientists that lacked close and recent observation of Pentecostals. Fortunately, newer research focuses on what the Pentecostal pastor deals with. In addition, scholars have shown the perfectionist quality of Pentecostalism: The demands are great; many do not succeed; individuals drop out or their pastors or communities expel them.

Almost no Catholics are expelled from their churches by their pastors. They can typically come back to worship after marital infidelities and other offenses without much fuss. Priests almost never keep written records of these lapses. In contrast, pastors in prominent Pentecostal groups, such as the Assemblies of God in Guatemala, have authoritarian control. Congregations have a rigorous code of conduct. Pastors keep track of offenses and list returning offenders in reports as "restored" to the community.

Even in Guatemala, the site of the most impressive Pentecostal growth, many have dropped out. Pentecostal scholar Everett Wilson found: "Many converts do not continue to attend church regularly and drop out of Pentecostal congregations. That many do not remain faithful is borne out in the Pentecostals' annual reports, which for given years, indicate as many 'restored' members (indicating a previous lapse) as conversions."[20]

Virginia Garrard-Burnett, in her masterful *Protestantism in Guatemala*, points out that backsliding, returning to the Catholic Church, and "recidivism into old habits proscribed by the churches, such as consumption of alcohol" occurred among many members.[21]

In contrast to their non-Pentecostal colleagues in Latin American history and social science, Pentecostal scholars are not surprised by the lack of observance among Pentecostals. They are especially aware of their own family histories and those of their denominations in the United States. A century after their founding, the Assemblies of God and the church of God in Christ (Cleveland, Tennessee) still have relatively small numbers of core practitioners. After a hundred years, Chilean Pentecostalism, too, shows the same history of many members cooling off.

Looking at statistics, Catholic leaders found their dominant position in Latin America diminishing. However, Pentecostalism has no magic wand that makes all its members fervent, as Poblete describes them. To imply that it has that power inflates the reputation of Pentecostalism. Poblete makes Pentecostals seem as if they are not part of the long march of Christians struggling against mediocrity or indifference.

Viewed at the grassroots, the panorama is more revealing than statistics. Choosing a religion to practice is increasingly a matter of individual preference, and a substantial number now desire to practice their religion. Religion can be seen as an ardent affair for many Latin American Catholics and Pentecostals.

Thus a complex picture of the Latin American religious world emerges and invites further examination. Still more features of the religious picture have come into clearer focus. In the last fifteen years, researchers have shown that Afro religions are booming among Brazil's white middle class. Virginia Garrard-Burnett and others argue that the newest religious movement in some Latin American regions is Mayan and indigenous religion, not Pentecostalism.[22] In addition, Mormons, Jehovah's Witnesses, and New Age practitioners are becoming more evident in many countries.

Is everyone in Latin America practicing religion? No, but the scene is lively. The view to follow offers greater insight into the Catholic Church in the competitive environment of Latin America. Contrary to superficial portrayals, the church has benefitted by competition. Many initiatives to invigorate the Latin American Church were undertaken decades before Evangelicals and Pentecostals began making millions of converts in the 1970s. I will show that the competition intensified internal reform rather than merely copying successful methods of rivals. Competition from Pentecostals, health-and-wealth Neo-Pentecostals, Mormons, and a host of African-based and indigenous rivals kept the Catholic Church focused in many, but not all, places on delivering word and sacrament in a way that generated vocations to the priesthood and deeper commitments for laypeople.

CHAPTER 1

Religious History and the Latin American Tradition

When the Latin American Church leaders and theologians returned from the Second Vatican Council, they were determined to interpret and to apply the Council's teachings in their own regions. In no other region of the world did the church experience a comparable systematic review and application of the Council to its context.

Enrique Dussel and other Latin American theologians emphasized that history should be used as a primary source of theology and not just of philosophy;[1] thus, Latin American Catholics, like others at that time, began to return to their "roots." In the course of this process, Latin American theologians and philosophers, especially Dussel and Gustavo Gutiérrez, reflected on their region's encounter between colonizers and indigenous peoples. The great figure of Bartolomé de las Casas served as a guide in theological and practical discussions by the way in which he focused his theologizing on the condition of the people to whom he had been sent. Initially insensitive to the plight of the native peoples, Las Casas was challenged by the Dominicans— one Dominican friar even refused him sacramental absolution because he neglected his duties to his native servants on Hispaniola.[2] Las Casas underwent a profound conversion, became a priest and a Dominican friar, and later, as bishop and theologian, became known as "Defender of the Indians," a title that he would have rejected since his goal was to empower the indigenous peoples to speak for themselves. From a theological point of view, his vision for later generations of Latin Americans had been somewhat forgotten by the nineteenth century. Gutiérrez, who spent seven years doing research in an attempt to clarify what Las Casas had accomplished, constructed a theological reflection on the history of his life's work, writings, and ministry as bishop. The result was a magisterial book that is a model for contemporary theologians.[3]

In southern Mexico, Bishop Samuel Ruiz García was stymied in his attempts to revitalize his diocese of San Cristóbal de las Casas where Las Casas had been bishop. Ruiz was a conservative organizational man who had attended Vatican II and was profoundly affected by the experience of absorbing a vision of the church different from the hierarchical ecclesiology with which he was familiar. He was determined to follow, as far as possible, the participatory theological vision of Vatican II. Ruiz's theological vision was that of *pastoral de conjunto*, the collaboration between lay and clerical ministers.

What followed was part of the birth of the indigenous church in Latin America. Mexico was one of the few Latin American countries that honored its indigenous past. While Ruiz was searching for ways to empower the laity, the provincial government unwittingly supplied the answer by promoting the First Indigenous Congress in San Cristóbal in October 1974 to commemorate the five-hundredth anniversary of the birth of Fray Bartolomé de las Casas. The congress was an event calculated to co-opt the indigenous into supporting the ruling political party.

After the Medellín Bishops Conference (1968), which established the policy of creating an indigenous church that honored cultural diversity, the goal of the church was to have catechist-leaders in every indigenous community.[4] The government, in contrast, was weak in indigenous community networks. Governor Manuel Suárez asked Bishop Ruiz to assist in convening the congress using diocesan structures. Bishop Ruiz hesitated since he did not want the government merely to sponsor a folkloric event to draw tourists and to strengthen the government's mobilization (rather than empowerment) of the indigenous masses. Instead, the bishop sought that, as Christine Kovic has said, "the indigenous would be permitted to give their word in public after living in silence for so many years."[5]

Thus the First Indigenous Congress was held in San Cristóbal de las Casas in October 1974. For the church and the people of Chiapas and Latin America, the congress became a wellspring of discovery that was a watershed event in the diocese's commitment to working with the poor, empowerment of the laity, and the political mobilization of peasants. Kovic judged:

> The importance of this congress cannot be overemphasized; it
> was the first opportunity in five hundred years for the four eth-

nic groups to unite and speak about their situation in public spaces that had been dominated by mestizos. Preparations for the congress began a year prior to the event and lay the groundwork for much of the organizing that would follow. Between October of 1973 and September of 1974 local, regional, and municipal meetings were held in indigenous communities to discuss the upcoming event. Initially, people met to "know our reality," that is, to talk about the situation of indigenous communities.[6]

The diocese was fortunate to have had, first, Dominican missionaries from California, and then Dominicans from Central Mexico. Both groups were well trained in theology and through their years of theological formation became aware of the life and work of Las Casas. Along with the indigenous, they would rediscover that heroic figure on his own mission ground.

More than 1,200 indigenous delegates from 327 distinct communities of the state of Chiapas attended the congress. Reflecting on Las Casas and on the openness of his current successor, Ruiz, they recognized the Catholic Church as a mediator for the poor, engaged in dialogue with them and supported their struggle for dignity. The participants at the congress discovered for themselves the pioneering work of Las Casas in his attempts to liberate the indigenous from Spanish subjugation. They discussed his work in relation to indigenous rights and saw clearly for the first time that they had rights. Las Casas became the focal point, a symbol of hope in the present state of affairs and source of motivation for the indigenous mobilization that was underway. If the governor had hoped that remembering Las Casas would strengthen the PRI's (Institutional Revolutionary Party) hold over Chiapas, the opposite occurred. The congress set in motion a new dynamic toward building a kingdom of justice, with demands on the state for the just provision of health and educational services. In a word, the congress helped create active citizens.

First, however, the indigenous had to de-emphasize their own divisions and pull together; then they could march toward a common future. The four linguistic groups attending the congress elected *hombres de buena palabra* (men of good word) as representatives to communities in order to continue the empowering work of the congress. The organization for continuity in the empowerment of indigenous was named Fray Bartolomé de las Casas. A year after the congress, one of the church advisers within the orga-

Opportunities to come together and reflect on God's word are an invaluable result of the modernization of the Latin American Church. Here a deacon leads a retreat for parish workers in the Dominican Republic.

nization asked the group members: "Who will be the next Fray Bartolomé de las Casas?" The natives responded: "We will. We are Bartolomé. Now we are beginning to speak for ourselves."

The diocese was well organized, especially through networks of lay catechists. With the "new theology" of Vatican II, the goal became building up the kingdom of God, that is, a more just world. For the indigenous, this meant that daily they were to affirm their own dignity as God's people despite living in a social order in which they were not treated equally. They rightfully felt they could lay claim to access to education and health. The diocese also linked them to other indigenous Catholics throughout Mexico and, indeed, throughout Latin America. Thus they viewed themselves as engaged in a common struggle.

As one observer described the theology of the indigenous Catholics of Chenalhó, "they see themselves as part of a global humanity and a global Catholic congregation."[7] This wider community of faith—*communio*—offered them a sense of solidarity. A major change in Latin American Catholicism was thus occurring: universalism, the shared sense of union with others in the region. This was in strong contrast to the fragmented Latin American Church of the 1950s, when it was common for Catholics only to know or care about their own parish and perhaps be acquainted remotely with the bishop of the diocese. A transformation occurred during the long preparatory process, during the congress itself, and during the years of pastoral activity and theological reflection that followed.

Before, there were no national conferences. Bishops in the remote areas where indigenous lived typically knew little of the nation or of the national church. The indigenous also discovered their connectedness through Bible study. Now that they were holding the Bible in their hands instead of only having sections read to them on Sundays, they forged a path to unity with other Christians. The Bible is a handbook for globalism through its universal images and its central message of breaking down barriers.

Roots of Change

We can see the religious thought that would become characteristic of the region in prophetic outline in Bartolomé de las Casas and the early Dominican missionaries, many of whom were bishops during the first century of Latin American colonization. Definitive historical research is lacking on important aspects of this first evangelization.[8] Vestiges continue, too, of the "Black Legend," of concentrating on the terrible things Spanish conquistadores and missionaries did. This was reflected in the politically correct statements of various church councils for the 1992 centenary.[9] However, recent and reliable historical work points to important innovations created by missionaries such as Las Casas himself in their encounter with another world.[10]

Las Casas, Antonio de Montecinos (a Dominican friar on Hispaniola, now the Dominican Republic and Haiti, who was the first clergyman to denounce publicly the oppression of the indigenous peoples), and other early missionaries were noteworthy for the theological method they pursued, which foreshadowed liberation theology. Their pastoral theology devoted great energy to describing the reality they encountered as the first step. By proceeding from describing the situation to judging it against Scripture and then to deciding on what actions to take, the theology of Las Casas turned the process upside down. Las Casas spent his life using this procedure to communicate what he saw to King Ferdinand and Queen Isabella and to other influential members of the elite who were open to what he had to say.

These missionaries in their moral judgments called attention to unjust social structures. In this they were ahead of their time, for moral thinking in that era tended to take social structures as a given and devoted full attention to individualistic moral questions. The basic moral question was: Did I give another person his or her due? But the early missionaries pursued their own intuitions and continued to raise serious objections about the system and not just about individuals.

For Las Casas and other early missionaries, Christianity especially raised a question of how to relate to the "other," a question that prefigures the current emphasis on trying to view ethnic or cultural groups distinct from one's own group with dignity and sensitivity. In the process of trying to establish the worth of the "other," Las Casas urged gentle persuasion rather than violent evangelism. For as long as could be remembered, Christians and others had traditionally joined religions through the conversion of the king or local ruler. As the ruler went, so did religious affiliation.

Beyond the content of their theology, Las Casas and the early Dominican missionaries modeled a communal process emulated by future theologians. Both the "original" and the present-day liberation theologians base their theology on their reflection on the experience of persons living at the grassroots. They describe what is taking place, then move to reflecting on scripture and then to deciding right and wrong. This took place locally, such as in Santo Domingo (Dominican Republic), Cobán (Guatemala), and Chiapas (Mexico). Perhaps the first community to employ this theological method in Latin America was directed by the Dominican friar Pedro de Córdoba (1482?–1525). Córdoba summoned the Dominican community into the chapter room in Santo Domingo to devise a shared theology about the Spanish treatment of the Indians. Thus, when Antonio de Montecinos preached what is regarded as a seminal statement of liberation theology, he expressed the community view. Montecinos charged that the Spaniards were living in sin because the system they created was sinful, again, an unusual idea for an era in which sin was defined as a situation in which an individual was out of order with the commandments. The doing of theology together, doing it at the side of the oppressed, and raising questions about economic systems were innovations of these early Latin Americans, innovations mirrored in the theology of liberation. Nonetheless, the early theologians did not have the full insight of the later liberation theologians. The early missionaries did their theology for, but not with, the grassroots.

These first grassroots theologians also consciously sought a transnational theological community, one centered in Salamanca. Systematic theology became a transatlantic effort with Francisco de Vitoria (ca. 1492–

1546), a founder of international law, as a major creator and spokesperson. (The history of Spanish theology frequently is divided into periods before and after Vitoria.) As one of his innovations at Salamanca, Vitoria opened the university term for many years with a public address on world problems. He employed a moral-legal perspective on these questions, especially those brought on by encounter with the New World. In a lecture highly illustrative of what he and his colleagues were about and subsequently published as *De Indis*,[11] Vitoria examined the legal titles Spaniards might use to justify domination in America. He questioned by what right the indigenous came under Spanish rule, what rights Spanish monarchs had in temporal and civil affairs, and what rights Spanish civil or religious authorities might have in spiritual affairs. Vitoria held that the indigenous of the New World had been in peaceful possession of their property and that they had to be considered as possessing valid ownership. In taking positions defending the rights of the native peoples, Vitoria not only was guided by the principles of Thomas Aquinas, but he also responded to descriptions and queries sent by his Dominican brothers in the Americas. Vitoria became a key player in communitarian theology. Ironically, authors from Protestant nations that undertook vast colonization efforts in North America and were also instrumental in starting the "Black Legend" of Spanish atrocities were strangely silent about the conquest of the Native Americans. While they could have built on the moral and legal basis that Vitoria established, or at least raised similar questions about the rights of the occupied, these theologians were, in contrast to Las Casas and Vitoria, most unquestioning.

Within one hundred years the influence of most of the theological innovations of Las Casas and others had decreased. But when Gustavo Gutiérrez and others in the 1960s re-embarked on the path toward creating a Latin American theology they found the blaze marks of Las Casas. Defense of human rights, too, was established as a minor but long-standing tradition within the Latin American Church.

Contemporary Issues

Liberation theology flowed naturally into other urgent concerns. The first tributary of this river of influence appeared as women's liberation theology. Presuming that a role within the intellectual framework of Christianity is fundamentally important, the activity of women in Latin

America and the United States in theology has been of utmost significance. To a considerable extent, women have not only taken their place in a profession that typically was dominated by males but they have also formulated the beginnings of a new ideology for women in the church and society. Just as their North American black counterparts were developing what came to be called womanist theology, Latin American women focused their efforts on *mujerista* theology.

Women from both north and south joined in this theological enterprise, especially Presbyterian theologian Letty Russell at Yale Divinity School, and Catholic theologian María Pilar Aquino at the University of San Diego. Two Catholic Brazilian women, Ivone Gebara and María Clara Bingemer, and a Protestant Mexican scholar, Elsa Tamez, achieved global recognition for their work.[12] Within a few years women's theology, based on ideas and methods from Latin America, took its place in most moderate-to-progressive theological circles, including universities in the United States.[13] Only slightly later did *teologia india* and Afro–Latin American theologies, already described, appear.

Care of the Earth: Peru and Chile

One of the newest developments, called by the Sierra Club "green theology," was slower to arise. Franciscan and other theologians from Brazil pioneered a theology of the environment in the 1990s, following the great buzz caused in the country by the UN Conference on Environment and Development, which was held in Rio in 1992.[14] The Brazilian Franciscans called this *una mística* because for them it was a spirituality as equally as it was a theology. But it impelled to action, as well; their representatives went to meetings in Europe to seek transnational support in representing Brazilian environmental interests. Ivone Gebara published a much-read volume on ecofeminism and liberation, showing the further extension of liberation thought through feminism to the environment.[15]

Green theology began taking center stage in Latin America in the first decade of the new millennium. The spark was the recognition at the local level of the gross environmental damage inflicted by modern technologies and fueled by global greed. In places as disconnected as the gold mines of Peru, the forests of Central America, and the jungles of the Amazon (touching five countries as well as Brazil), priests and laypeople began taking a stand against the uncontrolled harvesting of natural resources and consequent poisoning of water and air. They did so working from a theological vision and from the concerns of the people among whom they lived. Rodrigo Sierra noted that "indigenous communities in particular have grown stronger and can now hold states and multinational corporations accountable for their actions in their territories."[16]

Lay and clerical prophets found their own voices along with courageous bishops. Chico Mendes (1944–1988), the deeply religious Brazilian activist, became a symbol for those fighting (and being martyred) for care of the Amazon.[17]

Marilyn Snell, writing in *Sierra*, says that few Americans seemed to have noticed, that "a 'liberation ecology movement,' with the Church as its spiritual heart, has been taking shape from Chile to Mexico."[18] Father Marco Araña in San Cerillo, Peru, typifies the awakened opposition to irresponsible extraction industries and the theological impetus behind it. Newmont Corporation pulled some seven billion dollars worth of gold out of the earth in his area, using cyanide freely and leaving behind what the indigenous consider a trash heap. Thousands of local people lay siege to the mines because they see something sacred in the mountains, including the mountains as cradles of water—and of life for them in the arid environment. Father Araña formed the group to challenge the mine at Quilish and also acted as mediator. He negotiated the release of the protesters from the hands of police whose presence was likely bought by bribery (caught on tape) through the famous fixer Vladimiro Montecinos. Newmont backed off from its mine at Quilish, evidence that years of distrust and then focused protest by the indigenous had an effect.[19] The care of the earth as a God-given responsibility has become a clear theological charge. As a vivid example of the methodology typically employed, the National Commission for Pastoral Ecology of the Dominican Republic Bishops Conference began their "The church Observes an Environmental Crisis" with a diagnostic of forests, mining, tourism, waste materials, and water in the country; then reflected on the common good and responsibility; and concluded by speaking of needed actions to correct the unjust situation (in which authorities have helped out their friends and hurt those not so favored).[20]

These efforts were bolstered by extraordinary statements by Pope Benedict XVI as he arrived in Brazil in May 2007 for CELAM V. Again unnoticed by many, he strongly criticized unregulated capitalist ventures and their effects on the environment and spoke specifically of people's rights to protect their timber and land.[21]

The rising global backlash against the environmental and social costs of foreign firms and their technologies was also evident in southern Chile. The author was drawn to observe the work of another bishop who resembled Samuel Ruiz in southern Chile, Juan Ysern de Arce. Ysern, like Ruiz, was called "Tata" (Father) and Defender of the Mapuche, although he preferred to be thought of a brother and mediator-interlocutor or more simply facilitator for the indigenous to find their own voice. There the environmental issues focused on landfills and dumps that had a negative impact on the indigenous dwellers in the southern regions.

Care of the Earth: Central America

Outstanding among a new breed of clergy and lay leaders who have organized against environmental injustices is Father José Andrés Tamayo Cortez of Honduras. Fr. Tamayo, who was awarded the Goldman Environmental Prize, the world's largest prize honoring grassroots environmentalists, organized and directed the Environmental Movement of Olancho, commonly called the Wild West of Honduras. He put together a coalition of subsistence farmers and community and religious leaders to defend the land against uncontrolled commercial logging, which produced erosion and water shortages. Large landowners, logging companies, drug traffickers, and informal crime bosses control the area that lacks any effective authority. Fr. Tamayo's presence is greatly resented by the persons holding the controlling interests; they have tried to have him deported on the grounds that he was born in El Salvador (a youthful assistant to Archbishop Romero of San Salvador, Tamayo was advised by his mentor to leave the country to avoid likely assassination for human rights activity). Now he travels with military armed guards because his life has been threatened in Honduras for environmental activism. The most dramatic of his organized activities was the March for Life that drew 3,000 persons in 2003 to walk 120 miles from Olancho to the national capital. The march brought environmental debate to the national stage, inspired other communities to oppose illegal logging, and won for Tamayo an audience with the president and the National Human Rights Award that year.

Tamayo is far from the only cleric campaigning for environmental protection. Also in Honduras, Bishop Luis Santos of Santa Rosa de Copán convinced his thirty-nine parish priests to encourage their parishioners to join in protest of the extremely lax mining laws and practices that resulted in the contamination of Santa Rosa's drinking water. In 2006 ten thousand persons persisted in blocking the Pan American Highway until the president agreed to meet with Bishop Santos and his alliance leaders. Later Cardinal Oscar Rodríguez, archbishop of Tegucigalpa, the capital, joined in a dialogue with national leaders to seek a reform of the mining laws. He enlisted his frequent transnational ally, Caritas-Catholic Relief Service. The Canadian legislators lobbied the members of the Honduran Congress to reform the mining legislation, since a Canadian firm was at the center of the controversy.

In nearby Guatemala, Bishop Alvaro Ramazzini and many laypeople opposed the effects of gold mining at the large Marlin gold operation. After protests, impasses on roads, and shootings by government forces, the Guatemalan government appointed the bishop to recommend reforms to the nation's mining laws. He delivered his report to the Guatemalan Congress in 2006. Despite having no evident results, Ramazzini continues to push for reforms. He reads and rereads Pope Benedict's Christmas 2007 Address,[22] in which the pope reflects on respect for nature and the dignity of persons as part of the relations between individuals and nations. These are not theoretical statements for Ramazzini but are played out clearly in the lives of the poor he sees every day.

CHAPTER 2

Successfully Bringing Millions of Laypeople into Service in the Church

When bishops and archbishops returned to Bolivia from the final session of Vatican Council II, they passed through La Paz on their way to their respective dioceses, stopping off at the seminary to report on the Council to the repositories of the future, the few but precious seminarians who would become priests.

Despite the rigors of travel and of four years of attendance at the Council, the bishops were glowingly optimistic. They believed they had an excellent plan and a clear path to the future. What was that path? Bishop Armando Gutiérrez, then auxiliary bishop of La Paz and perhaps the best trained of the Bolivian bishops, summarized the thoughts of all the returning bishops: *Pastoral de conjunto*, or "lay involvement in the church." In fact, it meant much more, as will be seen.

The policy of *pastoral de conjunto* paid off handsomely for the Latin American church. Millions of laity became involved in the life of the church. The 1,200,000 who serve as lay catechists constitute a solid core around which parishes and communities are built. However, several million others serve in the church, or from the church to the world, without special title. The new policy also brought an increase in seminarians and religious sisters from families involved in this renewal.

While the first efforts to ground *pastoral de conjunto* in concrete projects were diffuse, they amounted to a gathering together of families and communities to begin to form a church that differed from the vertical one controlled and dominated by priests. The organization was to become a more horizontal one, grounded in the people of God. In this vision, all

24

shared in the priesthood; all worship and praise rose from them at the base to God through the ministry of the ordained priests. Priests acting without the active participation of the people no longer made sense. The theological emphasis was *communion*, joining together. Where this emphasis worked effectively, there was a strong sense of solidarity, a sense not only of meeting together but also of pulling together in a common enterprise.

The Latin American way is, if nothing else, to do things together. Two major consequences arise from doing things together and from having the church listen to ordinary people: first, a sense of ownership of the church by the laity, a conviction that lay and clerical together—and only together—form the church, and, second, small communities, an innovation that deeply marked the church. These will be taken up later in this chapter.

In the best case, Catholics came to a parish church expecting to proclaim (not merely read) the biblical readings at Mass and to hear homilies that incorporated their concerns and that carried them forward in their lives with hope. After services, some laypeople carried communion to the sick while others met to discuss the needs of their neighborhood, taught classes, or satisfied their need for biblical or spiritual reflection. This was their church. They made demands on the pastor, who was overworked but generally felt content within a busy family. Members of this parish typically were not very generous in terms of money (something to be explained later since it has consequences), giving a peso or two, but in most other ways they responded easily by giving their time and just by being present, part of the group.

Presence is a precious quality, perhaps more valued than money. Latin American generosity is striking in this regard. The difference between a North American and a Latin American Catholic can be seen in the decision of whether or not to attend a parish meeting. Typically, a North American will attend if he or she has something to contribute to the discussion but will otherwise try to avoid the meeting. A Latin American, on the other hand, will attend the meeting to bolster the solidarity of the group, regardless of his or her individual ability to say something significant, because that is what group life means to them.

By contrast, in the worst case, people in a parish passively watch a traditional and faintly Gothic Mass and do not sing the Gregorian hymns that are selected by a music director to be sung for them by a small choir. This is the Mass of the *beatas*, attended by old women and a few men, dressed in grey or black, absorbed in private devotions, ignoring the pleas of the pastor for help with widows or orphans. Young people were repelled by the ossified quality of this version of Christianity. In the last fifty years, millions of young and middle-aged Catholics who seldom or never attended Mass turned to Pentecostal, Evangelical, or other religious groups that engaged them in lively worship and a variety of responsibilities with the group.

Watershed Changes

During the debate at Vatican II about the role of the laity in the church, an Italian bishop argued boldly with colleagues. He summed up his position: "The role of the laity is to pray, pay, and shut up."[1] This, many agreed, neatly summed up the traditional view not only of the laity but of the vertical structuring of the church in much of the world prior to the Second Vatican Council.

Something new and dramatic began to occur in Latin America, however, evident even to foreigners. A European observer commenting on emerging lay leadership in the Latin American church wrote: "What is happening is a revolution in the Copernican sense of the term, a complete reversal. A switch [is being made] from a church resting on the point of the pyramid, in the person of bishop or priest, to a church resting upon its base."[2] The implications for changes in authority relationships, role definitions, attainment of status—all core social structures of the church—were enormous. The changes produced an effective organization, with not only lay participation but also ownership and a deep sense of belonging.

As important to the Latin American church as are its theology and the promotion of human rights, they are not the central mechanism of reform. The crucial issue, which received little attention in the mass media or in the opinion journals that tended to focus on the controversies of liberation theology or political activism in the church, was political—not the worrisome problem of politicization, but internal politics: the emergence of the laity, and the empowerment of laypeople for positions of leadership.

The greatest achievement of the Latin American church has been largely ignored: its empowerment of the laity to an extent unknown in most other regions of the world. Laypeople emerged in ways never dreamed possible; they were empowered for ministry in the church and for secular ministry. They performed functions previously reserved to priests and they created new ministries within the church.

Empowerment of the laity in Latin America has had more than religious implications. Here a missionary joins a village leader at a recently finished water project.

Laypeople also exercised ministries to society through social service (providing help to individuals or families) or through social action (activities aimed at making the system more responsive to the needs of "outsiders" or at changing structures). In the case of social action, lay leaders typically began with a project that addressed an urgent need of the community, such as land distribution, school construction, or water supply. Before long, they became aware of the larger realities of national, even transnational, economic and political life. Hence, an internal structural change in the church, empowerment of the laity, had larger social and political implications.

Based on reflection on their spiritual and temporal needs, laypeople and their clerical cooperators created new lay roles. While these new roles often match those described in the early Christian communities, contemporary invention bases itself on the needs and structures of new groups rather than on the imitation of ancient practice.

Lay leadership in the church is a larger and more complex issue than is the creation of basic Christian communities (to be discussed later). The empowerment of the laity for leadership in the Latin American church took place in many environments other than basic Christian communities. For example, the assembly of persons who worship at La Mansión in Santa Cruz, Bolivia—more a megachurch than a base community—numbers about

5,000. Either formally (by invitation) or informally (by initiative), laypeople at La Mansión assumed a whole range of roles, from liturgical music leadership to teaching groups of several hundred newer members ways to reflect on the Bible and to pray.

The modus operandi of La Mansión and other communities represents a remarkable change from the past and a key to understanding the relative success in organizational changes in Latin America. Most basic to the new spirit, in organizational terms, is a sense of responsibility. To a considerable but yet unmeasured degree, the confidence that Latin Americans have in the church comes from this sense of shared responsibility.

Responsibility is expressed by sharing according to one's abilities and talents. There are drivers, mechanics, teachers, prayer leaders, cleaning squads, and a range of other helpers. At La Mansión, members of the community gave money or other resources in a manner that was uncommon in Santa Cruz, Bolivia, or in Latin America as a whole. They were able to build and maintain an impressive community worship structure. Each day they provided prepared food for the Dominican community that typically numbered six priests and brothers, plus a surplus for other hungry persons. In fifteen years, the community only missed one meal.

As a result of these organizational changes, the number of what are commonly called "committed" laypeople grew. The new-style parish and community began sending students to seminaries to become priests and women to convents to become sisters. The increases appeared in statistics from about 1972, ten years after Vatican II and just a few years after implementation on a larger scale in Latin America.

In general, strong implementation of Vatican II and Medellín began earlier in South America and gained a foothold in Mexico and Central America almost ten years later. Hence, recollections of the timing and of the strength of reform implementation differ. Mexican observers declared that their conservative church needed to have the Third General CELAM Conference take place on their soil in 1979 before their bishops fully promoted the reforms of Vatican II. Central American informants reported simply that the region was a "theological backwater" and not then ready to absorb the conclusions of the Medellín Conference in 1968.

Need for Changes: The Background

To a degree not often recognized, the Catholic Church in Latin America lacked influence in the lives of its members. In most places, the rate of participation in church worship or social activities was low. Most Latin Americans received little formal religious education. Parishes were weak organizationally and in many places they had little impact on the lives of those who lived in their neighborhoods. In a word, the Latin American church failed to make contact with the majority of the people. Exceptions existed in Central Mexico and sections of Columbia and Central America. True, many Latin Americans were tied emotionally to their church; but in terms of participation, knowledge, and ethics, Catholicism was the religion of a minority.

The scarcity of Latin American clergy—due partially to assassinations, laicization of priests, and the return home of missionaries—exacerbated the weakness of the church. (This scarcity has been rectified, as will be noted.) In addition, the number of new priests was not keeping up with population increases.

The presence of many foreign missionaries created other problems, such as culture shock for the receiving church and confusion for many Latin Americans. This added to the flux and insecurity created by Vatican II and furthered confusion caused by political upheavals in a number of Latin American societies. Brazilian and Chilean Catholics, to name only more prominent cases, found themselves reeling from the impact of political and religious insecurities. In this context, foreign priests did not provide permanently for the full range of personal and organizational needs of Latin American Catholics.

Further, Protestant sects and naturalistic religious cults made great inroads in many Latin American countries. Whereas historical Protestant churches ministered to immigrant German- or English-speaking populations or attracted some middle-class Catholics, groups such as the Seventh Day Adventists, Mormons, and, above all, Pentecostals and Evangelicals have drawn masses of rural and urban poor, especially in Chile, Brazil, and Guatemala. Large numbers of Latin Americans practice spiritism, either imported from Africa or native to their region. Many indigenous people of the highland Andes or Guatemala continue the naturalistic religions of their forebears, often with an overlay of Catholicism.

How Latin America Saved the Soul of the Catholic Church

For every Latin American Catholic actively practicing his or her religion, in many countries an equal or larger number participated in some other form of religion.[3] This occurred especially "at the base" of the population. The poor and the working class were not abandoned by the church; many priests and sisters heroically attended to them. But the lower classes were not given attention proportionate to their numbers, especially in basic evangelization or education. The church perceived that its potential base was being eroded by the Protestants and by the practice of spiritism or other naturalistic religions.

In the middle class, competition for loyalty came from the secular left. The previous challenge of Masonic free thought or liberalism gave way to threats posed by socialism or various forms of communism. Universities, especially large, urban universities, became battlegrounds for conflicting ideologies. To meet challenges to the loyalties of the middle class, the Latin American church turned to imported—or in a very few cases self-initiated—strategies. They proved largely transitory and ineffective.

To meet these external threats, the church had to employ lay leaders. Not only were there not enough priests, but priests would not be accepted in secular circles in the same way that laypeople are. In the larger church, the issue became known as "the problem of the laity." Intellectuals, primarily articulate laypeople in Europe and the United States and the European theologians, began facing the problem of the legitimation and promotion of the laity. Many laypeople, especially the more educated, wanted a more active role. What place should they have in the church?

Church strategists were also aware of the pastoral challenge represented by largely passive masses of baptized Catholics in Europe. In contemporary life, persons who nominally belonged to an organization but had little intellectual or emotional involvement with it were likely to drift away, as many of the working class did in France and Italy. Moreover, serious external threats arose first from Protestants, then from anti-Catholics in revolutionary governments, and finally from communists and old-line socialists. Leaders within the church, such as Canon Joseph Cardijn and Father Adolph Kolping, created movements and structures to meet challenges to the loyalties of the middle and working classes as well as to meet demands for more active participation in the church by the laity. Thus a number of lay movements began in Europe.

What became obvious was that there was no ideology sufficient to support the movements: a theology of the laity (and hence an amplified eccle-

30

siology) was needed. Various factors influenced the genesis and direction of this ideology. First, the incongruity of masses of inactive Catholics in democratic countries where participation was expected became increasingly evident. Secondly, Protestant churches had already reformed the ideology, if not fully the reality, of lay participation. As Catholics and Protestants increased their interaction, especially in northern Europe and the United States, the Protestant model exerted an influence on Catholics, both clerical and lay. Finally, theological, biblical, patristic, and liturgical movements all pointed to the necessity of active lay involvement in the church. Historical and systematic scholarship began drawing the main outlines of a theology of the laity. Major theologians such as Congar and Rahner were attracted to the question because of their concern to rethink the nature of the church.[4] And the laity was demanding an adequate intellectual conception of its role. It was no accident that many theologians confronting the problem worked closely with worker-priests or laypeople.

What place was the laity to occupy in the church? Focus on the term *laity* led to nowhere. The laity consisted of nonclerics. They were called the faithful parishioners, a term without much meaning in the modern era. Instead, theologians focused directly on what it meant to be a Christian in

The age of the laity emerged when ordinary people were instructed and empowered to assume responsibility in the church. Here a missionary in the Dominican Republic leads catechesis before a Mass.

the world: the theology of the laity developed within the context of an evolving theology of the church at the service of the world.

Congar, Rahner, and others focused on and elaborated the central concept of the priesthood of the faithful, based on recent research into biblical and early church sources. Vatican II absorbed and diffused their formulations of the church and the place of the laity within the church. An ideology sufficient for the emergence of the laity had been created; laypeople gained legitimacy for assuming active roles in the church. Furthermore, the church was not to be turned in on itself but was to be at the service of improving the world.

One of the clearest signs of the radiation of the vital organizational life, sense of responsibility, and solidarity from the new style parishes and communities to the larger world is the Movement of the Landless (MST) in Brazil. This movement is the largest and perhaps most successful sociopolitical movement in Latin America. The connection between base Christian communities and Catholic parishes and the landless farm workers union is well recorded, as is the connection of MST to similarly renewed structures in the Brazilian Lutheran Church. MST members live arduous, communal lives for weeks or months in encampments. The success of these MST settlements depends on generosity and solidarity. Parish and small community experiences acted as basic training for these settlements.

In contrast to the haphazard life in the shantytowns or *favelas,* life in the settlement camps has a deliberate daily routine. Persons are placed in sectors, commissions, and other forms of organization. This brings people together, distributes power, and creates a strong experience of democracy. Parish and small community life offered basic training in such qualities.

Further, the two million or so members of MST stayed with the movement, many for more than ten years, even in the face of strong and sometimes deadly opposition. The same solidarity could be noted of the hundreds of thousands of members of small communities who faced martyrdom in El Salvador. It is the ordinary Catholic in the Latin American parish, however, who has his or her heart and soul supported and nourished in the church that most commands attention here.

The Crucial Latin American Invention: Small Christian Communities

For twenty years, emphasis shifted in the Latin American church from joining traditional lay organizations to focusing energies and resources on grassroots Christian communities. While not universal, these efforts were spurred by the new ideology and pastoral strategy enunciated by the church at the Medellín and Puebla conferences. Base Christian communities (CEBs—*Communidades eclesiales de base*) became the preferred but not exclusive pastoral strategy for the future. At Puebla (1979), the bishops reinforced what they believed: "We are happy to single out the multiplication of small communities as an important ecclesial event that is peculiarly ours, and as the 'hope of the church.' "[5]

With a new theology of the church in the world and a new ideology of inclusion and empowerment of the laity, Latin American pastoral leaders began a continent-wide discussion of how they might implement this inclusion and empowerment. *Pastoral de conjunto* remained a plastic term, applicable to myriad structures and roles. But *pastoral de conjunto* began evolving into *communidades de base* in a number of locations: Brazil, Chile, Paraguay, the Dominican Republic, and Central America.

Several factors were responsible for the creation and expansion of base communities, not all of which were operative in every location. At the beginning, the single factor within the church was the driving force of progressives who wished to emphasize social justice. This meant siding with the poor and working directly and extensively with them. Moreover, it was recognized throughout Latin America that no institution, whether political, social, or religious, would succeed without involvement at the base. Finally, the Pentecostal groups and naturalistic religions set an example of how to work successfully at the grassroots. Many base communities emerged in repressive political environments. The social control exercised by these regimes meant that the only "safe" place for activists, priests, and lay leaders was with the people, relatively out of sight.

Base Christian communities became a revitalization movement for laity and clergy alike. For individual members, the community brought about a religious experience. The community also fostered consecration and commitment. Life in the community brought with it a new perception of what it meant to be a Christian. Ultimately, commitment to a base community meant a kind of second conversion and fulfillment of Christian life for community members.

Other types of small communities have taken their place along CEBs. Another rapidly growing type is that formed by groups of Catholics who are part of the Catholic Charismatic movement. In Brazil and some other places, Charismatic small communities exist side by side with CEBs. Other types can be found, such as the Neocatechumenate, a much less prevalent form developed in Spain. In Cuba, where Catholicism has to attempt to survive as best it can in repressive circumstances, small communities are called house churches.

Worldwide, the different types of communities are referred to collectively as small Christian communities. They resemble the small communities of the first centuries of Christianity. What they have in common is that they resemble living cells in an organism newly coming to life. Generally, twelve to twenty persons make up a community. They usually come together in their neighborhood or village once a week to read sacred scripture, pray together, and sing hymns and to reflect on what the scriptures mean in their daily lives. That reflection frequently leads them to courses of social action to improve the living conditions in their barrio.

Association, Status, and Power

From a sociological perspective, the base community experience brought with it a new relationship to the church. By shifting from a parochial to an associational relationship to the church, church members made a deliberate choice to be a Catholic. This commitment was often missing in simply belonging to a Catholic society, but it was inherent in membership in a base community. That someone would continue to commit grave injustices while still belonging to a base community was repugnant to community members; eventually the offender dropped out of the base community.

In terms of status, another major shift occurred for base community members. Status as a Catholic was no longer "inherited"; it was achieved. Inherited status came from one's family, was beyond one's control or influence unless deliberately renounced, and was therefore neither merited nor especially rewarded. In contrast, achieved status resulted from one's own efforts, could be lost if these efforts were not continued, and was merited and rewarded in special ways.

Having attained new status as base community members, laypeople made new types of demands on the church. In a word, enhanced status brought new power to the laity in the church.

Newspaper and magazine accounts of the church often reflected common assumptions about power in the church as a formal organization. They portrayed the church as similar to a transnational corporation or some other type of tightly knit bureaucracy—less organized than an army but more so than a hospital staff. Power was assumed to reside at the top, filtering down from the pope, Vatican inner circles, and local bishops to local pastors. By the time power reached the grassroots, it was insignificant or more symbolic than factual, limited, for example, to reading liturgical texts or presenting liturgical offerings.

Such a conception overlooked the associational aspect of the church as it was evolving in Latin America. The base Christian community was an association "owned" by its members, each of whom possessed a portion of power. Many members of base communities could exert extensive and direct power by supporting or opposing the person or policies of bishop or pastor, attending or staying away from meetings, volunteering or refusing to serve, contributing or withholding financial resources. Members exercised ultimate power by withdrawing their personal involvement.

Church officials acted as power brokers as well as authorities. Pastors and bishops channeled power from individuals into programs and functions from which laypeople did not withdraw their power. The fact that power also arose from the base modified the assumptions of those who pictured the church as equivalent to a multinational corporation. The bottom-up view also helped to explain the power dynamics of the grassroots communities and new roles fashioned for and by laymen and laywomen.

Some measure of bureaucracy was and will always be maintained in the institutional church. A transnational agency in the contemporary world could not exist or function effectively without some formal authority, control, and lines of communication. Moreover, church superiors have sources of power not typically available to leaders of wholly voluntary associations. By office, bishops are guardians of long-standing traditions—that is, established ways to believe, worship, and practice. In part, they controlled the symbols and myths of the organization.

But the bishops controlled only in part. Not only did they need volunteers but typically they themselves were not experts in all these areas. They needed biblical exegetes, patristic scholars, systematic theologians, liturgical experts, and moral theologians to examine symbols, myths, and ideology. These three groups—superiors, experts, and laity—have interacted for centuries. Wielding of influence and the making of policy was thus a multifaceted enterprise, with influence in the church exercised at one time or another by each of the three groups. Interchange was usually cooperative but conflicts arose periodically on a variety of issues, including the widespread nonacceptance of birth-control restrictions. Potential for tension and conflict among the three groups was and is an ever-present factor in the life of the church.

Structural Changes in the Local Church

"Structural changes" refers to the way the local church was organized, the way power was exercised, and the availability and type of rewards for participants. The traditional local church had, first, a pastor who held centralized, diffuse power: He made decisions over many areas (finances, administration, education, and worship) without necessarily having expertise in each area. Second, parishes, and the the Latin American church in general, lacked accountability structures. In many places the church was so loosely organized and decentralized that pastors did pretty much as they wished and seldom had to make an account to parish members or superiors. This was true, too, of priests working in educational, relief, or social action agencies. Bishops typically stepped in to ask for accountability only under outside pressure. Third, the traditional church largely lacked meaningful rewards for grassroots members. Achieved status (by belonging to a respected lay organization) or positional status (by role) was available to the middle class. But for those at the grassroots, the rural and urban poor, such rewards were unavailable in most places.

The new church, as exemplified by the base communities, made crucial structural changes that affected the life of the laity:

1. *Scale of community.* The size of the base communities solved the problem of the virtual impossibility of developing full organizational life and a sense of identity among thousands of persons in an urban or rural parish. A membership level of about fifteen to forty persons allowed participants to "own" the group by sharing power and helping make decisions, by speaking up and being heard, and by being held accountable.

2. *Homogeneous groups.* As a rule those who belonged to base communities came from the same small village or urban sub-neighborhood. Not only were the members neighbors but they usually had the same economic background and subculture, typically peasant or working class. Base communities brought together neighbors who became involved with one another and became committed to the biblical Christ and the larger church. (Considerable difficulties loomed for the larger church because of the homogeneity and encapsulation of some base communities that engendered, ironically, "parochial" views.)

3. *Diffusion of power and division of labor.* In the new church, the priest shared power with the laity. Laypeople presided over or participated actively in worship; they taught new members, made decisions about their lives (no longer divided into spiritual and temporal spheres), and ministered to the sick or fostered projects such as the digging of a well, the construction of a road, or the obtaining of land titles.

4. *Accountability structures.* The lack of accountability structures that marked the traditional Latin American church generally did not exist in the new communities. Members were held accountable to other members for conduct inside and outside the group. Group membership entailed acceptance of group norms; in this case, members were presumed to be attempting to live up to a general understanding of the Ten Commandments. Grave or continued deviance was met by challenge, ostracization, or expulsion.

   Base community members made demands on the services of the pastor or bishop through group presidents or coordinators. Likewise the priest or bishop could challenge the group to new growth or activities or, through lay moderators, attempt to hold it accountable for dubious activities. Accountability of the small groups typically was not sought for authoritarian ends but rather to harness the resources of the laity toward the corporate goals of the larger church.

5. *Meaningful status rewards.* The church, traditional or revitalized, offered members considerable rewards, such as the promise of ultimate deliverance (if they are faithful) and certi-

tude of basic religious beliefs. These rewards might have sufficed for some self-motivated individuals, but most grassroots members needed rewards of higher status to become more actively involved in the life of the institution. Providing such rewards is a central concern for any organization that must enlist volunteers.[6] The base community bestowed achieved status on members upon entrance into the group and adherence to its norms. They gained further status through acceptance and performance of roles within the group.

6. *Legitimation and formalization of lay roles.* Although the group decided or helped to decide who would exercise certain functions within it, the pastor or bishop typically installed new office holders in a formal ceremony. As lay leadership emerged, legitimation became a key issue. Despite the bishop's or priest's acceptance of laypeople for roles within the church, some Catholics objected to accepting what they regarded as priestly functions from persons who were not priests. Accordingly, bishops and priests composed ceremonies of lay ministerial legitimation that resembled ordinations. In some cases lay ministers sent to other communities were required to have papers signed and sealed by the bishop, stating that they were empowered as ministers of baptism, the Eucharist, or whatever new function they were to perform. New ceremonies of office conferral tended to be simple and usually took place in a group prayer meeting or during the parish liturgy. In some places, such as Santiago de los Caballeros (Dominican Republic), assumption of the role of *presidente* of a community was treated as a weighty responsibility. Bestowal of full title was very formal and was granted only after an apprenticeship.

7. *Training and socialization.* From an organizational perspective, the weakest aspect of the new communities was the lack of training for some of the new roles. Some functions were simple in scope and required no special training. Some leadership roles could be performed by persons who already knew how to animate a group toward some goal. Persons with previous training, such as schoolteachers, were recruited, although such persons had only a sketchy awareness of the

38

history and content of the Bible and theology. Many dioceses recognized this problem and established permanent centers for training leaders.

Laypeople and Ministers

Military and other security forces closely monitored the progress and activities of laypeople who were members of base communities. The Vatican and CELAM, too, sensed dangers and problems. At times questions were raised about the teachings proposed by one or another base community. The main concern of higher officials was not doctrinal, however, but organizational. From this point of view, the base Christian communities offered many potential headaches, seemingly more than the Latin American church could bear. Could an already organizationally weak institution absorb more decentralization? Would diffusion of power from the center to the periphery— sharing the power of priest and bishop—mean potential disintegration? What would happen to the unity essential to any organization?

Perceiving the threats, Vatican officials flocked to the Puebla meeting in 1979. Pope John Paul II's central message at Puebla was a plea for unity, seeking a base from which to begin his long papacy.[7] As chief executive of an extensive transnational organization, he saw some ominous implications in the emergence of grassroots communities and of subsequent structural changes in the Latin American church. No president of General Motors would have acceded to a corresponding decentralization of functions and power within his corporation. Nonetheless, John Paul II and the Vatican approved the Latin American mandate for base communities and the emergence of the laity that it implied.

A major reason why the community movement was approved and actively encouraged in many places was that the demands of the laity in these communities were basically religious. For the most part community members sought enlightenment, spiritual growth, and the improvement of their human condition. Few laypeople in Latin America were demanding "citizen's rights," such as "one person, one vote." Moreover, where laypeople emerged in the church, they did so typically in an atmosphere of mutual trust between laity and clergy. Further, laypeople in these communities wanted to remain Roman Catholics; they were not seeking another church.

Finally, fifteen years of experience with base communities demonstrated that the communities usually continued to exist only where priests or religious sisters actively promoted them.[8] The pastor was largely responsible for creating the kind of climate in which volunteer workers flourish.[9] Without the pastor's blessing and active encouragement, lay groups tended to fade away.

The potential organizational threat posed by the base communities thus failed to materialize. Moreover, from a positive point of view, the grassroots communities and the emergence of the laity corresponded to a basic change in outlook in the worldwide church expressed at Vatican II. Finally, lay emergence and base communities reflected the global hierarchy's growing appreciation of the needs and aspirations of the rank and file.

Burning or Unresolved Issues

Because of the many appointments of conservative bishops under John Paul II (1978–2005), Christian base communities, especially the activist ones in Brazil, appeared to be in decline. The *National Catholic Reporter*'s series "Latin America: A Search for a Future" repeated the stereotypes about the decline of numbers and quality of life in these communities.[10] But these reports do not stand up to the research published by Luis Gomez de Souza, the Executive Director of CERIS, a research center in Rio de Janeiro founded in1962. In his work, *Do Vaticano II a um novo Concilio?* (From the Second Vatican Council to a New Council?),[11] Dom Luis states: "The CEBs continue to play an active role in society, from social assistance activities to mobilizations and involvement in associations, syndicates, and parties as well as in national campaigns."[12] As Robert Pelton made clear in his response to the *NCR*, the CEBs continue to be a vital work in progress.

Further, Brazil in the early 2000s showed a great increase in small communities of Charismatic inspiration. That the Charismatic Renewal (CCR) in many places instinctively chose the small community format rather than the Joel Osteen megachurch style popular with many Pentecostal congregations is noteworthy and indicates the high value and positive example of CEB creation in Latin America. The Charismatic communities exist side by side in parishes with CEBs, with some rivalry between Charismatics and non-Charismatics.

Some CEB proponents have emphasized the presumptive dichotomous nature of the two groups, citing the lack of a social justice orientation among Charismatics. In fact, the perceived opposition between CEBs and CCR is being reduced at the grassroots, at least in some places, as will be shown in the next chapter.[13] Another long-time Brazilian researcher, Alberto Antonunicci, believes that the time has come to discard depictions of types of communities as outdated and not useful and instead simply to emphasize small communities as vital to parishes and the larger church. He believes that some sixty thousand small communities exist in Brazil and that many of them flourish.

The emergence of the laity raised a whole series of questions, too complex and inchoate to discuss here beyond merely outlining the major ones. First, an active place for the laity meant an adjustment in the role of the priest. Indeed a "new" priest was emerging along with the new laity.[14] This new priest devoted more of his time to religious functions and less time to administrative and financial work. He needed time to keep up with the new religious ideology of the church and to follow the research in biblical and theological fields. He concentrated more on his own spiritual development as well as that of his lay collaborators. Homilies were much more demanding now that his listeners were reading the Bible and interpreting what they read and what they experienced in life. Some outlines of the new priesthood were thus being drawn.

Apart from Kenneth Serbin's valuable study of some seminaries in Brazil,[15] almost no systematic studies of seminaries have been done. The author looked at national seminaries in two different contexts, Guatemala City in the late 1980s and Buenos Aires in the late 1990s, chosen at random as windows into changes from traditional to modern. The first evident changes were expected: the much-increased size of the student body. Old walls could not hold the increases and a new seminary had to be built. In addition, the more advanced age of the seminarians was notable. But the most striking feature overall was the organizational structuring whereby seminarians were living in what amounted to small communities, groups of 12 to 16 students, with one faculty resident with them. Having to build a new seminary allowed for construction of these communities. The rector of the Guatemala seminary, himself a late vocation and a former dentist, thought the small communities offered a human scale, sense of responsibility, and a sense of solidarity more effectively than dorm living. Not only were the seminaries mirrors of improved parish life; in fact, they echoed what the bishops had written in 1968:

> The Christian ought to find the living of the communion, to which he has been called in his "base community," that is to say, in a community, local or environmental, which corresponds to the reality of a homogeneous group and whose size allows for per personal fraternal contacts among its members.... This community becomes then the initial cell of the ecclesiastical structures.[16]

Given the increased lay involvement in the Latin American church, observers from the United States and Europe invariably raised the question of the ordination of women or at least of the bestowal of greater status upon them. The Latin American church may work out those questions differently from the churches in the United States and Europe, given the cultural differences. Not only are women "starting from further back" in some ways, but the ways in which cultural and political conflicts are resolved in Latin America differ from Anglo-Saxon ways.

Notable in the first formulations of liberation theology was the lack of any mention of the role of women in Latin American culture and in the church. Theologians soon found themselves challenged on this point, especially in international conferences and in confrontations with women activists in Latin America. (Feminist theology, North or Latin American, owes much to liberation theology, as will be noted.) As a result, Latin American bishops also have been challenged on the issue, with an increasing sensitivity to the problem. Archbishop Marcos McGrath, chairman of the central steering committee at Puebla, observed that the church had only recently opened its consciousness to the problem, that advances had been made (as witnessed by the presence of women delegates and observers at that conference), and that further progress could be expected.[17] Clearly changes at the hierarchical level would proceed at an evolutionary rather than a precipitous pace.

At the local level, something of a revolution had already taken place in practice, if not in ideology. The Latin American church has been less fussy about lay/clerical distinctions with regard to status and functions than has the church in the United States. In Brazil and elsewhere, women perform many functions (preaching, baptizing, and giving communion) previously reserved to priests. Priests and bishops in Latin America have had the opportunity to note the effective work of women in such capacities. In a sense, then, some women in Latin America have made greater inroads than have most women in U.S. churches, Catholic or Protestant. The power of women in the Latin American church grew from practice, not because of decrees.

The place of women in Latin American culture and in the church showed some further subtleties, none more important than the question of how decisions are made.[18] To allow macho cultural stereotypes to suggest that Latin American women were relegated to the margins of effective participation in society and in the church is to overlook the residual power of women in Latin America. A glimpse of this extensive phenomenon is provided by considering what takes place in a base community: women, many of whom act as leaders in the group, contribute actively in decision-making; often women are the chief decision-makers.

In sum, influential leaders in the Latin American church moved the institution toward a new kind of organization. These leaders relied on experts to provide new ideology and directions for the church. The new ideology brought the laity greater prominence. It was an evolutionary process: the church did not immediately or completely empower laymen and laywomen, but it opened the door to new role definitions and conferred new status and power on the laity. The social background of the newest lay leaders represented another change. The men and women standing center stage in the 1980s were rural and urban poor; they upstaged the educated and middle class. By the 2000s lay leadership appeared to be diffused throughout social classes, at least as sampled in Chile and Mexico.

In general, churches fulfill several social functions, one of which is to provide a human community. The Catholic Church in Latin America failed to retain millions of indifferent Catholics in part because it did not provide the kind of community other churches provided. But especially after the 1960s, the church offered the promise of a new community, now fulfilled in many but not all places.

The emergence of the laity represented the greatest achievement of the Latin American church. Consequently, resources and energy only hinted at in the days before Vatican II have been released. Structural changes in the local church took place because of the movement. Power was shared, accountability structures appeared, and status rewards were offered to the people. As a leading Latin American bishop remarked, "We have set free the people of God to serve him."[19] A Copernican revolution has been taking place in the Latin American church.

Lay involvement implies much more than mobilization of members. The next chapter will explore the panoply of spiritualities that undergird this commitment to service. Later chapters take up major roles that lay-people now fill, cementing their central place in the revitalization of the church.

CHAPTER 3

Offering a Marketplace for Spiritual Well-Being

Catholic laypeople had at their disposal a wide range of spiritualities, from traditional and slightly modernized and family-friendly to esoteric, that reflected the general presence in Latin America of new and ancient religions from all over the world. This chapter offers a guide to that lively marketplace of spiritualities.

Communion has been the widely diffused theology that undergirds laypeople who assume responsibilities in the church. It is also a spirituality centered on holiness achieved in serving the people of God. Spirituality, or spiritual life, is here used to denote the Christian life, lived with some intensity[1]—a regard for things of the spirit, as opposed to regard for material things.

The spirituality of the church in the world, communion, also contrasts with the traditional devotional, otherworldly spirituality of the older persons who typically frequent churches, focus on begging favors from God, and yet display little interest in helping others. At the major Aparecida Conference in 2007 communion dominated as one of the three central themes. This spirituality continues as a groundwork upon which other spiritualities have been built. These include social justice, charismatic, and indigenous spirituality and, above all, popular religiosity, all of which thrive in Latin America, along with several other types.

Latin American Popular Religion

Virtually every journalist that comments on the civil wars in which the United States intervened in Central America in the 1980s remarked on the

45

deep religious sense of the people. Religion permeates Latin American culture. Its magical realism in literature and the everyday speech that incorporates references to God (*Si Dios quiere, vaya con Dios*, and hundreds of other phrases) witness to the widespread acceptance of a world of spirits. Even in Brazil, with its excellent economy and a highly modernized sector, 99 percent of the population believes in God. Cocktail conversations there include religion routinely and without embarrassment.

The soil in which much of Latin American religious sensibilities grow is popular religion. It may be more accurate to describe this not as *spirituality*, which focuses on a supreme being rather than routine practices, but rather as *religiosity*, the habit of carrying out religious practices.[2] *Religiosity* also implies a continuum, ranging from persons for whom religion is primarily a source of favors to those who are awed by the source of the favors.

The history of this religiosity also helps explain a paradox: most Latin Americans do not regularly attend church. In a word, one must understand popular religion in order to understand the soul of Latin America. It is not the whole soul but it is an essential component for probably the majority of Latin Americans. "Popular religion" refers to religion as practiced by ordinary Catholics in contrast to official religion delineated by religious elites (bishops and theologians). At the heart of popular religion is concern with the material world: "with bodily nourishment and healing, with birth and death, with mundane concerns, as getting a job or having good fortune on examinations, with warding off misfortune," as Cristián Parker has described it.[3]

In many ways, Vatican II marked a major shift away from traditional religion on the part of the institutional church. It forced church policy makers and pastoral leaders to decide which traditional elements to safeguard, modify, or discard. What differentiates the soul of the Latin American church from that of the churches of the North Atlantic is that the Latin American church held on to popular religion, albeit after considerable controversy. Novenas, processions, devotion to Jesus the Miracle Worker, Mary, and the saints continue.[4]

Popular religion attained its comfortable position in most national churches only after fierce debates. From the end of Vatican II in 1965 through the 1970s, progressive leaders and theologians argued that popular religion encouraged fatalism, conservatism, and excessive emphasis on life after death while largely ignoring the building of a just society in this world. The debate also became confused because one aspect of popular religion, fiestas, were sometimes occasions of binge drinking and resulting in violence, including sexual violence and aggressive macho competition between men. Concern about the drinking and violence continued, as exemplified among Catholic Mayas who have become teetotalers in Chiapas and Catholic Aymaras in Bolivia's altiplano. The debate about the main aspects of popular religion moderated, however, as theologians began noting the positive aspects of popular religion, including its potentially liberating aspects. By the time of CELAM III at Puebla (1979), bishops were noting the good as well as the bad.

Shrines and Pilgrimages

Probably nothing is more expressive of popular religion than *el santuario* and *la peregrinación*. The shrine and the journey to it, pilgrimage, furnish pageantry, physical test and voluntary suffering, movement, mystery, hope, resignation, and the pleasure of an outing.

National or regional shrines exist in all countries. Bolivians of the high plateau, for example, are drawn to Copacabana, where the natural grandeur of the setting takes the place of a splendid manmade basilica, while Bolivians at lower altitudes seek out Our Lady of Cotoca and similar provincial shrines.

In Argentina, one has only to go to Luján, the national shrine, an hour's drive from Buenos Aires, to see the mix of gender, classes, and age that frequent such a shrine. On an ordinary Sunday afternoon, at three o'clock, between 30,000 and 40,000 persons can be found moseying slowly through the very large basilica church and surrounding shops. People are not there to attend Mass; it will be celebrated later in the afternoon.

They walk around and take in all the aspects of the church, including the family names of the basilica's benefactors, images of Jesus and various saints, and at the center a curious and somewhat homely image of Mary. This image, like those in other national shrines, was created by an unknown lower-class artisan, was lost, found, and discovered to have miraculous powers, thereby inspiring individuals and families to contribute to the building of a magnificent structure. The shrine thus came from the grassroots, from within the people, not from episcopal edict; nor did theological experts vote on which image or saint was more appropriate for devotion. God seems to have chosen.

People pause and pray at various times in their stroll around Luján's basilica. Crowding together also seems essential, in contrast with North America, where people cherish their individual space. Being at Luján renews a sense of belonging. Nuestra Señora de Luján is not just a national shrine; it is part of many Argentines' Catholic identity.

This relationship of Argentines to their shrine was cemented by more than thirty national pilgrimages. While the shrine itself has grown over more than a century, national planned pilgrimages are a newer phenomenon. The first national pilgrimage occurred in 1954, when young Argentines were challenged by their Catholic chaplains to walk 60 kilometers from the outskirts of Buenos Aires to Luján. The trip, mostly on foot, places demands on urban young people beyond what they normally would attempt. It takes most people twenty-four hours, with little sleep, and typically demands prior conditioning. While some may have undertaken this journey to go along with their friends, the danger of failing because of lack of endurance is real, so even physically passive persons attempt to tone up beforehand. In 2004, the annual October pilgrimage drew more than a million, including many young men and women, in a nation of 40 million.

The national patron and shrine of Peru were barely known outside the country until recently. Peruvian migrants are changing that.[5] In the course of three hundred years the image of Jesus as Señor de los Milagros (Lord of Miracles) grew into part of Peruvian collective consciousness.

The image appears hanging on a cross in a shrine near the colonial center of Lima. This distinctly Catholic image was carved by an Angolan slave in the mid-1700s, and eventually the place where the image was venerated became a national center of prayer. The image is carried throughout Lima with a million participants several times in October and again on Good Friday.

In 2005, the archbishop of Lima, with Vatican approval, named the Lord of Miracles as patron of Peruvians who reside in other countries. Several million Peruvian emigrants have taken with them the yearly custom of an October procession. In more than thirty capitals or large cities from Stockholm to Washington, Peruvians process in October, carrying replicas of el Señor de los Milagros. It was no surprise then that the *New York Times* in October 2006 carried a very large photograph (without an accompanying story) of the principal procession in Lima as a major cultural event.

The relation of Mexicans to Our Lady of Guadalupe is legendary. Most non-Mexicans cannot fathom the depth of this relationship, but through books or photographs, some have tried to convey the notion of *una nación guadalupeña*. That Mexican Catholics fought under the banner of Guadalupe helped to cement this relationship.[6] There are other shrines in the country as well. In the first years of the new millennium, 16 million Mexicans, in a country of 100 million, went annually on pilgrimage to four principal shrines.

The relation of Cuban Americans to Our Lady of Charity (Nuestra Señora de Cobre) is more complex than that of Mexicans to Guadalupe. Before Castro, Cuba was perhaps the least Catholic country in Latin America in terms of church attendance, which barely registered on any scale; in the late 1950s it was about 4 percent. After fleeing the island, however, many Cuban families practiced Catholicism more fervently or professed to be Catholic, even if not *muy católico*. Religion became part of their identity, in defiance of the hated godless revolutionaries. A shrine of Nuestra Señora de Cobre was created in Miami and, for some, is the geographical center of their religious identity.

Women and Popular Religion

From the colonial period of conversion to Christianity into present times, women played a crucial part in shaping the practice of religion. Major elements of popular Christianity—the religion of the people as contrasted to institutional religion—have been fostered for centuries via early socialization at home, primarily by mothers. This maternal role intensified when three-quarters of the clergy left Latin America after independence from Spain was won in the wars between 1810 and 1825. From a ratio of some seven hundred Catholics per priest, the ratio went to several thousand per priest in rural areas. City parishes still had a decent ratio of priests to Catholic population but many large open-country areas had no priest resident in the territory.

Thus, the distribution of priests in Latin America was highly irregular. Some areas had an abundant stock of priests but other areas and countries had only a few. In part, this distribution reflected Spanish homesteading interests. Much of Cuba, Puerto Rico, Venezuela, and Central America were bypassed as having few resources to attract the first generations of Spanish settlers. The church tended to send or to allow its more talented or better-prepared clergy to choose such countries as Peru and Mexico. Less talented, less well-motivated clerics filled in the less desirable places.

In vast areas of Latin America, the few available clergy attempted to carry on minimal administration of the sacraments during annual patron saints' days. However, the sustained instruction necessary to achieve an acceptable level of religious knowledge and practice was virtually impossible. In many places, Latin America became a land without priests.[7]

In priestless areas in Latin America, mothers filled in as the main agents of religious socialization, even beyond the early childhood years. In much of nineteenth-century Latin America, religious practice was almost entirely carried on in the home by women: mothers, grandmothers, and female servants. Cuba exemplifies what occurred in many other countries, at least in the rural areas from 1830 to the mid-twentieth century. Most Cubans remained outside the reach of the Catholic Church. As noted, only a tiny fraction of Cubans attended church weekly. Many Catholics—including Fidel Castro in his childhood—went for months, sometimes years, without even seeing a priest, much less talking with one.[8]

Women used religious practices already at hand, improvised new practices, and copied from one another. For many Catholics, praying at home, whether daily or occasionally, replaced attendance at church. The rosary became the main devotion in many regions. Home altars, still in houses in the Caribbean or New Mexico, became a center within the home. Walls and tabletops supported images of Jesus, Mary, and the saints. Not all of them— St. Lazarus, for example—were recognized by the church. But this was religion as practiced by ordinary people, not as dictated by the institutional church.

Until recently, Catholics with this type of popular spirituality comprised the main type of Catholic found in most Latin American countries.[9] They learned from their earliest days that the *santos*, the holy ones, including Jesus, can be venerated at home altars, in churches or chapels, or, at special times, at local or national shrines. The visible representation of Jesus, Mary, and the saints is all-important. No wonder, then, that statues of San Cristo, Santa María, San Martín, or San José still find their place in Latin American buses and taxis, with a small Christmas-tree bulb below, acting as votive light.

Without priests and with the few churches that were served by clergy far from their homes, most Latin American Catholics never attended church regularly. By contrast, Pentecostals, Catholicism's main challenger, define their own faithful practice by church attendance. (In this respect, Pentecostalism also contrasts with major global religions for which church or temple attendance is not especially important.) For Pentecostals church attendance once a week is considered minimal; twice or more times a week is common practice.[10]

Women were the carriers of this religion nurtured at home. With minimal tolerance for rosaries and other home devotions, many men wandered from the house at prayer time at the earliest age tolerated.[11] Others, however, were imbued with faith, prayer, and at least a minimal loyalty to the church, giving them a sense of identity that thereby included Catholicism.

The thrust of this religion tended toward the miraculous, the obtaining of favors in difficult or nearly impossible economic circumstances from a powerful saint who could, if he or she wished, beg (and often obtain) divine favors. God or the saints also delivered *castigos* (punishments) when deserved. On ordinary days (assuming every day did not bring a crisis), saints were asked for commonplace blessings: rain when needed, success in exams, luck in dating, victory for one's sports team. In fact, both the truly extraordinary (instantaneous healing of cancer) and the ordinary windfalls are thought of in the same way: something that exceeds the realistic possibilities or capabilities of the devout person, because of the person's low social level or the bad economic or health conditions under which the majority of Latin Americans live.

Many studies have raised questions about popular religion. These include surveys of popular Catholicism purporting to show that the "faith" of many practitioners is somewhere between magic and religion. This assessment is also made of neo-Pentecostalism. Anthropologists regard magic as practices that imply manipulation of the sacred to control moral or cosmic forces for personal ends, without concern about one's own ethical conduct. Religion, on the other hand, looks to a supreme being with praise and honor, asks for divine aid, especially to sustain an ethical life, and hopes to bring one's life into conformity with accepted moral behavior. Many average Catholics surveyed vacillated between the two poles. Faced with this prevalent form of religiosity, the million-plus lay catechists in Latin America were believed to have a formidable task of re-education.[12]

Two great changes impinged on this form of Latin American Catholicism. First, beginning in the 1950s orthodox Catholicism received marked emphasis, especially with the great influx of foreign religious personnel to Latin America and with the simultaneous improvement in the level of education for native priests and a sector of active laity. Second, systematic religious education, which conflicted strongly with the popular religion of the home underpinned by devotion to *santos* in priestless areas, became more common.

Even more, the emphasis toward an educated and modern spirituality received a great impulse when the Latin American bishops and their theologians absorbed the spirit of Vatican Council II (1962–65) and applied it to Latin America in the watershed Medellín Conference of Latin American Bishops (1968). The bishops could not avoid focusing directly on popular religion, which they described as a religion of "vows and promises, pilgrimages, numberless devotions, based on the reception of the sacraments, especially baptism and first communion, received more for social implications than a strong influence on the living of a Christian life."[13] This popular religion appeared to be the direct opposite of a "reformed Catholicism."

The church devoted a whole document to popular religion at the Medellín Conference but the reception of the conference among Latin Americans was uneven. Progressive sectors of the church and its liberation theologians largely ignored cultural considerations, including the popular religion of the majority of Latin Americans, and thrust the church toward a life dedicated to justice and peace. In many reformed places, devotions were barely tolerated.

The *Aggiornamento* of Latin American Catholicism

If *pastoral de conjunto* was the dominant thought carried home by the bishops from Vatican II, as mentioned previously, then the church needed to furnish a theology that would guide the new policies and practices. This shift in ideology (meaning theory with implications for practice) toward universal holiness, a century in the making, appears especially in the Second Vatican Council's Constitution on the church (*Lumen Gentium*), a central document for reform that deals directly with the church. It clearly states: "Therefore, all the faithful of Christ are invited to strive for the holiness and perfection of their own proper state" (no. 42). This came as a surprise to many who believed that their main obligation was to avoid serious sin.

The spiritualities that were available to Latin American Catholics before Medellín were largely limited to three sets of spirituality: sacramental and church-going piety, a home-based popular spirituality, and a small sector with a militant spirituality. Only the latter had a strong element of social justice; the other two were mostly otherworldly.

Liberation Spirituality

Vatican II and Medellín brought forth new possibilities for millions of ordinary Catholics. As the Vatican Council was closing, the first steps toward liberation theology were being taken. Liberation theology grew from a desire to interpret the council for Latin America. It was almost immediately recognized in Africa and Asia as applying to them, *ceteris paribus*. Before long there were also Irish, Jewish, and other national liberation theologies, plus women's and black theologies of liberation. European publishers began referring to this new field of thought as contextual theology, for two reasons: "Liberation theology" became a favorite target of rightist Catholics and thus books in which that term was prominent were less likely to draw readers. More substantially, contextual theology called attention to the method of the new theology that began with describing and reflecting on the context, which made it appropriate outside of as well as inside Latin America.

Rooted in the option for the poor, liberation theology served as the ideology for thousands of priests and millions of lay people. The ideology was clear in its intent: to create the beginning of a kingdom of justice and peace in this world. To commit oneself to such an orientation demanded courage. Observers, especially ethnographic ones, believed that such a commitment and change of heart amounted to a religious conversion. Gregory Stanczak in his *Engaged Spirituality* explored ways in which spiritual experiences sustain activist involvement.[14] Jim Wallis, the editor of *Sojourners* and author of many books on evangelicals and political action, has been the North American who had made the best case for this conversion.

A major vehicle for carrying liberation theology has been Christian base communities. Over the last thirty years probably 20 to 30 million Catholics in Latin America participated for a few years in these communities, especially in Brazil and Central America. As previously noted, these Christian base communities were like living cells within the larger parish, and in terms of spirituality they served as incubation spaces for acquiring a

Base Christian communities have been an important means of lay empowerment in Latin America. Here a catechist leads a base community meeting.

sense of discipleship and for challenging and encouraging other community members. This sort of personal challenge was typically missing in the large parish church setting. While megachurches flourish in the United States and among Pentecostal Protestants in Latin America, the small community has been profoundly important for the revitalization of Latin American Catholics.

The deeply rooted convictions within the soul needed for a justice-based orientation, however, seemed to many persons, but not all, to be missing, at least in the early days of liberation theology. After some initial criticism for this deficiency, the main pioneers of liberation theology—Gutiérrez, Boff, Segundo, and Sobrino—all attempted to produce works on spirituality. Thus, they put forward contemporary versions of ancient spiritual themes: living in the desert, following Christ, living on the side of God's poor, viewing other persons as neighbor, resisting state repression as a form of martyrdom.

Liberation spirituality can be seen in the lives of some of the greatest Latin American Catholics of the twentieth century. In the minds of many, Archbishop Oscar Romero of El Salvador tops the list. There he is joined by Jean Donovan, Ita Ford, Maura Clarke, and Dorothy Kazel, also killed in El Salvador. Virtually every country had outstanding examples: Cardinal Arns,

Archbishop Câmara, and the hundreds recalled each year in the assemblies of base communities in Brazil.

What was essentially new after Vatican II was searching the Bible, as liberation theologians did, for resolute ways to live in a hostile or suffering-filled environment. Whatever renewed spirituality would be Latin American, the odds were that biblical reflection would be part of it in the latter half of the twentieth century and into the twenty-first century.

Out of these reflections, accompanying the poor and the vulnerable became a major theme in Latin American theology and praxis. Novices entering religious orders in Latin America learned that being with the poor on their life's journey was now a guiding principle for whatever pastoral work they would undertake. Many activists were sustained by a hope that they were contributing to the Kingdom. Sister Michael Mary Nolan, for example, a criminal lawyer in Brazil who attempted to bring social-cleansing killers to justice in the 1980s, worked for street kids and landless farm workers, combating a flawed justice system in which criminals who killed children she knew well went free. She summarized her spirituality as "accompanying those in need." Whether such activists were successful was, they felt, beyond their control; it was enough to live on the side of the oppressed. The theme also motivated many lay persons and was carried to other regions of the world.[15]

Indigenous Spirituality

Following the Medellín Conference in 1968, many priests and lay people in Latin America looked for alternatives to liberation theology for the basis of their spirituality. Another clear strain of influence on spirituality came from the sector of priests and lay intellectuals working on cultural identity. These culturalists were led to an intense examination of indigenous cultures and their religions. Simultaneously liberation theologians, especially of the second and third generation, were expanding to this sector. Thus culture and liberation were incorporated in the newly vitalized field of indigenous theology in the lands of the Incas and the Mayas.

Some forty million indigenous are concentrated largely in two areas: Mexico-Guatemala and Ecuador-Peru-Bolivia. Largely living on the margins of mostly racist societies, they managed to maintain key elements of their traditional religions. The Catholic Church changed its policy toward dealing with indigenous populations from paternalistic to participatory, from *indigenista* to *indígena*, from integration to diversity. *Indigenista* policies supported the mainstreaming of indigenous children in Spanish-language schools, for example, while *indígena* policies sought the teaching of native languages and of carefully prepared cultural histories.

The description and analysis of indigenous religion especially took place in academic centers described in chapter four. Out of these efforts was being born a *teología indígena* that serves as the rationale for indigenous spiritualities and inculturated sacramental practices.

Indigenous spirituality offers a vision useful for contemporary times because it is based on a cosmology that differs from Eurocentric cosmologies. Typically, indigenous worldviews present God as male and female, have room for utopia and justice, and expect care of the earth as part of religion. While reverence, awe, and beauty are transcendental concerns of this spirituality, it is also mundane and earthy.

Afro-Brazilian Spirituality

African Latin American spirituality, highly important as a spiritual anchor for this sector of the church, has received little attention. Its promotion flows from the sparsely studied *pastoral do negro* of the Brazilian Catholic Church. Of all the expansions of liberation theology to specific sectors, one of the most successful was Afro-Brazilian spirituality, a spirituality that also undergirds political action initiatives. This spirituality took form, improbably, as a part of a tiny social movement with a small chance of success.

While visitors to Latin America and the Caribbean believe, based on their observations, that there must be large numbers of blacks in the region, probably equal to the 40 million indigenous, color means little. For a recent Brazilian census, only a small percentage of respondents said they were *negro*. Ten times as many think of themselves as *pardo* (brown). While being brown and of African descent in the United States usually meant being black, it did not in Brazil.

The vast majority, more than 80 percent, of African Brazilians practice Christianity. In a national survey in 1994, 71 percent of self-identified blacks were Catholic and 10 percent Pentecostal. Despite these majority percentages, anthropologists describing the black religious experience in Brazil typically emphasize African-based religions such as Umbanda and Condomblé rather than inculturated Christian ones.

Black movements, virtually all with strong ties to religion, have taken hold in Brazil, although at the beginning this hold was precarious.[16] Many differences exist between Brazilian black movements and those of the United States, where the black movement achieved both a wide base of support among whites and basic legal changes. For one, in Brazil little seemed to be gained by identifying oneself as black in a society that encourages passing into whiteness. (This is changing, as young blacks are encouraged to enter universities *as blacks*.) The first national magazines honoring blackness only appeared in recent years. Moreover, Brazil has a very weak tradition of defending the rights of minorities. Further, many Brazilians continued to indulge themselves in the myth of racial equality. What, then, would be gained by presenting oneself as black? Hence, only 4 to 10 percent of Brazilians identify themselves as black for census purposes, while general information sources show 35 percent of the population as black. Probably some 66 million out of 190 million Brazilians in 2007 could claim African heritage.

Within the sector of persons for whom being black is a strong personal issue, the best known groups turned their backs on Christianity as the religion of the oppressor and emphasized Brazilian versions of Afro religion as a major source of their identity. These religions did not typically generate black political activism, except for freedom to practice their religion.

There are, however, both Catholic and Protestant black identity movements. The Catholic initiative was wider than those of the Pentecostals. As noted above, inculturation, the effort theologians describe as incarnating the Gospel in national culture and in subcultures, has received a major impetus since Vatican II. It was a major stated goal of the international agenda of the church and was incorporated into Latin American church documents, largely with indigenous culture in mind. Major missionary organizations and religious orders, such as the Jesuits and Dominicans, took inculturation for granted as a major task for themselves worldwide.

In fact, the drive toward inculturation was nothing new within Catholicism but was a phenomenon that now received a renewed emphasis. The process of adaptation generated by the encounter between Christianity and traditional cultures began as early as New Testament times, when the Apostle Paul released Christians from Jewish ritual obligations. It has continued ever since, sometimes successfully, as when Gregory the Great encouraged his missionaries to respect the practices of the Northern European pagans they were evangelizing, and sometimes not, as during the eighteenth-century Chinese Rites controversy, when Rome forbade Chinese converts from continuing their social rituals of ancestor veneration.

In Brazil, as in most historical cases of adaptation, the impetus for black Catholic rites came from grassroots activists—seminarians, priests, and their lay allies. They created and emphasized "the Inculturated Mass" ("Black Mass" was already appropriated by satanic sects). This hybrid of real and imagined African elements and Catholicism was presented rather rigidly as black Catholic worship. There was a strong measure of willfulness in the creators of this black liturgy: to those black Catholics who wished periods of silence at sacred moments of the Mass, the promoters of the Inculturated Mass replied that the African drums had to keep beating continuously; thus they ignored the variety of practices in African Catholicism.

The Inculturated Mass belongs to a line of modern liturgical adaptations to various cultures (probably most of them successful). The Missa Luba from the Congo was well known and loved worldwide forty years ago. Other inculturated Masses, such as the Misa Criolla, Misa Flamenca, and Misa Nicaragüense, are more recent creations and, in the case of the Misa Criolla, have gained a wide following.

History of Change

In the mid-to-late seventies, the enthusiasm shown by a large sector of Brazilian Catholics for themes of liberation theology generated an interest in black consciousness among black seminarians. Liberation as a theme debated within the church intersected with discussions of racial justice within fledgling black movements in Brazil. Seminarians and laypeople lobbied the bishops. At that time, the Brazilian bishops were debating the preparatory documents that would serve as the basis for the landmark Third Latin American Bishops Conference to take place at Puebla in early 1979. Given the late date of the black pressures before the Puebla meeting, the bishops accepted from movement advisers an appendix to the basic preparatory document from the bishops for the CELAM meeting. The black Catholic movement then went through several phases of decline and advance, typical of fledgling social movements. By 1983 *agentes de pastoral negro* (APNs) emerged. In that year, they convinced the Brazilian Bishops

Latin American Catholics have enthusiastically embraced Charismatic spirituality, and praise and singing are an important part of Charismatic worship.

Conference to make the 1988 national Lenten program that of a Brotherhood Campaign. Thus in the centennial year of the abolition of slavery in Brazil themes of racism and black identity occupied center stage in Catholic parishes.

The majority of Brazilians were ready neither for the politicized tone of the campaign nor for the challenge to the Brazilian myth of racial equality. If political visions were ignored, cultural themes had greater appeal. APNs in the Rio de Janeiro region championed a Black Pastoral with the Inculturated Mass. Despite the elaborate logistics—this Mass took two to three hours to perform and required that trained drummers, musicians, and dancers make commitments weeks in advance for long periods of their free time—performances of the Mass occurred with increasing frequency in select regions and then more extensively throughout Brazil.

Thus, in contrast to the view that modern societies would become more secular and less tolerant of prolonged religious rituals, many of the fastest growing contemporary religions or emphases within traditional religions in Latin America, not only in Brazil, devote two to four hours for services on Sundays and long sessions on weekday nights as well. The Sunday services of these groups are locally organized extravaganzas. Sound, movement, color, and large casts of participants are all ingredients for performances. Pentecostal Protestants, Catholic Charismatics, Umbandistas, and Mayan spiritual groups differ in their religious understandings but not in their promotion of worship as performance. In many Brazilian neighborhoods, every one knows somebody who has been to a performance. A person attends with hopes of being engaged, of being drawn into an *experience*. The twentieth and twenty-first centuries are the Age of Enthusiastic Religion, of personal contact with God, and of religion as performance, and are aimed at generating a strong identity. And Latin America is leading the way. Two major trends for this form of religion are Pentecostalism and its closely allied trend, Catholic Charismatic spirituality, and Latin America, both Catholic and Protestant, is in the forefront of both of them.

Catholic Charismatic Renewal and Other Spiritualities

Popular, indigenous, and Afro spiritualities are derived from long traditions, are thriving, and are clearly Latin American. Another thriving spirituality came from North American roots and is more clearly global. The Catholic Charismatic Movement is part of the Pentecostal movement, the fastest growing segment of global Christianity today. With estimates of some 73 million adherents, Latin America leads all Catholic regions of the world.[17] Sometimes called Catholic Pentecostals,[18] Charismatics appear to be the Catholic answer to its stiffest challenger in the region, Protestant Pentecostals, who number some 30–35 million members. It has struggled to gain acceptance by the organizational church while at the same time exerting a wide influence on worship styles and parish participation.

The Charismatic movement is part of a second wave of Pentecostalism, a Christian religious movement centered on the gifts of the Holy Spirit. church historians hold that Pentecostalism began with Charles Parham in Topeka, Kansas, in 1901 but typically cite the preaching of William J. Seymour at Azusa Street Baptist Church in Los Angeles from 1906 to 1913, an event known as the Azusa Street Revival, as the starting point for Pentecostalism in the United States, which initiated a stream of influence that spread to many countries.[19] Charismatics are Pentecostals within mainline Protestant churches or the Catholic Church. They differ from Classical Pentecostals and from third-wave neo-Charismatics (the latter to be found especially between the independent and indigenous churches) in ways that will be shown later.[20]

The Charismatic movement began in an Episcopal church in California and spread quickly through Methodists and Presbyterians to Catholics in a matter of a few years in the 1960s. Jack Hayford and David Moore describe what followed as part of the "Charismatic Century" and show the enduring impact of the Azusa Street Revival.[21] Almost all written histories of the Catholic Charismatic movement recount its beginning at Duquesne University in Pittsburgh in February 1967. This is misleading because a similar event occurred in 1972 at Bogotá, Colombia, with no connection to Duquesne.[22] (It is also misleading because a major figure in the United States and in initiating the movement in Latin America was Francis MacNutt, who was not drawn into the movement by ties to the Duquesne experience.) At both Bogotá and Duquesne, participants claimed to have experienced baptism in the Holy Spirit and spoke in tongues. At the time, baptism in the Spirit and speaking in tongues were considered the threshold experiences for entry into the Charismatic movement. Some have described this baptism in the Spirit as a peak experience; that is, a detachment from pedestrian concerns and a time of wonder and awe.[23]

Francis MacNutt came as an itinerant preacher to Bolivia in 1970 to light a spark that led to the beginnings of the Catholic Charismatic Renewal (CCR) in the Andean countries of South America. Another major force in starting the CCR in the west coast countries was Javier García Herreros of Colombia. Like MacNutt, García Herreros received baptism in the spirit through Protestant colleagues and not through Catholic sources. One of these colleagues in Colombia was Sam Ballesteros, of Mexican descent, from a Pentecostal Baptist church in Chula Vista, California. García Herreros's reception of the Spirit in Colombia in 1972 ignited the movement that spread through an already existing Catholic community, Minuto de Dios. García Herreros was soon joined in his efforts by another Colombian priest, Diego Jaramillo, who became probably the best-known promoter of the movement in the west coast region of South America.

These two streams of influence became more unified through the First Latin American Leadership Conference summoned by MacNutt and held in February 1973 at Bogotá, Colombia.[24] By then the movement had spread to the Dominican Republic, Mexico, Puerto Rico, and Venezuela, and those countries sent representatives. The meeting concluded with the creation of the ECCLA (Encuentro Carismático Católico Latinoamericano), a major organizing force for Latin America.

The main focuses of the Life in the Spirit retreat as practiced by MacNutt and others became conversion and physical and spiritual healing, rather than primarily speaking in tongues or other major emphases typical of classical Pentecostalism. At least at the beginning of the movement, however, speaking in tongues was considered a sine qua non sign of entry. In many ways, the directions and the emphases placed for future efforts in the Spanish-speaking countries were consolidated at the Bogotá meeting. Itinerant preachers would go on for many years to promote conversion and healing in other countries. The best-known Charismatic missionary traveled from his base in the Dominican Republic. Emiliano Tardif, a Canadian priest, went as a missionary for the movement to seventy-one countries. When he died in 1999, the president of the Dominican Republic declared a national day of mourning for the man known as the apostle of healing.

Brazilian Catholics also began to become Charismatic through the international network that grew from the United States and Canada; but the movement acquired a Brazilian imprint, was absorbed within Brazil in taking care of the great growth of "converts," and continued on a somewhat separate path from ECCLA and the Spanish-speaking countries. Beginning in 1972, two priests from the Jesuit province of New Orleans, Edward Dougherty and Harold Rahm, carried the movement to various parts of Brazil.

The Struggle for Church Acceptance

The Catholic Charismatic Renewal movement is a revitalization movement that offers a clear and popular alternative to liberationist Christian base communities (CEBs). Its numbers match or exceed those of CEBs in a number of Latin American countries. The Catholic Charismatic movement places definite demands on new candidates, in contrast to some other movements that do not have initiation criteria and tend toward inclusion rather than exclusion. At least in the early days of the Catholic Charismatic movement, one had to speak in tongues and believe in healing. Once having been taken over by the Holy Spirit, once having spoken in tongues and believed in healing through prayer, converts could advance to a higher plane of Christian life.

When first faced with these "requirements" and the unusually emotional religious ceremonies employed by the movement, bishops recoiled. Just as mainline Protestant churches before 1960 opposed speaking in tongues and Charismatic healing, the Catholic Church for some time first found these practices difficult to accept. In Latin America, leaders from the progressive wing, especially theologians and lay leaders, threw their weight against the Charismatic Renewal. Theologians and lay leaders committed to the CEBs lobbied mightily with the bishops' conferences and with influential bishops to keep the Charismatic movement at the margins of church influence.

One of the first to attack the movement was Leonardo Boff, the best-known Brazilian liberation theologian. The CCR had begun in Brazil in the early 1970s. By 1978, Boff was urging the Brazilian Bishops Conference to withhold official approval from the CCR in its present state.[25] Progressive bishops and theologians succeeded in calling attention to serious flaws in the Charismatic Renewal. In 1994, the Brazilian bishops belatedly approved a policy statement about the Charismatic movement—long after Rome, European countries, and the United States had done so. Some bishops continued to express their grave reservations about the movement after 1994.

Limited Acceptance and Wide Expansion

One of the first Latin American countries whose bishops approved the Charismatic movement was Guatemala, the country with the highest percentage (estimated 25 to 30 percent of the national population) of Pentecostals. In 1986 the bishops issued "Guidelines for Charismatic Renewal," in which they noted the fruits of the action of the Holy Spirit in terms of deepened spiritual lives of lay persons and priests.[26] They repeated the commonly expressed fears that, without close supervision on the part of authorized chaplains, Charismatic groups would easily go off the tracks into such practices as unorthodox kinds of prayers, exclusive attitudes (non-Pentecostal forms of prayer were frowned upon), and overemphasis on emotions.

Back in Brazil, the battle against CCR was being lost. Talented Brazilian priests caught the Charismatic spirit. Padre Marcelo Rossi, Padre Zeca, and others interpreted the Charismatic movement in their own dramatic ways, and Brazilians followed in droves. Bishops, too, took note that the Charismatics were fulfilling one of the episcopal conference's goals, that of having a TV channel and satellite network, Redevida.

The unexpected innovation of the Brazilian Charismatic Renewal has been priest performers, of whom none exceeds Padre Marcelo Rossi.[27] Fr. Rossi looks like an incarnation of an evangelical televangelist, only better. He has drawn two and a half million persons to a Charismatic celebration, which needed a racetrack because a soccer stadium was not large enough. "He drew as many people as the John Paul II did when he came to Brazil," a middle-of-the-road Catholic priest reported. Rossi's message is one of personal conversion in an atmosphere of joy and hope.

The CCR's solid place in Brazil was indicated by its two television enterprises, Rede Brasil Cristão (Christian Brazil Network) and Redevida (Life Network). Behind Rede Brasil, the first of the Charismatic TV efforts, lay the strong personality of Padre Eduardo Dougherty, a New Orleans Province Jesuit. He represented a generation of Catholic Charismatics before Padre Marcelo. One of the major concerns of Charismatics, especially families, was the maintenance of Christian values in an increasingly secularized society. These reinforcement efforts in television and other media were aimed at helping people to become more deeply Christian. Estimates of the amount of Charismatic programming on Redevida ran from 60 to 80 percent. The primary TV audience was the "Charismatic" type, middle-class, with no advertising for alcohol, tobacco, or other products not in line with Christian family life.

Life for many Charismatics was lived out in small communities. It was there, along with the larger parish church, that conversions were fostered, life-changing decisions supported, pneumatic gifts received, and God praised. These communities were sometimes called prayer groups, but this description is too mild for the intense religious life experienced in the communities that, for many, became extended families. Without the communities, the Charismatic Renewal would not exist. CCR, at heart, was not a Mass following of Father Marcelo or other evangelists; it was life lived out in a neighborhood, with community and parish as its pillars of participation and support for weakness amid alienating stimuli (temptations). Conversion, conceived as a lifelong process of adhering to the precepts of God with increasing love and devotion, involved daily discipline and vigilance. For Catholics, participation in the sacraments, centered in the Mass, was a principal source of strength. The community itself was seen as a space through which the Holy Spirit acts.

Erosion of Opposition and Grassroots Synthesis

For some time liberation theologians and prominent religious journals in Latin America largely ignored the Catholic Charismatic Renewal, apparently holding it as beneath the dignity of serious theological investigation. (Pentecostalism has struggled to develop a systematic theology.) A change occurred in 2000 when Clovodis Boff (Leonardo Boff's brother), a major and highly respected Brazilian theologian, wrote with appreciation of the Charismatic movement.[28] With millions of Brazilian members and still growing, the movement had not only gained numerical importance but also achieved acceptance or tolerance from the majority of bishops. This represents an erosion of the caution the Brazilian Bishops Conference expressed in 1994 when it viewed the Charismatic movement with "serious reservations."[29]

Even Leonardo Boff pictured the Charismatic Renewal becoming "a singular expression of Christianity in the Twenty-First Century."[30] Many Catholic leaders remained adamantly opposed to the Charismatic movement, however. While some, such as ecumenist Jorge Atilio Silva Iulianetta, would like to see good on both sides, another religious intellectual, Pedro Ribeiro da Oliveira, viewed the conflict as a war of titans. As a thinker favoring dialectical analysis in appositional terms, Ribeiro saw CEBs and the Charismatic Renewal as dialectical contradictions that would compete until one became dominant. He wrote in the heavyweight *Revista Eclesiástica Brasileira*: "Probably they will coexist for some time until one of them shows greater plausibility, incorporates the other, and creates a new Catholic synthesis for the Twenty-First Century."[31]

The perceived opposition between CEBs and CCR was, in fact, being reduced in practice at the grassroots, at least in some places. Margo de Theije, an anthropologist, found in her Brazilian field studies that Catholic lay participation in the two movements overlapped and participation in one group informed the other.[32] Thus, for example, CEB members who became Charismatic considered themselves "more Catholic" than they were previously. Further, membership in the Catholic Church was integral to their identity, salvation, and loyalty.

CERIS, the respected Brazilian research organization, surveyed small communities in two major regions of Brazil and found that aspects of Theije's study were replicated, showing that the celebratory style of CCR was permeating the daily practices of CEBs through its music, fervor, and spirituality. Younger members especially were drawn toward giving testimonies and prayers of praise. This influence occurred in regions even where CCR had not established communities, presumably through television, word of mouth, and other means.

From the beginnings of the movement, at the founding of ECCLA, some participants came from CEBs and activist–social justice backgrounds and found that the CCR movement supplied for them and their collaborators a strong spiritual basis that they felt had been missing in their activism. In a word, transforming society demanded a new attitude and a new mindset for the new structures of justice and equality to be effective. Personal renewal would help to bring societal renewal.

The growth of the CCR has had several effects, one of which has been a notable reinvigoration of religious practice at the grassroots. This included more personal participation, such as through testimonies given during the Liturgy of the Word, and lively musical selections. Second has been a remarkable increase in priests, seminarians, sisters, and, above all, lay people dedicated to work in church ministries, as already noted.[33] These increases cannot be only attributed to CCR, but clearly CCR and other revitalization movements have had a positive impact on the Catholic Church's workforce. Third, CCR has reinforced Catholic identity and adherence to the church. Further, Charismatics typically respond to questioners by saying not only that they are Catholics but that they are happy in the church. Fourth, a distinctive feature of the Latin American church has been the high level of confidence in the church as demonstrated in various polls over time and across different countries.[34] One could argue plausibly that satisfying spiritual needs and providing community, as CCR does, contributes to this confidence.

Despite the impressive numbers and its evident vitality, the Latin American bishops and the Vatican chose no delegate from the movement for CELAM V, although delegates were chosen from movements with far fewer numbers. Nor were the themes favored by CCR emphasized in the meeting documents. The movement is still the invisible giant.

Conservative Spiritualities

Two spiritualities that have taken hold in Latin America clearly represented the preferences and desires of conservative Catholics in the region. Both the Legionnaires of Christ (Legión de Cristo) and Opus Dei approximated total institutions, were authoritarian, but managed to appeal to sectors of the modernizing elites, especially the managerial class.

The clerical Legión de Cristo (Legionnaires of Christ) and their lay arm, the Regnum Cristi, were a Mexican creation while Opus Dei, founded in Spain by José María Escrivá, integrated laity and clergy. Father Marcial Maciel created Legión de Cristo within one of the deeply rooted Mexican Catholic traditions, that of defending the church and professing loyalty to Rome. He gradually gained support from the Vatican. The group included 650 priests, 1,000 major seminarians, 65,000 lay members, nine universities, and numerous other institutions.

The Legión recruited successfully among the upper social strata in Mexico. The sons and daughters especially of upper-level Monterrey society were eager candidates, but its influence had a long reach. The group also enjoyed the support of the world's richest man, Mexican Carlos Slim, who is not known as a regular churchgoer but lent his name and his resources to fund-raising for the Legión. In a New York City event that honored Slim, Wall Street supporters raised $700,000 for the group. The Legión also reached out to the poor through evangelization. So striking are these efforts that they merited full treatment in the *Wall Street Journal.* The group weathered the banishment by the Vatican in 2006 of its founder to the sidelines because of repeated allegations of sexual misconduct.

Opus Dei by now should be well known through documentaries and commentaries devoted to this organization during *The DaVinci Code's* brief period as reigning theme in North American and European popular culture.[35] Opus Dei has a more gradual and elegant history than the Legión. Like the latter group, this secular institute defends the faith, is loyal to the Vatican, and its lay members work in secular professions to radiate Christian influence out to the world of work or within their families. Both Legión and Opus Dei members pledge themselves to pursuing sanctity, typically through prayer, sacraments, and a disciplined life.

Communitarian Spiritualities

Both movements appeal to Latin Americans in part because of a communitarian spirituality. More moderate lay movements with a strong communitarian emphasis also grew in Latin America in the last quarter of the twentieth century. These include such global movements as Comunione e

Liberazione and Sant'Egidio and more regional movements, such as LaSalle, Don Bosco, and Dominican Family movements. The movements favored by the Holy See could be seen in the selection of delegates only from these movements to the CELAM V meeting.

Within these movements, Schoenstatt stands out as a vivid example of what is occurring in Latin America. A European-based movement with a modest and deeply loyal following in Latin America, Schoenstatt was an example of both the modernizing and the traditional appeal of the type of spirituality described here. Thousands of persons associated with Schoenstatt have been drawn to finding in Mary, the Mother of Jesus, "the force of the grace of Christ to see their life as part of the plan of God and the energy for an apostolic commitment."[36]

This spirituality was quietly effective. One of the persons who illustrated the Schoenstatt way was Chilean General Juan Emilio Cheyre. When he became head of the army in the 2000s, the Chilean armed forces were still under the influence of the former dictator, General Pinochet. The military maintained institutional silence about its part in state-sponsored oppression (1973–1990) for more than thirty years. Cheyre took two important steps in a mediating role in improving military-society relations. The first was apparently insignificant: he encouraged the annual anniversary Mass for the death of leftist General Carlos Prats and his wife, who were killed by Chilean secret agents, to be held at the National Military Academy instead of in a remote parish church. But the central mediating move in army-society relations was his public admission that the army as the main military force in the country killed and tortured illegally. After wide consultation, Cheyre apologized for the institution.

These were major steps in the consolidation of democracy in Chile—healing steps undertaken by a layperson as an expression of his spirituality, one aimed not at confronting but at mediating and unifying.

At the National Meeting of Catholic Laity in 2004,[37] Cheyre and other lay leaders spoke about faith and commitment to public service in a multicultural Chile. While expressing a longstanding assumption by many military men and women that faith in God and military service are naturally linked, he added the Latin American touch to the relationship: our "faith also in the Holy Virgin, the Captain and General of the Chilean Armed Forces under the title of the Virgin of Carmen."[38] Cheyre described the chaplains as looking out for the spiritual health of servicemen and women, their families, and the domestic service workers in their homes. Thus, the religious instinct of Latin Americans seems irrepressible, its soul still alive and able to express itself even within an institution with a very recent history of killing and torturing and of actively keeping silence about its record.

Conclusion

The Latin American spiritual scene is lively and diverse, enriching the church and society. These spiritual lives undergird what was described in the preceding chapter as *pastoral de conjunto*, lay participation and creativity in the church. Thus, both lay involvement and lay spirituality act as twin sources of revitalization of an institution that lay moribund in many areas at the middle of the twentieth century. If there is a new man or woman emerging in Latin American society, this spiritual area offers a major place to look.

CHAPTER 4

Embracing Diversity: Encounters with Non-Christian Religions

Latin America has on various occasions been described as the region of many colors. Not only do its mountains have every shade from pink to purple, but its people, too, seem to come in every hue, including shades of yellow-black of Chinese Blacks in the Caribbean that yields exotic beauty.[1]

The shock of two races meeting when Columbus and the Iberians arrived in the Americas had a much greater impact on the peoples of Latin America than did anything similar on the peoples of North America and the English Caribbean. Since some Spaniards and Portuguese were already "dark" after centuries of Moorish and African contacts, more was involved than new colorations.

The year 1492 marked an encounter of civilizations. Clearly Hernán Cortés and Francisco Pizarro knew, when they viewed Cuzco and Tenochtitlán (now Mexico City), respectively, that they were dealing with great civilizations. In North America, in contrast, explorers and colonists treated the indigenous people not as inheritors of a civilization but as inhabitants of a foreign land, and not particularly civilized inhabitants at that.

When overlooking Tenochtitlán, Spaniards viewed an orderly city sparkling with beauty and cleanliness. With a population of more than 150,000 inhabitants, this was one of the largest metropolises in the world at the time. No city like that confronted the English, Dutch, or French in North America; although they did learn about new crops and agricultural techniques from the Native Americans, these North Europeans preferred to coexist rather than understand the wisdom contained in another culture.

70

Above all, Iberians and indigenous each appreciated that something new in humanity was being created. In his influential 1925 essay *La Raza Cósmica*,[2] José Vasconcelos argued that the New World had a new race. Most Latin Americans became *mestizo*, with a culture that was no longer wholly Iberian, not an admixture but a hybrid. Even if one's family managed to maintain European bloodlines over twenty generations, a Latin American person would be living in a hybrid culture. One of the main cultural forms in Latin America, its literature, includes the literary expression of the highly developed indigenous civilizations conquered by the Spaniards. Over time, hybridity became incorporated into Latin American thought, with a rich and complex diversity of themes, forms, creative idioms, and styles. It is not surprising that magical realism or utopian thought now seem natural to many Latin Americans.

African views and cultural preferences added to the rich mix of cultures. Vasconcelos' views of the Cosmic Race needed correction through the recognition of African contributions to Latin American culture. To a considerable extent, indigenous and African influences help to explain the Latin American propensity for believing in the world of the spirit. A similar world of spirits, good, bad, and mischievous, existed in the Old World but was greatly diminished there. Why is it still alive in Latin America, informing both religion and literature? Why did middle- and upper-class Brazilians from the modernizing sector of society recently become adherents of Afro-based spirit religions? Both indigenous and African cultures and religions enjoyed a resurgence through the 1980s and 1990s.

Accepting cultural influences is not, however, the same as placing high value on being indigenous or African. Latin American society has been deeply ethnocentric and racist, and the preference for whites has diminished very little over time. Indians suffered through five centuries of discrimination. The myth of racial equality has diminished in Brazil since approximately 1988, the centennial of the abolition of slavery in that country. Heightened examination has uncovered racial discrimination at many levels of Brazilian society.

Against this background, the church was impelled to dialogue with other religions in the region, in part because Vatican II gave an impetus toward greater understanding between religions. In the late 1960s, most observers of Latin America took this to mean Protestants and a new way of relating to them: ecumenism. The other religions of Latin America, indigenous and African, had millions of practitioners, but they practiced in the shadows, on the edge of society; moreover, these religions had achieved many levels of mixing with Christianity. The amount of hybridity depended on the person and the local context. Further, neither indigenous nor Afro religions in the 1960s were consolidated movements with identifiable leaders or central spokespersons.

Thus, the dialogue with non-Christian religions has been slow and tenuous. However, church activists at the grassroots pushed for engagement of Catholicism with persons and cultures from both indigenous and African-based religions. Therein lies our story: it is the story of what the church calls inculturation, the process by which elements from other religions are incorporated into Catholicism, especially into worship and popular piety. The church needed to adapt thought and practices—Gregorian chant and the notion of God as male are only two examples—that had evolved from European roots to local cultures. Thus, to the surprise of many, indigenous and African spiritualities became part of the Latin American church. In addition to ministering to the needs of its own indigenous or African members, the church is still searching for dialogue with non-Christian indigenous and Afro–Latin American religions.

The following sections deal first with church-indigenous relations, because the indigenous were the original inhabitants and because the church has given much more attention to indigenous culture and political activism. The church's involvement with Black Africans in terms of spirituality and activism has been much more recent, both because the history of Africans in Latin America is more recent and because the African presence in most Latin American countries is less widespread than the indigenous presence.

Two distinct perspectives exist on the major non-Christian religions of Latin America, indigenous and African. In one, many social scientists and journalists hold that these religions are thriving and are active competitors with the Catholic Church, which they almost invariably describe as losing its religious hegemony in the region. The other perspective views the Catholic Church as engaging these religions and including them within Catholicism in some fashion, often with great success. Both perspectives are included here. The Latin American church pursued two goals: first, moving toward the creation of indigenous theology and, second, creating inculturated Afro worship and spirituality. The two processes are not parallel and need to be described separately.

Indigenous Theology

Liberation theology can claim two important contributions to present-day theologizing throughout the world: method and context. Both are salient here. Like the thought of the early Christian fathers, liberation theology emphasizes an inductive method: begin with a description of the world and the church within it, reflect on the situation from a biblical perspective, and act to bring the world and the church more in harmony with this biblical vision. Liberation theology also took the lead in what is today called contextual theology, which takes into account the cultural environment in order to express Christian faith in distinct languages, thought patterns, and other cultural expressions. Contextual theology is of utmost importance to many missiologists.[3]

One cannot speak of the existence of a comprehensive Latin American theology before 1964. When the father of contemporary Latin American theology, Gustavo Gutiérrez, began to formulate his theology in terms of the indigenous cultures, he turned to the thought of his compatriot José María Arguedas. Arguedas portrayed Latin American culture as *Todas las Sangres*: in sum, all racial bloods (and all life) find their union in Latin America.[4]

In the best account of indigenous movements as a transnational enterprise, Alison Brysk found that liberation theology "played a critical role in establishing indigenous movements and remains a key referent in that area."[5] Liberation theology radiated out from its academic setting to the empowerment of the indigenous people of Latin America, and missionaries were crucial to this process.

The Missionaries and Liberation Theology

The proportion of Catholic missionaries in some countries was extraordinarily high, comprising between 70 and 80 percent of all the clergy.[6] Missionaries contributed greatly to the resurgence that has taken place in the Latin American Church. Missionaries from Protestant and other churches also flooded into Latin America. In the 1960s perhaps as many as 160,000 missionaries worked in the region at one time.[7] Although the number of Catholic missionaries has declined since the early 1970s, a significant core has remained. Their prolonged presence accelerated the activism of the indigenous peoples and revealed to the church the religious vision of the

Missionaries to Latin America have helped to empower the marginalized, the poor, the indigenous peoples. Here a visiting missionary blesses an older couple.

indigenous. While Catholic missionaries were not, largely, creators of liberation theology,[8] they were among its main consumers.[9]

Some forty million indigenous are concentrated largely in two regions: Mexico-Guatemala and Ecuador-Peru-Bolivia. Living on the margins of mostly racist societies, they managed for centuries to maintain key elements of their religions. Here we examine more closely the main sectors of the indigenous populations that at the end of the twentieth century existed mainly away from urban centers, specifically a concentration of millions of Aymara- and Quechua-related populations in altiplano Peru and Bolivia. To a considerable degree, this region is an epicenter of indigenous Latin America. The developments to be described have also taken place to greater or less degree in Ecuador, Guatemala, and southern sections of Mexico, the five countries with the greatest Indian populations.

Clashes of Religious Ideology

A religious ideological war has been waged on the Andean altiplano for more than thirty years. (The word *ideology* is used here in the sense of theological vision leading to action.) The thousands of square kilometers of upland Peru and Bolivia in which the majority of the inhabitants are natives contained areas so remote that few signs of modernity were present: no graded roads, no clinics, and few tax collectors. Yet before 1970 a great influx of ideas coming from outside was taking place. Nor were the people of the altiplano passive peasants. By the 1960s, many altiplano and other rural Indian men and women lived part of their lives in towns and cities, sustaining themselves by raising crops in a rural area, which they then market in a town. Thus, they typically lived Saturday through Tuesday in one place and Wednesday through Friday in another. Many served in the military, traveled to other parts of their countries, and listened frequently to radio with news of the outside world.

Two classes of religious ideology flooded into the altiplano and clashed there, especially beginning in the early 1970s. First, Seventh-Day Adventists, Mormons, Pentecostals, and a wide range of churches, sects, and cults brought conflicting religious messages, claims of "true faith," and various promises. The Adventists especially fostered indigenous empowerment. The impact of "foreign" religions on many indigenous persons was, however, confusion and division.[10]

The second religious conflict took place within Catholicism. The presence of clergy in the remote areas of Peru and Bolivia has waxed and waned over the five hundred years of Catholicism in these countries. When the first modern missionaries reached remote Andean areas in the early 1940s, they found few priests ministering there. Missionaries mostly from North Atlantic countries began assuming responsibility for many parishes and whole dioceses in the region. As the church gained organizational strength, it multiplied jurisdictions and responsibilities. To traditional indigenous religion, missionaries counterpoised orthodox Catholicism. Where missionaries had a steady and substantial presence, their impact was often strong. Anthropologist Hans Buechler has described the changes they affected in the altiplano as "reform Catholicism."[11]

Vatican Council II (1962–65) and the Latin American Bishops' Medellín Conference (1968) led to further changes in the pastoral approach to the indigenous, this time toward modernity and away from vestiges of traditional practices. Bishops, priests, and catechists began taking harder stands against traditional practices that, in their view, had little to do with essential Christianity. At least one diocese in the heart of Aymara country, bordering on Lake Titicaca, forbade the celebration of Catholic masses within certain traditional celebrations, such as Carnival in the period before Lent. For a period of a few years, meetings to plan church strategies were often marked by strong disagreements.[12]

During this period, liberation theology became *un paradigma hegemónico*, a hegemonic paradigm, for many missionaries. Theology of liberation, as a modernizing and rational element in religious thought, was understood by many missionaries not only as looking down upon traditional practices as out of touch with a modern understanding of Scripture but also as portraying traditional practices as the continuation of the dominance of mestizo political and economic control and the subordination of native peasants. Further, leading liberation theologians in their early formulations opposed the concept of human rights, a major consideration for indigenous populations.[13] Peru's Gustavo Gutiérrez had not one reference to human rights in his major statement, *A Theology of Liberation*. His counterpart on the Atlantic Coast, Juan Luis Segundo, accused Western countries of manipulating human rights discourse to justify global maintenance of economic systems.[14]

Although liberation theology was the dominant theological paradigm, it guided only a sector of missionaries and native religious leaders. Others were aware of liberation theology but did not follow its principles closely. Instead, they were driven by another impulse, that of forming an indigenous church. This overarching policy was shared by most liberationists working in a large part of indigenous territory. As we have previously noted, the church changed its policy from an *indigenista* to *indígena*, from paternalist to accompanist.[15]

Thus, the main thrust of missionaries and other religious personnel working among the very large indigenous populations of Peru and Bolivia was the creation of an indigenous church. This represented a major change of emphasis: instead of working to incorporate the indigenous within a unified culture, the church turned to provide the basis for other than Eurocentric cultural expressions of Christianity. In attempting this, missionaries and others found the basis for an indigenous theology.

Further, those involved in the monumental task of creating an indigenous church were deeply concerned about the lack of what they called "religious knowledge." Left without benefit of clergy for decades, many indigenous peoples did not have an orthodox understanding of Christianity. Questions increasingly arose about whether native communities (and many other Latin Americans) had ever been properly instructed in fundamental aspects of Catholicism.[16] Out of this discussion came the conviction of the need of a New Evangelization. This became the policy emphasis of John Paul II and the Latin American bishops at their Santo Domingo General Conference (1992).[17]

Long before the Santo Domingo meeting, those interested in establishing an indigenous church had focused on training native teachers, catechists, to begin this epic task. Thousands of catechists were educated in myriad centers. To extend geographically the efforts of the catechists, to reinforce their teaching, and to increase such survival skills as improved farming methods and health precautions, Catholic and Protestants alike employed citizens' media, especially low-range radio stations and radio schools, described below.[18]

At root, the policy shift to an indigenous church meant, first, promoting native languages for worship and instruction. It also meant supporting political self-determination, equipping communities for contact with outsiders, recovering cultural memory, and stimulating alliances. All these objectives had implications for political involvement.

Intellectual Resources for Indigenous Peoples

Indigenous religion was truly in crisis, in danger of being overwhelmed by the avalanche of foreign religious imports and torn by internal divisions among Catholics. Despite the remoteness of the altiplano, the indigenous peoples had experienced other invasions and internal divisions. The invasions of Inca rulers and then of the Spanish were only two of these incursions. What distinguishes this period from others in which Indians were assaulted by outside influences and what consolidated the Catholic Church's presence in indigenous areas were, in the author's view, intellectual centers placed throughout or near the altiplano in the larger Andean region. In a word, indigenous religion was given the intellectual, theological resources it needed to articulate itself under assault from other religious thought systems.

These centers grew from the conviction that each culture has its own integrity. This culture must be known and respected by missionaries. The centers grew up especially in the Andean region of South America and in Guatemala in Central America. There bishops and missionaries hoped to form native religious leaders for an indigenous church.

Thus much more was at stake than finding indigenous translators of contemporary theology. Indeed, some missionaries and even more bishops had neither the personal inclination nor the time to absorb theology. Rather there was a confluence of interests in an overriding goal: the formation of an indigenous church. Lacking a native clergy, at least this church could have catechists. Therefore, in important ways, these centers became something similar to indigenous seminaries. There or in smaller centers closer to home, catechists could receive training especially in biblical understanding.[19]

For at least fifty years in the Andean region the ideal has been growing of having a native catechist in each rural settlement area. ("Village" implies more organization than the Andes people typically can muster.) Under the impact of missionary presence, religious life has changed in many areas of the Andean region. The hegemonic hold of fiesta sponsorship (see Chapter 7) has diminished to a considerable degree; in some areas, it is gone entirely.

Both progressives and conservatives among Catholics have promoted access to the Bible. In some important places, the number of Spanish or native-language Bibles sold to Catholics continues to be high. Reflection on the Bible takes place at Sunday liturgies or, more commonly, in weeknight meetings of small communities. Catechists, *presidentes de la comunidad*, or leaders of the Word of God facilitate the meetings, but everyone in attendance is expected to offer their interpretation of the Bible passages.

These communities are by no means all Base Christian Communities promoted by enthusiastic followers of liberation theology. Nevertheless, for the sake of argument, let us presume the case of small community where the catechist and members have picked up ideas from liberation theology. Many observers would concur with Barry J. Lyons that "exposure to the Bible and the exposure of liberation-theology-oriented pastoral agents in interpreting it certainly contributed to indigenous Catholics' political consciousness in the late 1980s and early 1990s."[20]

Whether or not small community leaders are liberationists, however, the indigenous interpret the Bible in more complex ways than does liberation theology. Their biblical reflections are more than folk liberation; the indigenous churches have cosmologies that guide them to interpretations that are distinct from liberation theology. (It has become commonplace to note that within global Christianity, Christians of the South are reading the Bible with fresh eyes.) Thus is being born a theology of inculturation and, sooner or later, indigenous theology.[21]

Remarkable centers grew from missionary efforts in the region and within the revitalized Catholic universities in Peru and Bolivia where missionary anthropologists centered their activities. Seven well-placed centers anchored a theological and pastoral indigenous revitalization. Five began as free-standing centers near Puno, Cuzco, and Sicuani, in Peru, and La Paz and Oruro, in Bolivia.[22] Two others were not so much centers as well-defined emphases at the Catholic University in Lima, headed by Marcel Marzal, and at the Bolivian Catholic University's theological campus in Cochabamba, with Hans van den Berg, Luis Jolicoeur, Juan Gorski, and Frank McGurn.

The major figures staffing these centers were principally missionaries. Many had advanced graduate training in anthropology or religious studies. A large part of their own and the centers' financial support came from their overseas congregations or foreign-mission collections. All made masterful efforts to include indigenous members as part of their team, anticipating the day when the centers would be conducted fully by native talent. Members of these centers have been extraordinarily productive.[23] The academic nature of their work and their influence on a wider world can be seen in the long lists of their works that are routinely collected at the libraries of Harvard University and the University of California at Berkeley and the Library of Congress.

The centers conducted anthropological and historical research and engaged in theological reflection. To a greater or lesser extent, members absorbed the method of liberation theology, taking seriously the first step of liberation theology: to describe the universe in which the indigenous people lived. To do this, members of the centers had to listen to the natives describe religion as they experienced it. The second step of liberation theology is biblical reflection. Researchers and indigenous peoples spent thousands of hours in discussing the Andean or biblical understanding of native religious practices. Individual researchers have spent ten to thirty-five years in this process. The director of the Andean Pastoral Center, María José Caram, OP, described the effort of the noted Southern Andean Church as cultivating "a spirit of contemplation and listening" and trying to put aside paternalistic and materialistic attitudes.[24] This Peruvian emphasis contrasted with the more activist promotion goals of the La Paz and Oruro centers.

The major figures differed considerably in how they came into this enterprise. As a theological student in Chile, Diego Irarrázaval internalized an earlier, leftist version of liberation theology. A member of the executive committee of Christians for Socialism in Chile,[25] Irarrázaval was forced to leave Chile in the 1970s and thereafter dedicated his life to working among the Andean Indians. Given his theological acuity and writing talents honed at the University of Chicago, Irarrázaval became an anchor for the Institute of Aymara Studies at Chucuito, near Puno, Peru.

Irarrázaval had seen at first hand and early in his life (he was a deacon and not yet ordained priest when he left Chile) how leftist Catholics had failed. He recognized, for example, that the movement of Christians for Socialism did not sufficiently acknowledge the extent to which it generated divisions within the church. In Peru, where he worked as a missionary, Irarrázaval emphasized listening rather than organizing and built up an impressive body of work on indigenous religion based on what he observed.[26]

Irarrázaval never lost his enthusiasm for liberation theology. It was the driving force that led him to the poorest of Latin America. "Here [among the indigenous] liberation theology has borne its fruit: believing communities and men and women missionaries who are fully committed to the cause of the continent's poor."[27] By the 1980s, he began seeing indigenous religion as inculturated liberation: communities finding salvation from evil and sin and confronting local customs that cause self-destruction. He also saw this as the church of the poor becoming missionary itself, including sending priests and lay people to other countries.[28] For him, all this was a way of reworking the preferential option for the poor.[29]

On the Bolivian side of the Andes, Xavier Albó has become what one longtime observer has called a "twentieth-century reincarnation of Bartolomé de las Casas," "a one-man publishing industry," and "the country's most intellectual activist in the area of indigenous issues." [30] As a Jesuit, Albó's journey differed somewhat from that of Irarrázaval. Jesuits in Latin America responded to the Society of Jesus' goal in the late 1960s to establish social study and action centers in each Latin American country. To prepare himself for establishing or working with an indigenous center, Albó, a Catalan priest, obtained a PhD in anthropology and social linguistics at Cornell University. For the most part, he eschewed working with other professionals, choosing instead to mentor talented native activists and intelligentsia. In sum, he began with a people and discovered a theology that would encourage their empowerment.

After his contacts among indigenous communities where he had done doctoral research, Albó began gathering around him native speakers and investigators to form CIPCA (Centro de Investigación y Promoción del

Campesinado—Center for Investigation and Promotion of Peasants). This activist think tank nurtured the Katarists, a core group of Amara intellectuals. In turn, the Katarists spawned a family of parties and movements. When possible, Albó submerged his talents, hoping that others would take leadership positions. The CIPCA group included Víctor Hugo Cárdenas, who became a major figure in Bolivian politics. Cárdenas translated and familiarized himself with North American and European anthropologists and historians who wrote about the Andean region. This gave him the capacity to make a more profound critique of Eurocentric development paradigms that predicted the disappearance of indigenous from modern society.[31]

Simultaneously with these efforts in or near La Paz, Oblate priests from French Canada established INDICEP (Instituto de Desarrollo, Investigación y Educación Popular Campesino) in the mining center of Oruro. CIPCA and INDICEP strongly nurtured and supported the Katarists. With the Oblate priest Gregorio Iriarte as adviser, the Katarists appeared dramatically on the public stage at Tihuanaco, the premier indigenous site in Bolivia, with a carefully crafted statement called the Tihuanaco Manifesto. Cultural assimilation and education in the Spanish language were all condemned. Because of the military dictatorship in power when the manifesto was "announced" in the Latin American fashion, the national media gave little attention. With the help of the progressive church and some clandestine groups, the manifesto received serious attention at the grassroots.

The manifesto appeared in 1973. A few years later, with state authoritarian controls decreasing, Albó helped young Aymara leaders found the Tupac Katari Center that fostered an enlarged Katarista movement. Within a relatively brief time, the movement took over most of the government-sponsored peasant unions and organized its own union. Aymaras asserted themselves with a degree of political sophistication and independence not seen since colonial times. They also broadened the labor movement to bring together urban and mineworkers with rural workers. They had a much larger target than labor rights, however; they took aim at the state, presenting their demands about unequal treatment from the state for agricultural prices, credit, education, and health. They proposed a series of revindications about the nature of ethnicity and the basic racial definitions of national society. The Katarists helped move what had been in Bolivia a cultural awareness movement to one with political goals.

81

Missionaries in other countries also acted as midwives for indigenous identity. Ecuador furnishes the strongest example of churches fostering indigenous movements. This is a great surprise since forty years ago Ecuador seemed to be the last place whose natives would move away from their stance of quiescence. Nonetheless, Ecuador proved to be the nation where the indigenous people most forcefully confronted governments and their policies. Italian Salesians in the country helped establish a noteworthy publication center, the Abya-Yala Center, with Juan Bottasso its best-known collaborator.

Catholic and Protestant missions in the Bolivian and Ecuadoran Amazon gave external support to the foundation of indigenous Amazonian associations, helping to bridge differences among indigenous groups, teaching literacy, providing radio and air transport services, and helping to organize against land seizures. Catholic and Protestant churches with strong missionary histories also formed pivotal networks in Chiapas, Mexico.

Emerging Theology of Inculturation

Missionaries were strategically placed to have a major hand in shaping a theology of inculturation. They sought out remote areas where 90 percent of indigenous people live. Missionary groups remained there long enough to hear and understand native languages and conceptions of God and Jesus, death and resurrection. Missionaries had intellectual and economic resources for drawing in teams of experts and for organizing activities. Further, as foreigners they were acutely aware of the need for cultural adaptation, whereas national clergy frequently did not conceive of the indigenous as "the other," a concept central in dealing with cultural change. Finally, foreign missionary orders and congregations involved in establishing the centers under question have a long tradition of attempting to be sensitive to local culture.

Under the hand of missionaries, liberation theology began to take a decided turn. In a sense, missionaries and indigenous spokespersons forced theologians of liberation to reconsider traditional forms of thought as expressing the face of God in imperfect but important ways.[32] Traditional indigenous religions were seen as having strongly positive as well as negative qualities.[33] On the part of the indigenous, liberation theology had to be extended to include cultural liberation,[34] a major element missing from early formulations of liberation theology.[35]

Three larger aspects of liberation thus emerged in missionary/indigenous discussions of liberation. First, development of all forms of life to their full potential is liberating. Second, liberation would strengthen community solidarity, not weaken it, as Christian churches have done by bringing division to communities. Third, in the case of the Aymara people, liberation would mean liberation of the Aymara nation. For his part in this enterprise, Gustavo Gutiérrez spent many years writing his longest work on Las Casas and the defense of indigenous interests.[36]

Out of these efforts has been born a theology of inculturation that promoted notions of the dignity of all persons, the worth of native cultures, a political role for all in society, and justification for presenting one's interest in the political arena. Theology of inculturation is not a theology of culture that in the developed world would focus narrowly on values, Christian or secular; rather, it is "the thought of the church in our peoples."[37]

This thought can be found embedded in indigenous spirituality, which is only now emerging into view for a larger world. It offers a vision useful for many persons beyond Latin America because it is based on a cosmology that presents God as male and female, has room for utopia and justice, and expects care of the earth as part of religion. Reverence, awe, and beauty are transcendental concerns of this theology. This is also a mundane, earthy spirituality[38] that typically includes care of the earth. Further consideration will be given indigenous spirituality under the treatment of "green theology."

African-Based Religions

Among the major challengers to the Catholic Church, African-based religion has expanded in new and important ways. Not only has the religion attracted larger numbers of black followers, but the religion has drawn in notable numbers of white practitioners. It has gained much more open acceptance in Brazilian society than it enjoyed for centuries. African-Brazilian religion has also spilled across the borders to cosmopolitan Buenos Aires and Montevideo. African-based religions also prosper in the larger Caribbean region. The church made great progress in meeting this challenge by actively engaging African religions, incorporating elements of these religions into worship and spirituality, and fostering black identity and activism toward racial justice.

Two areas of greatest concentration, hubs from which these religions radiate, are Brazil and Haiti. The African-based religions of these countries bring with them a host of questions for Catholics and Protestants alike.[39] How serious is the challenge, particularly with regard to Brazil, the major player in this challenge? Probably 20 percent of the population practice one or another of the African religions found all over the country. If they practiced African religion on a regular basis, they would equal or exceed the number of Catholics who attend church weekly. The challenge is even greater in Haiti, where 90 percent of the population is mostly black, the main form of African religion, Voodoo, is firmly entrenched, and the church has fewer resources to deal with challenges. Given the weakness of the Haitian church and the almost collapsed state of government, Haiti is treated here as an exception in the generalized pastoral effort of the church.

These African challengers are long-standing ones for the Catholic Church. Brazil has had African religion for as long as Brazil and other countries have had slaves—that is, since the early 1700s. Since this religion had to be practiced in some secrecy in the shadows of *la casa grande* (the plantation master's house), the religion took on different forms within Brazil and thus became a variant of African religion; but Brazilians, with their celebrated capacity for creating cultural forms, including religious ones, have invented new forms, notably Kardecism (spiritism), that Africans would barely recognize. And in privileged sections of Rio and São Paulo, Afro religion, once solidly rooted in the need to touch earth, now has a new face, as worship leaders lead their congregations from airy lofts in uptown condominiums.[40]

In the 1980s, the practice of African-based religions spread in Brazilian cities and the countryside, removing barriers of race and class. Some middle-class white Brazilians enthusiastically spent a sizable part of their income practicing one or another (expensive) form of African religion—a religion that used to be hidden from public view and limited to lower-class Brazilians—in plain view of their neighbors. However, urban and affluent Brazilians are not alone in discovering the attractions of African religions. African-based religions spread noisily to neighboring Argentina and Uruguay, primarily to two of the most modern cities in Latin America, Buenos Aires and Montevideo. No one predicted that this would happen.[41]

Within Brazil, as noted, some 20 percent of the populace practices Afro-based religions. The 2000 Brazilian census showed less than four million practitioners, but several million more practice from time to time. No one knows with precision their number.[42] Until recently the practice of African-Brazilian religion tended to be veiled, so that judging the magnitude of its practice was more difficult than was the case with established religions. Social scientists had to walk around and count *terreiros* (temples) in crowded neighborhoods or go to authorities and look at registers, probably missing some religious centers in the process. If one uses the example of Salvador da Bahía, one of the larger cities of Brazil and said to be the soul of the country,[43] in the 1930s, 67 houses of worship were entered in the registry at the Union of Afro-Brazilian Sects. In 1968, Vivaldo Costa Lima reported 768 houses. In 1972 ethnomusicologist Gerard Béhague found more than 900 houses officially registered with the city police department. Estimates for 1989 run to more than 2,500 centers.[44] Other indicators exist of greater numbers and of greater institutionalization and sophistication.[45] Rather than perpetuating the myth that Brazilians are Catholic, Thomas Bruneau and others studying "Catholic" Brazil have long suggested that for every practicing Catholic there is an equal or larger number of non-Catholics practicing African or Protestant religion.

Such a view, however, overlooks the practice of many Latin Americans who dip into other religions and at various times in their lives go to Catholic Mass, Umbanda ceremonies, or Pentecostal services. The boundaries between religions are certainly not well fixed at the level of everyday practice, for either the poor or the rich. Hybridity has long been a feature of Latin America's religious practice. At the beginning of the twenty-first century, it is much more open to view.

Africa in Latin America

African religions came to Latin America when slaves were imported from various regions of Africa. These diverse geographical roots help in part to explain the diversity of religions in Brazil, but cultural origins do not explain the changes in African-based religions that have taken place in that country or the hold of these religions over the lives of many Brazilians today. Without appreciation of the background of these religions, many present-day controversies about African religions would be unintelligible. For example, how could Bonaventura Kloppenburg (until his death an influential bishop in Brazil), as a young Franciscan friar and social scientist, describe these religions as pagan, fetishistic, based on superstition, and encouraging of generally loose and permissive sexual attitudes? For him the African religious heritage turned religion into mere superstition.[46]

Philip Curtin estimates that about half of the New World's slave trade went to South America, and about three-quarters of that number, about 3.65 million persons, arrived in Brazil. Joachim Piepke's estimates of 15 to 18 million African Brazilians presumably refers to the number of black slaves in Brazil in 1888, when slavery ended.[47]

Africans going to Brazil came from slavery or freedom[48] within two large culturally distinct groups: the Sudanese from West Africa and the Bantu, a cultural range from Cameroon to Mozambique. While blacks from various areas of Africa spread all over Brazil through internal migration, until thirty years ago they were especially found in the north and northeast. Further south, such as in the state of São Paulo, they comprised 10 percent of the population.

African Minorities and Spiritualities

The overall black population of Latin America and the Caribbean is estimated at about 5 percent of the total population, with very large numbers counting themselves as mulatto. Contrary to practice in the United States, in Latin America one drop of African blood does not constitute being black; nor do mulattos see themselves as black. So, most Latin American baseball players of color are surprised to find themselves treated in American society as black.

By far the largest segment of African Latin Americans lives in Brazil. The second largest segment resides in the Caribbean, but virtually all countries have some blacks within their population. The following section focuses on Brazil, where the church has been actively involved in promoting racial identity and efforts to reduce discrimination in the country. Aside from Haiti, smaller numbers of black citizens reside in countries other than Brazil. These groups, too, are becoming active in pursuing their identity and in reducing the effects of the pervasive Latin American racism that Carlos Aguirre, writing about Peru, calls the "wound that never stops bleeding."[49] Noteworthy efforts by the church to assist these minorities have been made along lines similar to those in Brazil. This is true even in Mexico, where Mexicans of Black African descent received little attention by Mexican politicians or social scientists.

African-Catholic Political Activism

APNs moved from the issue of preparation of blacks for advance to leadership positions in the church[50] to the external issue of equality for blacks in higher education. They began by increasing the blacks' chances of being accepted in public universities through the crucial college entrance exams. The preparation for these exams, commonly called *pré-vestibular*, was carried on for blacks by seventy groups in Brazil that trained some 3,300 high school graduates. From 5 percent of African-Brazilians at public universities in the 1980s the percentage grew to at least 20 percent in 2000.

The next step in the political process was the successful lobbying, in 2003, for the reservation of 40 percent of all places at public universities for *pardos e negros*. At the very least, a further step toward destigmatizing African ancestry had been taken. The process affected young *negros* and *pardos/morenos* who began to feel pride in both African and Portuguese blood.

Brazilian Catholics reaped a harvest for their *pastoral negro* efforts. They produced theologians such as Father Toninho A. da Silva, organized intellectual and cultural institutes such as Instituto do Negro Padre Batista in São Paulo, initiated websites such as www.pastoralafro.org, and intensified loyalty to the church.

Expansion of African-Catholic Efforts

In countries beyond Brazil, small but notable efforts were made at first largely by individual priests and not by the institutional church to promote African identity. Largely unnoticed centers began operating.[51] The Italian Comboni congregation's Centro Cultural Afroecuatoriano opened at Quito in the early 1980s. By 2007, the center had grown into a vital enterprise with a strong publishing arm. Other African-Catholic cultural centers opened in Colombia and Mexico. In 2003, the Latin American Bishops Conference organized its first secretariat dedicated to the African–Latin American pastoral effort. Grassroots efforts in the region supported the first Encuentro

Continental de Pastoral Afro in 2007 and were sponsored by the Latin American bishops at Quito.

The vitality of these efforts at the grassroots resulted in the founding of two small seminaries that prepared young persons to be missionaries from Latin America to Africa. Thus, the flowering of the indigenous and black ministries not only contributed to a Latin American soul of many colors but also led to a newly found missionary spirit, to be described more fully in the last chapter.

CHAPTER 5

Emphasizing the Poor and Vulnerable

A long with *pastoral de conjunto* (communion in mission), the option for the poor was the policy of the Latin American church that most changed the direction in which the church was to advance after the Medellín conference (1968). Here the church developed its policy on the lines firmly established by the council fathers of Vatican II, especially as set out in *Gaudium et Spes*. The Pastoral Constitution on the church in the Modern World, as this document's official title implies, sets the Catholic Church squarely within the situations and issues that confront the contemporary world. The chapter on "The Church and the World as Mutually Related" (nos. 63–72) intentionally builds upon the tradition established by the great social encyclicals of the past, going so far as to offer pointed criticism of those who, "in underdeveloped areas, ... gravely endanger the public good ... [by depriving] their community of the material and spiritual aid it needs."[1]

Option for the Poor and the Global Church

Vatican II and Medellín forged a new view of poverty as an evil to be eliminated that replaced the view of the poor as an object of charity. By the turn of the millennium, the concept of "option for the poor" had attained a firm place in the church's documents and discourse.

The bishops of the United States made the most complete use of the term in their pastoral letter *Economic Justice for All* (1986). Joseph Curran, in his dissertation on the document,[2] argues that the bishops used all the modes of moral discourse delineated by James Gustafson: prophetic, narrative, ethical, and policy. Curran believes that only such a wide view shows the full depth of meaning of the term under discussion. The preferential option was meant to guide personal decisions, such as choices about giving alms, as well as policies of governments.

Economic Justice for All and its use of option for the poor provoked severe criticism from some quarters. William E. Murnion, a respected author with a doctorate from the Gregorian University in Rome, writing in the *Journal of Business Ethics*, found that the underlying social justice principle in the pastoral was "actually socialist, indeed communist in nature." The intemperate reactions died down as the focal point of the debate shifted to a more global outlook than that supplied by some Catholic philosophers and neoconservatives in the United States. As noted, the confluence of biblical scholarship and social teaching also bolstered the acceptance of the concept.

Option for the poor entered into the wider social teaching of the church, especially through the writings of Pope John Paul II, who incorporated the documents of the Latin American Bishops' Medellín and Puebla conferences, and thus option for the poor, into the body of the church's teaching. This was ignored by some conservatives, although at times the Pope was explicit; in his major address *Ecclesia in Asia* (2001), n. 34, he was clear about this option. Citing Matthew 25:40 as a reference, he stated, "In seeking to promote human dignity, the church shows a preferential love of the poor and voiceless, because the Lord has identified himself with them in a special way."

Biblical scholars, for the most part, had no problems in finding evidence of God's special concern for the poor in both the Old and New Testaments. Indeed, a central message of the Old and the New Testaments is that God has a special concern for the poor and expects all persons to do likewise. There were two problems about understanding this in the social teaching and its implication for public policy: biblical scholarship was being developed in the Catholic (and Protestant) traditions on a separate track from the social doctrine and the social gospel. Not until the 1990s would these streams begin to converge.

With the passage of time, option for the poor found a central place in Catholic social teaching. Father Albino Berrera and other scholars describe option for the poor as a major building block of the church's social teaching.[3] The Augustinian Friars called the option the fourth principle of Catholic social teaching on the obligation of Christians in today's society: "We are called to emulate God by showing a special preference for those who are poor and weak."[4]

Option for the poor now permeates Catholic Church recommendations for public policy. The phrase is in the policy declarations and statements of priorities of both the national bishops' conference of the United States and various state conferences of Catholic bishops. It is also in documents of individual ecclesiastical jurisdictions, such as the archdiocese of San Francisco. Usage in the United States and, in general, in English-language documents tends toward such phrases as "the poor and the vulnerable" or "the poor and the weak" as translations of *pobre* since the Spanish word, especially when used in a biblical context, has a wider meaning than a person who is penniless.

Unknown to most U.S. Catholics, a vibrant advocacy for the poor by their church is being carried out at the state level.[5] Imperceptibly both policy issues and federal money have moved to the state government level, where debate about issues—abortion, same-sex marriage, stem-cell research—and about dispersal of funds for welfare, health, and education programs have increasingly taken place. In states where the Catholic Church has more than a token presence the bishops maintain lobbyists as representatives of state Catholic conferences.[6] The fuller extension of this discourse could be seen in Britain, where Cardinal Cormac Murphy O'Connor highlighted the need to help women "who are poor, vulnerable, and open to exploitation" as a major challenge to the church today.[7]

Latin America

The Medellín Conference and its pronouncements shook the ground upon which people and institutions had been built. As earthquakes do not affect all equally—some are on bedrock, others on gravel—so Medellín especially affected those already disposed to reform. Religious reform was already under way in Brazilian and Chilean sectors before Vatican II and Medellín. Concern for the perceptions of the wealth of the church or concern for the poor had intensified in some regions in the 1940s and 1950s. Such visionary figures as Juan Landázari Ricketts, archbishop of Lima, took the lead in insisting at mid-twentieth century that private Catholic schools (among the best in Lima) also conduct sister institutions in poor neighborhoods. In La Paz, the archbishop instituted a policy of granting free tuition to at least ten percent of the student body in Catholic schools. Bishops and religious orders in countries like Peru and Bolivia quietly divested themselves of the remnants of land holdings and servant-workers from their Iberian past when land grants supported the church.

After World War II, missionaries, especially from richer countries such as the United States, Canada, and northern Europe, who were drawn or assigned to areas with mostly poor people, reinforced these Latin American initiatives. They came with egalitarian values and with questions raised by their missionary mentors about serving the rich.

Alignment with the Rich?

Despite the extent of the church's work among the poor, the humble parish priests and others involved in this service were mostly out of the constricted view of historians who usually focused on the ruling elites: hence the prevailing notion that the church was aligned with the rich. This perspective became most common after independence, when the church lost most of its economic support from the state and depended increasingly on private benefactors. Further, most of its clergy who had been supported by European church bodies went into exile.[8] Between 1830 and 1950 the hospitals, schools, and other institutions of the church largely depended on the patronage of the rich and middle classes. A notable positive turn for the church occurred after World War II when a large influx of missionaries and foreign aid resources brought renewed strength and enabled new initiatives for the poor.

Indeed, the renewed care for the poor necessitated a major reorientation in the focus of religious orders and institutions—first in South America and the Dominican Republic and later in Central America, especially in Guatemala—as they discussed the fate of schools, hospitals, and other institutions run primarily for the middle and upper classes by religious orders or missionary diocesan priests. The affluent classes could pay fees for school tuition or hospital care. Perhaps 10 to 20 percent of poor students or patients received free tuition or health care in their institutions, but many institutions catered primarily to the privileged.

Having read and discussed statements that emerged from the Medellín Conference, religious communities were faced with decisions about the thrust of their educational outreach. Famous Latin American high schools closed down, the best known being the Colegio Dominicano in the Dominican Republic. This *colegio* (high school) for women, run by highly

The option for the poor often entailed a shift in educational focus from elite schools to teaching the poor. Here children line up for class at a mission church.

competent sisters from Adrian, Michigan, educated the "cream of Dominican society" in Santo Domingo, the capital of the Dominican Republic. After the school closed, the sisters, who included upper-class *dominicanas* among their number, devoted themselves to working among the poor, side by side with socially active Jesuits, in evangelization and adult education in some of the poorest sections of the capital.

In another treasured school for the middle-class and privileged, that of the Maryknoll Sisters in Guatemala City, teachers such as Sr. Miriam Peter, later Marjorie Melville of the activist Catonsville Nine, had attempted to raise the consciousness of students. School administrators, however, chose a more drastic choice, closing the school so that teachers could work directly with the poor. The Sisters of Loretto from the United States also elected to close their first-class school in La Paz, Bolivia, to devote themselves to work among the poor. Lay faculty from the school continued a similar but reduced establishment in an exclusive neighborhood.

Most elite Catholic schools continued in operation with a new or renewed emphasis on social justice education, missionary work during vacations, and volunteer work during the school year. One of the persons who led the transformation of his institution was Gerald Whelan, a Midwestern

Holy Cross missionary, who helped reorient St. George's College, one of the three best prep schools in Santiago, Chile. Whelan has been hailed as a hero for his emphasis on social justice and his opposition to military rule. Although he died prematurely from cancer, his spirit was captured in the popular Chilean film, *Macuca*.[9]

In Córdoba, Argentina's second largest city, the rector of the Catholic University, Miguel Petty, SJ, incorporated a missionary spirit into the university by recruiting students for summer evangelization projects among isolated peoples of Patagonia.[10] The Patagonian project was one of many projects to inject concern for the poor into mostly middle- and upper-class university students.

The volunteer spirit that North Americans take for granted—half the high school students in some states have community service as part of their school program—had been missing in much of Latin America. The option for the poor furnished a new focal point for fostering volunteer community service among students. The community service work was designed not only to aid the poor through activities such as tutoring but also to afford opportunities for the privileged to see for themselves the living conditions of less fortunate persons and to listen to their aspirations and the obstacles that stood in their way.

The option for the poor began changing the composition of religious orders as well. The Jesuits were the best-known religious congregation in most of Latin America, except Brazil, where Franciscans were more numerous and more influential as bishops. In 1975, when I asked an employee at a Jesuit institution what background the Jesuits came from, he replied, "Vienen de la clase pudiente" ("They come from the influential elite class"). When I asked the same question in 1990, I was told that Jesuits came from all classes, including the poor.

Changes were made in the service focus of religious orders of brothers, priests, and sisters, including the Jesuits. Members of religious orders number about 175,000 men and women and serve in schools, hospitals, and parishes. Religious sisters especially work in Latin American barrios and favelas. Their spirituality has been characterized by their major coordinating group, Conferencia Latinoamericana de Religiosos (CLAR)—the Latin American Conference of Religious Men and Women—as "accompanying the poor and vulnerable on their journey."

Poverty and Think Tanks

What was equally needed, besides a tilt toward the poor, were good data about the condition of the poor, analysis of the reasons for their condition, and a public voice for their advocacy. Option for the poor and the more general goal of social justice led to two institutionalized responses within the church. The first was an innovation, a Latin American Catholic variation on a think tank. Such institutes grew up to furnish a vision for renewal of the church and society. These organizations usually were run by religious orders and were created in Latin America as well as in Asia and Africa. They included three basic functions: research, theological reflection, and adult education. The research included both socioeconomic and socioreligious research. In Latin America, Jesuits created centers often called CIAS, *Centro de Investigación y Acción Social.* They instituted one in each country, unless a similar center already existed, in which case Jesuit experts joined in a cooperative effort with others. Following the lead of the French Dominican Louis Joseph Lebret, Dominicans in Argentina, Uruguay, and Bolivia founded centers based on economics and humanism. Both Jesuit and Dominican centers operated as development centers, collecting data and doing investigations; training teachers, cooperative and credit-union officials, and persons collectively known as "change agents." Many change agents became organizers within movements, some of which coalesced and grew in the twenty-first century, such as the impressive movements for the landless or for educational equality for those of African descent. Typically, the centers also had theologians on staff or as consultants. The centers were modern-day carriers of the social teaching of the church.

Two of the best-known development centers, CIDE (Center for Investigation and Development in Education) in Santiago and CEE (Center for Educational Studies) in Mexico City, centered their activities on investigating and improving education, especially of the lower classes of their countries. They operated with notable foreign aid from a variety of sources, including the Ford Foundation, USAID, and European church aid agencies.

Accurate knowledge about the world of the majority poor was lacking because at that time governments largely functioned for the benefit of the economic elites; they certainly were lukewarm or inept in collecting data about the marginalized. The development institutes thus provided data that governments in the developed world routinely collected, such as data on wages; educational access, success and failure in schools; epidemiology and provision of health care. This was but the first step. Theological and philosophical reflection was needed to respond to the question "So what if many are excluded from this or that?"

The godfather of these institutes and one that best exemplified what was being attempted in the 1950s and 1960s was Centro Bellarmino in Santiago, Chile.[11] Its core resource was a team of experts in economics, sociology, and theology. A network of persons surrounded the core group. These networks included "convinced" lay members and their chaplains from various movements, such as Catholic Action and labor; political parties, primarily of Christian democracy; and Catholic spiritual movements, such as the Jesuit Sodality and the Cursillos de Cristiandad.

The heart that pumped life into this large body was the church's social teaching. Virtually everyone involved was concerned in one way or the other with participation of the church in public life and with questions of social justice. Since Chile was mostly comprised of Christians, many of whom were not churchgoers and few of whom were educated in social justice, the persons associated with Centro Bellarmino acted as carriers of visions to improve Chilean society through social justice–oriented vision.

Catholicism depends heavily on ideas. Its twenty centuries of philosophy and theology built a reservoir from which to draw up plans and policies for a more just society. The men and few women associated with the Centro Bellarmino, however, lacked a Latin American vision of how the region and specifically Chile might look.

What they had on hand was European: the social teaching of the church and Thomistic philosophy and theology as formulated and expressed mostly by French and German philosophers. French Catholicism, then in full revival, mediated many central ideas from these traditions, not only for the Center but also for the Santiago archdiocesan headquarters. Virtually everyone in these middle and upper levels of the church seemed to read and to speak French. Intellectuals and activists went to Chile and lectured in French to Center and chancery personnel, including bishops, who in turn attempted to dialogue in a mixture of French and Spanish. The mixed discourse was symptomatic of the change yet to take place in Chilean religious thought. Catholicism would have to express its social vision through a Chilean, not a Eurocentric understanding of the social order.

Fortunately, the methodology was at hand for a Latin American theology within Catholic Action: describe the situation in which Christian Chileans live, reflect on the biblical message that applies to the situation, and act to make the situation most just, that is, more in line with what God intended. This transition from a largely otherworldly piety to a this-worldly consciousness was both difficult and energizing.

The Discovery of Poverty and of a New Discourse

The first step of describing reality was especially difficult because long-practiced denial blocked an honest appraisal. Most Latin Americans and Iberians looked at the poor without focusing on them. The biblical passage "The poor are always with you," understood as "always will be with you," expressed what many felt. Liberation theologian Jon Sobrino said that he and his fellow Jesuits who came from Spain in the 1950s looked on the poor as an unobserved part of landscape, as many other others did at the time.

New views on poverty took hold in twentieth-century Latin America, because of the ferment caused by the intense debates over what political and economic paths—socialism, communism, state-led capitalism—Latin American nations should follow. In Chile, politico-philosophical debates have been a vital part of public discourse for decades. Probably a third of intellectuals and political leaders favored socialism, in either its moderate European or communist forms. A third of Chileans from conservative parties were strongly opposed to socialism. A third position, neither capitalist nor socialist, took root among Christian Democrats of the time. These debates arose during the ascension to power of the relatively new party of Christian Democrats in 1964 under the first Eduardo Frei. They intensified with the fateful election in 1970 of a Marxist socialist (not communist), Salvador Allende, as the first freely elected Marxist president of any country in the world. Both parties made great efforts to reach out to the poor: Christian Democrats to the poor in the countryside, the Allende Socialists to the urban poor. How to bring the situation of the majority of Chileans— the poor—into intellectual focus for policy and practice?

The situation of the poor was clearly more than just a lack of money or possessions. The first attempts to create a Latin American phenomenological or systematic description of the poor were tentative. Before long, though, a word was created and then popularized by the Centro Bellarmino group and others to characterize their situation. It was an awkward word in Spanish and English: *marginal*. The majority of Chileans—indeed most Latin Americans—were *marginados*, living on the margins of society. They often lacked the benefits of education and health that the middle and upper classes enjoyed. Many were illiterate and unable to join in many of the economic and cultural benefits of society.

Marginal was criticized for not being a word derived from the scientific discipline of economics or at least a word with which economists felt comfortable. Nonetheless, the Bellarmino group felt that they were on the track of a concept that furnished a vision of two Chiles, one that received the social and economic benefits of the nation and the other that did not share well or at all in those benefits.

In the United States in the early 1960s, a somewhat similar discovery of poverty was taking place. Americans accustomed to thinking of poverty as existing in war-torn Europe or in the Third World were reading Michael Harrington's groundbreaking work *The Other America: Poverty in the United States*,[12] and it came as a revelation. The book influenced first the Kennedy administration and then Lyndon Johnson's War on Poverty. It also inspired the mobilization of millions of volunteers for community service in the inner cities as well as in remote areas such as eastern Kentucky. Harrington himself had first discovered the U.S. poor through his work at one of Dorothy Day's Catholic Worker houses.

Latin American social scientists, influenced by anthropologists, began shifting linguistic usage from *marginal* to a stronger word, *excluído*. The poor were not just on the sidelines; they were excluded from the benefits of society, often for reasons of class, race, or gender. Physical security, minimal health and educational resources were the rights of all, but, in fact, many were excluded. Through the focus on *excluídos*, religious people were beginning to see that their own society was not the one described in biblical visions of the Kingdom.

A major vehicle for communicating this vision of the poor was *Mensaje*, the monthly magazine of the Chilean Jesuits, who were then closely associated with Centro Bellarmino. Lay activists and priests in various countries passed it from hand to hand until the cover fell off and pages disintegrated. Nevertheless, the image of the red cover of an issue with the single word MARGINAL remained emblazoned in many memories.

These efforts to frame the social and ethical issue of poverty took place in the early 1960s in Chile and elsewhere. In the waning days of Vatican II and leading into the Medellín Conference, a core group of some thirty Latin American theologians was creating a theology that would help apply and interpret Vatican II for Latin America. Poverty was very much on the minds of these liberation theologians. They were applying the theological advances of the recent council to their own region.

Vatican II did not take up poverty systematically. Cardinal Lacaro forcefully proposed the topic for the Council agenda, but it was dropped. Vatican II was primarily a European council in which themes such as faith within a secular world had priority over poverty and human rights, the main concerns of the Third World. Nonetheless, the council furnished a vision for peoples in other regions. Vatican II was a transitional council to a future with a Global South. Theologians at the time understood well that the next council might be in Lima or Lagos.

While the issue of poverty attained, in Gustavo Gutiérrez's view, "a tiny presence" at Vatican II, poverty was the key issue three years after Vatican II at the Medellín Conference.[13] The exact phrase *preferential option for the poor* is not used in the documents of the conference but the idea clearly is there. Liberation theologians refined the phrasing in the ensuing years and the exact phrase occurs in the documents of the subsequent Puebla Conference (1979) that confirmed and amplified the Medellín documents.[14]

Those who opposed the preferential option for the poor resisted the idea that the church should show preference for any group. This, they argued, went against the egalitarian nature of the church, in which distinctions in reference to salvation were voided in the new dispensation that recognized neither Jew nor Gentile, master nor slave, rich nor poor. The argument raged over "option for the poor" for some years. The Legionnaires of Christ, a conservative group working especially with Mexico's elite Catholics, assured members that they too deserved special attention.

The negative reaction of the conservatives to preferential treatment for the poor was fueled by the closing of some prominent elite high schools, the threat of more closings, and the implication that the rich were no longer worthy of attention. In their minds, the rich and middle class had kept the church afloat financially and shielded it during anticlerical regimes after independence from Spain (1810–1825).

The controversy over preferential option for the poor spread among conservatives to Europe, with the Vatican as target. A conservative European-Latin Alliance was formed to oppose such Latin American innovations as liberation theology and its trademark preferential option for the poor.[15] Gustavo Gutiérrez, among others, did not back down but insisted that the rights of the poor were true rights, not optional objects of charity.

That his views won out became clear in an Instruction approved by John Paul II: "The special option for the poor, far from being particularism or sectarianism, manifests the universality of the church's being and mission. This option excludes no one."[16]

What increased the appeal of the preferential option was the biblical basis for the option. Before Vatican II and Medellín, the vision of poverty among activists was built almost exclusively on social doctrine. The social teaching at that time proceeded on a separate path from the Catholic biblical renewal that began in the early twentieth century. As John Donahue notes: "In the post–Vatican II period the social teaching of the magisterium began to be more explicitly theological and scriptural."[17] This anchored the option for the poor in the Old and New Testaments, where God's special concern for the poor seems to be evident on every page.

John Paul II made repeated use of biblical references to the poor, his favorite being the parable of Lazarus used at Yankee Stadium on October 2, 1979, and elsewhere. By the time of his later teaching in *Centisimus annus* (1991), he wrote of "evangelical duty that the church feels called to take her stand beside the poor, to discern the justice of their requests."[18]

Cooperation with the State: Faith-Based Initiatives

Fe y Alegría marks another prominent change in direction toward work for the benefit of the poor. This large educational movement began in 1955 through a visionary Spanish Jesuit who wished to reverse the long-standing focus of Jesuit education toward formation of elite members in Latin America. Whereas half of the twenty-eight U.S. Jesuit universities in the 1950s had labor institutes with close ties to working-class movements, Jesuit universities in Latin America typically lacked such connections. In Venezuela, José María Velaz, in his first steps as a Jesuit priest, focused on the poor of the country and viewed education as a major transformative instrument that would take them from being a dominated, vulnerable people to a people that would be proactive in their own destiny.

Using the energies of university students and recent college graduates as teachers and aides, Velaz created from primitive buildings at hand primary schools for the most impoverished and excluded sectors of the population, with a view toward empowering them in their personal development and their participation in society. From the start of his activity, Velaz foresaw a movement that would include as goals nutrition, housing, and cultural learning.

These goals would never be achieved on a large scale without financial aid from the state. Further, the obligation to educate its citizens fell on the state. In country after country in Latin America, agreements were reached whereby the state would provide buildings, maintenance, and salaries while the church would train, recruit, and supervise teachers and helpers. Generally, Jesuits have acted as administrators, recruiters, and animators. For the Jesuits this meant a monumental commitment in terms of personnel and energy. For national societies, this meant a contribution from a group with almost five centuries of notable educational experience. As the Latin American church began using the phrase "option for the poor" in the late 1960s, the Fe y Alegría movement easily assumed this perspective into its discourse.

This cooperation of church and state was highly unusual in Latin America, especially in more secular countries such as Venezuela, where many unchurched Europeans immigrated in the nineteenth and twentieth centuries. The Fe y Alegría program expresses what became known under Presidents Clinton and Bush as faith-based initiatives, preceding by some forty years those initiatives of church-state cooperation and avoiding many of their pitfalls and aggravations. Opposition by secularists, competing religionists, freemasons, and Marxists has been remarkably muted in most Latin American countries. However, opposition from long entrenched anticlerical groups probably means the movement will not take hold in countries with deeply embedded anticlerical traditions, such as Mexico or Uruguay.

By 2003, 1.2 million students were participating in Fe y Alegría programs in fourteen countries. This represented a fivefold gain in little more than twenty years from 1981. Movement leaders extended educational activities to the secondary level in selected areas and used radio to broadcast instruction to sparsely populated areas. The rapid expansion faced new obstacles. The government resources available to Fe y Alegría faced contraction. The fuller entry of Latin America into free-market capitalism brought cuts to federally funded programs in the 1980s and 1990s.

Not surprisingly, the Latin American Jesuit provincials took a stand with a joint statement against what were called in Latin America neo-liberal reforms. They declared that the globalized economy was bringing new hardships to the vulnerable majority of Latin America's population. The superiors saw, through means of Fe y Alegría and other programs, the drastic impact on the poor of reduced government spending for education and other outreach. They later modified their stand to acknowledge the dominance of the market system. If one wished to measure the change of the Latin American church toward the poor, one could trace the policies and practices of the Jesuits in the region.[19]

The central assumption of the contemporary thrust to aid the poor was maximum involvement of the poor in having a hand in their own destiny. Contrary to the objections of the rich about handouts to the indolent, the poor were not to be the subjects of either temporary handouts or perpetual doles. Looking at this situation of the poor in the late 1950s and early 1960s, Catholic lay leaders came to two conclusions about the peasants in Brazil, the subsistence farmers who formed the core not only of Brazil's poor but of virtually all of Latin America's destitute. First, these people represented a serious obstacle to the plans for *grandeza* shared by Brazilian planners and activists. Brazil and Latin America could not become a developed region that exploited its great natural resources as long as the poor lacked the skills and attitudes needed in the modern world economy. They were fatalistic and illiterate. Second, to help create a new man and a new woman, to achieve this self-reliance, another major emphasis for aiding the poor became literacy. In the Brazilian literacy programs, the goals were much more than learning to read and write. The key influence in the programs was Paolo Freire. His great contribution was literacy as consciousness-raising.

In the 1950s and 1960s the majority of Latin Americans peasants were presumed to be fatalistic, accepting what life gave them.[20] Freire and his many followers emphasized empowerment through self-reliance. The prototype of this thrust was Brazil's Movement for Basic Education with which Freire and other Catholic Actionists worked. Freire's seminal works, especially his *Pedogogy of the Oppressed* from that period, reached around the world. His key ideas were viewing the learner as active agent rather than as a passive object and creating a sense of the forces working against justice.

This push from above for literacy and social change met the newly awakening desire among the poor for literacy and for a better place in society. This yearning came to them from the diffusion of global images and ideas through the new media of television and of cheap radios not dependent on electricity that was unavailable in remote areas.

The next crucial step in the empowerment of the poor began under military dictatorships. Freire and other activists began their efforts before military rule. Once the military dictatorships were established, the church became virtually the only public agency left with a measure of freedom. Armed with a new vision, the church would help to care for the poor, but not paternalistically. The Movement for Basic Education attempted to act as a companion, funneling foodstuffs, legal aid, etc., but not robbing the poor of their own agency.

The difference between the United States and Latin America can be seen in soup kitchens (*olla comunas*). In Chile and elsewhere, the Catholic, Lutheran, and other churches helped supply neighborhood groups with foodstuffs to add to what neighbors contributed. The neighborhood women and their children then took over, preparing the main meal and distributing the meal to households of the neighborhood. In the United States, activists and volunteers from the "haves" usually run soup kitchens, serving food and a measure of companionship to the "have-nots." The dynamics are in sharp contrast.

Not only do Latin American common-pot kitchens under the care of the church tend to emphasize self-reliance, but the project is conducted as a communal activity with shared responsibility. The fuller message of the church is empowering people to act for themselves, to pull together. The theology of communion is operative here.

The Church as Agent of Socioeconomic Development

That the church should be involved in socioeconomic development was a foreign idea for an otherworldly, understaffed institution in Latin America in the 1950s. Missionaries thought otherwise and sought ideas from other parts of the world. Many chose the path of credit unions and cooperatives, well known in Canada and the United States as instruments of development.

Credit unions and cooperatives seemed like safe paths when, in fact, they became dangerous for religious and lay promoters and even more for participants. These modern efforts indirectly contested traditional arrangements. The new marketing techniques and credit arrangements challenged *mestizo* and white middlemen and capital-providers. Racist prejudices against the indigenous entered strongly into this combustible mix.

In the documentary *Our Houses Are Full of Smoke*, Thomas Melville recounts how the truck owned by the cooperative with which he was associated was run off the road and the driver almost killed by vested interests. Others associated with the cooperative movement were not so lucky. Many priests, sisters, and laypeople were murdered. While most died in the 1970s, the killing continued in the twenty-first century, claiming the life of Sister Dorothy Stang, a North American religious in her sixties.

The many accounts of this conflict would fill a small section of a library, including its film section. More recent efforts at socioeconomic development, in which the church has been involved, are microcredit or support for microenterprises. Hundreds of thousands of Latin Americans— especially women—received small loans for equipment, generally something like a loom with which to produce goods to be marketed in the global economy. The number of persons involved is unknown but reaches into the millions. Microenterprises or microcredit efforts have become a major expression of the church's twenty-first-century thrust at empowerment of the poor.

The church depends on its transnational character for provision of credit. Catholic Relief Services (CRS) has been very active in supplying credit. Most countries have national social service agencies called Caritas, founded mostly in the 1950s to administer aid from richer countries. They also collect money and other resources and move quickly into disaster relief, since earthquakes, hurricanes, and flooding routinely batter the region. Greater sophistication prevails at CRS and in Latin America about reduction of poverty than was the case after World War II, when distribution of food and clothing was emphasized. By contrast, the contribution of the church now is based on changing the attitudes of the poor to being proactive.

The agencies of Caritas thus offer the church a national structure that it did not have for centuries. It is now able to reach out to the poorest in an organized fashion, a major improvement over the previous haphazard dispersal of charity. Further, the image of effective aid that Caritas enjoys allows the agency to teach a national audience about option for the poor as a Christian value.

This consciousness-raising was a clear change on the part of the poor. CRS's role of acting as mentor for this process of empowering the poor includes: insisting on household savings, participatory management, emphasizing scale and self-sufficiency, and planning for permanence.

Was the Option for the Poor a Failure?

Some have argued that the option for the poor has failed, because, despite the church's focus on the poor, the poor have elected in very large numbers to join Evangelical groups. Latin Evangelical spokespersons assert that, at heart, the poor prefer a church that promises or guarantees healing or health and wealth to an institution that acts as advocate for government programs or offers the accompaniment of religious men and women on their journey.

The Latin American church shows no sign of weakening in its commitment to the poor. The precise words "preferential option for the poor" (Gutiérrez's favored expression) or "option for the poor" occurs fifteen times in the Final Document of the CELAM 2007 meeting at Aparecida, and the concept appears many more times in the document.[21] As several commentators have noted, the option for the poor still permeates the church in a society where statistically their presence is less but their faces are still to be found in the alleyways and other corners of society.

CHAPTER 6

Transforming Theology from Hyperintellectualism to Concerns of the People and the Care of the Earth

That Latin Americans would create theologies that would draw world attention came as a rude shock to intellectuals used to the dominance of Eurocentric theology in the twentieth century, up to and including the Nouvelle Théologie (New Theology) that served as the basis for the modernized church promoted by the Second Vatican Council.

The great names of the front rank behind the Council—Karl Rahner, Yves Congar, Henri de Lubac, and Edward Schillebeeckx—were northern European Jesuit and Dominican theologians. In addition, almost all the second rank—Joseph Ratzinger, Leo Suenens, Marie-Dominique Chenu, Gustave Thils, and many others—were European except for a handful of North Americans, including John Courtney Murray, Avery Dulles, and Bernard Lonergan. No Latin American theologians were then recognized as being in these front ranks of experts.

Until the late 1960s, Latin American theology was derivative. Its theological books were largely manuals based on European thinking or translations from European works. Then young Latin Americans, most of whom did extensive graduate theological study in Europe, burst onto the theological stage with the creation of liberation theology. Their work was admired and reproduced worldwide, from the United States through Africa and Asia. Liberation theology was recognized as one of the most important theological movements of the twentieth century. Senior European theologians varied in their reaction to it, ranging from laudatory (Schillebeeckx and Congar) to questioning (Moltmann) and to dubious (Ratzinger).

While some question the current viability of liberation theology, the important place attained by Latin American theology and its theologians in academic theology is not in doubt. Ivan Petrella in his brilliant if not fully credible *The Future of Liberation Theology* demonstrated a vigorous present and predicted a strong future.[1] More than 900 dissertations and theses have been written in major North American schools about aspects of liberation theology.[2] Hundreds more theses have been completed in Latin America, Asia, and elsewhere. Theological journals and books flourish in Latin America. So, too, does the theological enterprise as it faces up to new issues.

Latin American theologians, both Catholic and mainline Protestant, have moved on to a wide array of themes to include women, indigenous, African–Latin American, and, especially the environment. Thus, liberation theology is not frozen in its early 1970s form but is much expanded. Latin American indigenous intellectuals have combined liberation insights with cultural considerations that liberation theology ignored. Cuban and Chilean theologians, thousands of kilometers apart and facing diverse situations, have emphasized communion as a core theme. Hence, it makes more sense to refer to "Latin American theology" in its various emphases rather than to concentrate on "liberation theology" as such.

Latin American theology continues to be different from European theology and is therefore disappointing to some; yet for some purposes it may be better. The reader will have to judge. Some theologies, especially European ones, tend to be overintellectualized. Rooted in philosophy, many academic theologians have been occupied with building systems—deductive systems, in which the foundations are clearly stated and sections grow from the foundation. Care is taken that sections and foundation are all logically related. Close to what modern science attempts, this theology is thus characterized as systematic theology.

These are important enterprises and have been pursued by great intellectual talents. But this kind of deductive theology, important as it is, is not the only type of theology; nor perhaps is it the most needed. The fathers of the church, such as Augustine, Ambrose, and Cyril, were more interested in the urgent questions they and other fourth-century Christians faced, such as how Christianity related to the Roman and Byzantine empires. They used the inductive method to reflect theologically upon issues that faced a church emerging from the catacombs into the public square. A major contribution of Latin American theology has been its refinement of the inductive approach.

Methodology of Latin American Theology

Latin American inductive methodology takes a three-step approach: describe as accurately as possible the reality in which the church resides; reflect on this condition using the Bible and tradition; plan for action to improve the situation. It is also called the *see-judge-act* method, since it derives from the methodology of the Catholic Action movement.

Catholic Action and its method of analysis have been present in Latin America for almost eighty years. It is woven into the consciousness of most Latin American Catholic leaders, clerical and lay. See-judge-act has been employed routinely, except for part of the pontificate of Pope John Paul II, for national and regional meetings since at least 1968.

From the 1940s through the 1960s, the method was practiced mainly within the Catholic Action movement itself. University students, workers, and farmers from the three branches of specialized Catholic Action used the methodology. The objective was to analyze and to move toward improving the milieu in which they operated. This was the era in which Christians hoped to have some impact on an increasingly secular world. Young priests who acted as Catholic Action chaplain-advisers became adept at using the method. Especially noteworthy is the number of Latin American theologians (including Gustavo Gutiérrez) who spent a long apprenticeship with laypeople dealing with worldly and urgent issues.

One of these young Catholic Action priests was Hélder Câmara, who went on to become the organizational architect in 1954 of the famously innovative Brazilian Bishops Conference (CNBB). This structure, in turn, became the model of the Latin American Bishops Conference (CELAM) that was founded in 1955, as well as being the model for many new national bishops' conferences in the region.

Thus, by the mid-1960s, as Latin American Catholics were forming effective regional structures, see-judge-act became a common way for conducting meetings. The method was ratified for them at Vatican II when the Constitution on the church in the Modern World followed a similar method. By the time of the Medellín and Puebla conferences, the inductive method of see-judge-act had been consolidated by the bishops, their theological advisers, and lay associates the method had been consolidated into the preferred way to proceed. At the CELAM Aparecida meeting in 2007, journalists simply referred to see-judge-act as though the method were something innately Latin American.

Similarly, the historic meetings of the church at Medellín and Puebla were important not only for setting a previously otherworldly church on a path of justice and worldly caring but also for consolidating the use of see-judge-act. To the consternation of many Latin Americans, Pope John Paul II pushed aside this methodology at the succeeding meeting of Latin American bishops at Santo Domingo (1992). The method clearly resurfaced at the 2007 Aparecida Conference of bishops, so that delegates and observers were constantly asking whether see-judge-act had returned as the major methodology.

See-judge-act has an unusual dynamic. It focuses on issues, especially those facing ordinary persons, it invites biblical and theological reflection from all participants, and it moves toward action to correct or improve an environment. The method acts like an electric dynamo, generating new energy. Every one in Catholic Action cells is expected to contribute to analyzing, reflecting, and proposing. So, too, all the participants in ecclesial meetings are expected to contribute. Also specially prized within the meetings are experts on analyzing (social scientists and economists), on reflecting (biblical scholars and theologians), and on proposing actions (bishops and pastoral planners). One has only to contrast the final documents of the CELAM General Conference I (Rio, 1955) with CELAM General Conference II (Medellín, 1968) to note the difference between the perfunctory statements of Rio and the dynamic documents of Medellín, especially those on justice, peace, and poverty.

The conciliar fathers in *Gaudium et Spes*, the architects of Medellín and Puebla, and liberation theologians themselves consistently follow the same three-step methodology. The first step, a description of the church in the world, involves the use of sociology and economics. And in the case of Latin Americans, their analysis includes structural analysis, deriving in part from class and dependency analysis.

The second step is biblical and doctrinal reflection on the situation described. Thus in the case of Latin America, scriptural and church teachings led the bishops at Medellín and Puebla and the theologians of liberation to reflect on a society in which justice would prevail: a society, that is, in which human dignity is respected, the legitimate aspirations of the people are satisfied, and personal freedom and access to truth are guaranteed. This type of society, built upon Christian principles, conflicts with oppression by power groups and elites observed by bishops and theologians in Latin America. "[These] groups may give the impression of maintaining peace and order," they claim, "but in truth it is nothing but the continuous and inevitable seed of rebellion and war."[3]

In the third step, pastoral conclusions follow the biblical and doctrinal reflections. Some conclusions that consistently appear in CELAM documents and in the writings of theologians of liberation include defense of the rights of the oppressed, a healthy critical sense of the social situation, and promotion of grassroots organizations.

The father of liberation thought, Gustavo Gutiérrez, and other liberation theologians contrast their theology with traditional (largely deductive) theology. They emphasize that theirs is a second act or step, not a first act, as is the case in traditional theology. Liberation theology is elaborated in making reflections on reality; it develops out of praxis.[4] This praxis is the core of understanding how liberation theologians conceive their methodology.

Praxis is for them a somewhat vague term with unfixed parameters. At times it refers to the activity of the hierarchy, clergy, and other church professionals. At other times, it is used to designate actions of the entire ecclesial community in conformity with the message of the Gospel: this is usually referred to as orthopraxis. Sometimes praxis refers to the conduct of the believer within an essentially social dimension.

Praxis is used in a larger sense than it has had from the days of the Greek philosophers, and especially larger than its Marxian usage. Praxis is a way of knowing. It means learning by reflecting on experience. This is exactly how Gutiérrez defines theology: critical reflection on the activity of the church.

It is important to note that this is not detached reflection by an analyst poring over facts gathered by academics. The first moment or act for Gutiérrez is charity—doing justice in action; then theology can be practiced as a second act. Juan Luis Segundo is even stronger in drawing out the practical inferences for the doing of this new theology; it cannot be learned, as traditional theology was, behind seminary walls by teachers and students isolated from the day-by-day struggles of the church in the world, meaning especially the poor in the world.

Hence, not only does theology have a new meaning; so does "church." Until Vatican II, traditional theology described the church as believers

Empowerment of the laity has meant training in ordinary skills as well as teaching religion. Here a catechist teaches people in the Dominican Republic to read.

organized in a hierarchical, institutional body. Liberation theology, using both class and scriptural analysis, sees the church and the world in terms of class; within the social classes, the poor are the most favored by God. For liberation theologians, this option for the poor is a biblical imperative.

The first moment or act of the liberation theologian is action on the part of the poor, on the side of the poor, in the sense that one identifies who are the poor, locates where they are, and advocates for them. This understanding of theology differs from the meaning it usually has in North America and Europe. In practice, liberation theology may not be that distinct, but liberation theologians have found it useful to define themselves clearly and often in contrast to traditional theology.

Praxis

The understanding of praxis is more specific in liberation theology than the learning-from-experience described by the philosophy of John Dewey. Liberation theology means learning from the experience of the poor.

Far from being over intellectualized, Latin American theology has stressed orthopraxis.

First, practice should match vision or beliefs. Thus the church should be more concerned about orthopraxis than about correct intellectual tenets. The second perspective is on orthopraxis as efficacious love. Theology bases itself on praxis, on commitment to justice. This means a theology rooted in service to others, especially the neediest.

This theological theme is not only meant as a corrective to academic theology, which may hold itself apart from the real world; it was also addressed to the large numbers of Latin Americans symbolized by the *beatas* (blessed ones) of the lower classes or the *muy buenos católicos* (very good Catholics) of the upper class who turn their backs on the needy. The theologians felt that the Latin American church had been especially guilty in sheltering churchgoers instead of challenging them. At Medellín, the church accepted the judgment of history on her chiaroscuro past and acknowledged the existence of "a lamentable insensitivity of the privileged sectors to the misery of the marginated sectors."[5]

Paulo Freire

Key ecclesial leaders, clerical and lay, spent their formative years refining for themselves the see-judge-act method. Two of Catholic Action's most famous alumni are Gustavo Gutiérrez and Paulo Freire. Freire made clear that not only was contemporary Latin American religious thought different in method, but its manner of communication also differs from Eurocentric forms. Education is seen as a liberating process. This insight owes a great intellectual debt to Freire.

As a junior professor at the University of Recife in the 1960s, Freire's area of interest was the history and philosophy of education. What he was searching for was a philosophy to serve as the basis for a practical program for training adults to read and write. Together with a number of other young Catholic intellectuals, he joined Catholic Action, thereby becoming involved in adult education especially for those who were illiterate or had no formal schooling, as was the case in the 1950s for millions of Brazilians especially in the northeastern part of his country where he worked.

Freire was interested in far more than functional literacy. He wanted to empower illiterates, to raise their consciousness of their own fatalism, and to motivate them to take charge of their lives to a greater extent. It was no wonder then that his literacy program was considered revolutionary (questioning of the status quo) or that the Brazilian military dismantled the program when it came to power in 1964.

Some critics have argued with Freire that it is better *not* to tell the poor the truth about themselves. Freire, of course, disagreed. So did many Latin American theologians. It is only a slight exaggeration to say that their whole effort has been to tell the poor (and the nonpoor) the truth about poverty and disenfranchisement. Further, they argue that education is never neutral. Left to itself, conventional education socializes students into the values and the worldview of the dominant culture and its elite members.

Freire thus viewed traditional literacy training as a mechanism for adjusting the illiterate to a given society. Its methods treated disadvantaged human beings as objects into which superior beings poured knowledge. For Freire this was debasing and dehumanizing. The human person, for him, is not an object but a "subject," one who works upon and changes the world.

Freire proposed a critical, active method for adult students that would overcome fatalism and resignation. The critical capacity of the illiterate grows out of discussions about situations that "mean something" to them, and to which they themselves have something to contribute. The teacher serves as facilitator and catalyst for this dialogue.

Freire's method, too lengthy to describe here in detail, can be read in his *Pedagogy of the Oppressed.*[6] What is important and what has been seized upon in other parts of the world—and by pioneers in other types of liberation theology, such as black or feminist liberation theology—is that groups of oppressed people need to reflect on their own cultural, economic, and social situation and to begin to become masters of their own lives. This process of *conscientization* (consciousness-raising) won a place for itself at the heart of Latin American theology.

Concientizâo (the Portuguese version of Freire's method) continues as a living and widespread practice among the several million members of the Landless movement in Brazil. In MST (Movement for Landless Rural Workers), the activist strategies and cooperative farming enterprises have been conducted along the lines Freire endorsed to enhance empowerment, even though the process takes up much time since all, including adolescents, are expected to contribute their energies and points of view.

CHAPTER 7

Emphasizing Evangelization and Empowering 1.2 Million Lay Catechists

In recent Latin American history there have been two waves of catechists among Catholics. The first wave occurred well before the evangelizing initiatives of Popes Paul VI and John Paul II,[1] when a missionary crusade to Latin America that began in the 1950s and intensified in the 1960s[2] brought in its wake a revival of the ancient office of catechist, indigenous persons assisting missionaries.

Considerable numbers of missionaries arrived in Latin America from Europe, Canada, and the United States. The Latin American church in many places was in grave crisis, with few Catholics practicing their faith and with a dire shortage of human and economic resources. Typically, the twentieth-century missionaries were assigned to remote areas where there had been few priests and very little in the way of organizational resources.

These remote areas contained large indigenous populations. Thus foreign missionaries assumed pastoral care of the majority of the indigenous peoples—some forty million people—who lived in two geographical concentrations: the Central American regions of Guatemala and southern Mexico and the Andean countries of Ecuador, Peru, and Bolivia.[3] These regions had been the seats of the advanced Mayan, Aztec, and Incan civilizations. Their descendants, who often lived in extreme poverty, had managed to retain core elements of their cultures, including their languages, through five centuries. Their religious practices included vestiges of Catholicism mixed with native religious beliefs and practices.

Despite the efforts of national governments after independence from Spain (1810–1825) to integrate the indigenous peoples into national society, they remained apart, marginalized from the benefits of society by racist discrimination. Thus, the new set of missionaries encountered Central American and Andean cultures four hundred years after the first Spanish missionaries had done so. European and North American missionaries were to have a strong hand in the resurgence of the indigenous[4] but first they needed mediators for intercultural understanding and interpreters for the hundreds of languages. They also needed native allies who would counter the civil-religious hierarchy (the dominant elites who controlled native religious practices) and correct widespread unorthodox religious beliefs. These they found in the catechists.

First Wave of Catechists: Indigenous Populations

It was not widely understood that the Catholic Church had largely lost control of native religious practices. Large areas of Latin America had had no priests for generations.[5] Beginning in the early 1800s, clergy left indigenous regions in large numbers. Spanish clergy, affected by the Wars of Independence, went to other parts of the world. Anticlerical governments in some regions, such as Central America, were determined to maintain a reduced church influence. Guatemala, the largest of the Central American countries, restricted the number of Catholic clergy to about one hundred between the late 1870s and the 1940s.[6] As a result, indigenous areas had very few resident clergy, and visiting clergy typically came only for yearly celebrations of local fiestas.

These fiestas, central to the religious culture of the indigenous, were increasingly organized without priests by what anthropologists called the civil-religious hierarchy, who ensured that *la costumbre* centered in yearly religious celebrations was carried out. Thus the *cargo* or sponsorship system passed from loose church control to native religious leadership. Under supervision of the civil-religious hierarchy, members of the local communities routinely assumed *cargos* (sponsorship) of fiestas. These responsibilities implied great economic hardship. Assuming the role of *patrón* for a fiesta meant that Indians exhausted their slim economic surpluses to maintain a traditional religious system.[7]

Thus the native religious system rebuilt itself in the absence of priests. It was this civil-religious hierarchy of native religion that offered opposition to the Catholic missionaries of the twentieth century. When Maryknoll missionaries from the United States began sending missionaries to Guatemala instead of to China in the 1950s, they found no priests resident in the rural areas where most of the natives lived. Rather, they and many other missionaries encountered passive-aggressive opposition to their presence by the civil-religious leaders, who viewed the Catholic priests as usurpers.[8] Maryknoll missionaries expected to take over abandoned churches and other buildings left unused by Catholic priests for decades. Instead, native leaders, sacristans, and majordomos resisted turning over church keys, prized images of patron saints, and use of buildings. Not only was the *cargo* system a religious enterprise, it was an economic microsystem as well, and the missionaries were viewed as challenging it.

Thus, the Catholic Church found itself in a deeply pitched struggle to regain the hearts and minds of some forty million indigenous souls.[9] The struggle was titanic. The stakes were high in this religious competition. The church could have lost millions of indigenous to the practice of native religion. Orthodox Catholicism, as understood by North Americans, Spaniards, and other Europeans, was pitched against the heterodox understandings of Christianity that were thoroughly blended with traditional religious practices that had returned or intensified in the absence of priests.

Thus, this mid-twentieth-century battle meant that the Latin American church was faced with the challenge of indigenous religion. The struggle was a fitting prelude to the challenge of Pentecostalism that has intensified in the present century. In both cases, catechists were central actors. The missionaries who took charge of the church in indigenous areas had to engage in a renewed evangelization of these peoples. This they did through training indigenous evangelizers. More commonly called catechists, these persons not only had to teach their peoples in native languages but they also were responsible for Catholic worship and other aspects of church life, such as care of the sick, in their communities. In the interaction of catechists and missionaries, it became clear that the Christian faith had to be made understandable to the members of the culture being evangelized. In turn, the missionaries began their own theological valuing of the indigenous

Catechists have been a vital and essential force in the spread of Catholicism in Latin America and have frequently assumed roles beyond the teaching of religion. Here a woman catechist leads the baptism rite.

religious experience and of its cultural expressions. Cultural adaptation, commonly called inculturation in the Catholic Church, was taking place.[10]

The catechesis had a scriptural content reflective of the biblical renewal in the Catholic Church in the twentieth century. This gave it evangelical dynamism and the capacity to sustain a renewal. Further, as John Gorski notes, Latin American missionary resurgence (Latin Americans becoming missionaries) had its roots in the grassroots challenges of the indigenous ministry.[11]

The role of the catechist in the indigenous resurgence that has taken place is highly instructive for understanding evangelization and renewed religion as a catalyst for social change. These leaders saw in their religious beliefs the sacredness of the human person as the basis for seeking their social and political rights. In the 1960s and 1970s many catechists were community leaders and in key positions within indigenous groups. In Central America, especially in Guatemala, catechists became special targets of the military repression that took place because catechists were reputed to be agents of change, albeit peaceful and mild change. In the gross tactics typical of repressive militaries dealing with presumed opposition to the government, villagers were murdered, towns burned to the ground, and survivors moved to newly constructed hamlets.

One indigenous catechist typical of many others was Señor Alejandro Atz,[12] who was a community leader among the Cakchiquel, a major cultural group of Guatemala, as well as a catechist. Señor Atz lost his wife, several relatives, and most of his possessions through actions of the military. He was not alone in his suffering. Bishop Gerardo Flores Reyes of Alto Verapaces estimates that 5,000 catechists were murdered by Guatemalan armed forces. The true number is probably much higher, as the names of murdered catechists now fill the pages of written accounts of the Guatemalan ethnocide that took place from 1954 to 1996.[13] "Catechists were the chief targets of persecution," stated Señor Atz.[14]

Two types of catechist can be noted here. Señor Atz represents the several hundred thousand who have been working in the special field of the indigenous church. The author estimates their number as being around 400,000.[15] They deserve the special title of catechist because they mainly deal with evangelization among peoples of non-Christian religions. The Vatican Congregation that deals with this type of evangelization calls them catechist-leaders, implying a role and status in their community beyond that of mere teacher.

The other catechists—perhaps 800,000—are mostly working as adult religious educators among the 90 percent of the population of Latin America who are not indigenous. The majority of this sector of catechists became active in the New Evangelization. They tend to be roughly similar to Sunday teachers of adults and children, without necessarily implying community leadership. But, in Latin America, they do share in the missionary function of the church.

A discussion of what catechists represent institutionally must begin with the role of the more traditional catechist, the one who works among the indigenous peoples. A monumental task of the Latin American church in the last half of the twentieth century was creating an indigenous church. For centuries, the church attempted to assimilate its indigenous populations into a standardized western mold. But a major shift in policy occurred at Vatican Council II: the church wanted to respect non- European cultures to the degree that "the seeds of revelation" were thought to be present in other cultures. At the very least, Christians in contact with other cultures would have to look for expressions of the divine in those cultures.[16]

In Latin Americanizing its theology, major theologians from Latin America created liberation theology. Despite this Latin American thrust, liberation theology at the time did not address major cultural issues. Further, some missionaries and even more bishops had neither the personal inclination nor the time to absorb liberation theology. Rather, virtually all missionaries and bishops agreed to the formation of an indigenous church. Another theological stream within Latin America pursued cultural themes. The two streams, liberation thought, on the one hand, with its emphasis on contextualization, and the cultural emphasis on the other hand, merged in the beginnings of *teología india* or inculturation theology.[17] This intellectual basis served as the basis for the new catechesis of indigenous populations.[18]

Lacking a native clergy, the indigenous church could have catechists. Catechetical centers trained persons especially in understanding the Bible. These centers became something similar to indigenous seminaries. For at least fifty years, the practice grew of having a native catechist in each rural settlement area.

Under the impact of the missionary presence religious life has changed in many areas of the Central American and Andean regions where most indigenous reside. Missionaries and their catechist collaborators conducted intensive educational campaigns to re-evangelize the natives. These modern efforts often included such innovations as rural Catholic Action with small cell-like study and prayer groups and cooperative and credit union membership; that is, they comprised strategies that included political action or socioeconomic betterment. Kay Warren, Hans and Judith Buechler, and other anthropologists noted the effect of missionary work in the shift toward a more orthodox Catholicism.[19] They called this religion either folk Catholicism or reformed Catholicism, in contrast to *la costumbre*, indigenous religion that centered its practice in fiesta sponsorship. The fiesta or *cargo* system had maintained a hegemonic grip on community life in much of Central America and the Andes for decades. The hold of fiesta sponsorship has diminished to a considerable degree. In some areas, it is gone entirely.

Further, Warren and others traced changes in the consciousness of indigenous peoples that resulted from their new openness to acculturation and participation in development projects. The Catholic Action groups, called by Warren "study groups," were small groups that compensated for the lack of priests and decentralized the large territorial parishes and the settlements tied to parishes. Catechists were typically community leaders trained for evangelization and leadership within Catholic Action. These Catholic Action cells were in direct opposition to the civil-religious hierarchy that controlled the religious beliefs and central rituals of the indigenous brotherhoods, the *cofradías*, that perpetuated unorthodox religious beliefs. Catholic Action was only one of the challenges to the power of the civil-religious hierarchy. Modernizing forces of various origins were taking their toll on traditional indigenous authority, especially twentieth-century style political parties that made incursions into indigenous territories to organize electoral politics.

The contemporary history of the indigenous areas has been played out in an entanglement of local and global forces.[20] Indigenous ethnic groups are interacting with national political forces as well as penetrating an international market. Fundamentally the situation touches upon personhood and identity, an interaction of religion, persons, community, nation, and the parts of the larger world that affect Central American and Andean agriculture, commerce, and economic lives. Viewed from the grassroots, catechists are a major factor in the processes that affecting the recent and current changes in personhood among indigenous in these areas.

Catechists are lay specialists, mostly volunteers in Aymara, Quiché, and other indigenous communities. Missionaries have been important in indigenous revitalization but catechists are equally important. Catechists recruit and lead. They act as intermediaries between missionaries and communities. They act as a new layer inserted between the original layers of a religious organization, that is, between priest and congregation. They have become increasingly important actors in the wide, intense, and influential discourse of ethnic identity that has been taking placing in the indigenous resurgence occurring in Latin America.

Catechists began to see themselves as protagonists of their interpretation of Christianity rather than as objects of evangelization. In doing so, they discarded their role as buffers between larger society and communities to become translocal intermediaries. In a word, religious actors joined or fostered, to a degree no one knows, the liberation of indigenous communities from isolation to occupying a contentious public space. They became vernacular intellectuals, interpreting a universal message within a particular culture.

Basic conceptions of personhood and agency are important in this transformation toward political activism. Catechists have been helping Aymaras and others to define their personhood proactively as persons capable of interacting with the state instead of hanging back fatalistically from

120

full political participation as citizens, or, more accurately, operating only in their own world, more or less apart from a citizen's participation in the nation. Equally, the catechist-led reinterpretation of "community" is important for indigenous who, to a greater or lesser extent, define themselves through their participation in a community. Thus, Aymaras and other ethnic groups began conceiving themselves as a people on the march toward greater independence or autonomy within the nation.

In sum, catechists helped reshape indigenous ethnic groups by leading small groups to reinterpret their place in society through the Bible and through their ethnic cosmologies.[21] Further, in some areas of the Guatemalan or Bolivian highlands, catechists formed networks within their own circle of catechists. These networks helped to overcome the antagonism between indigenous communities that built up over centuries of feuds over land and other issues. They have become meta Aymaras or Quichuas.

While the missionaries utilized indigenous catechists who, in turn, interpreted their organic place as mediators between the layers of society and the church, a newer type of catechist among the indigenous has appeared in Mexico and elsewhere. The "classic" catechist was typically a leader embedded in his or her community. Newer catechists among the indigenous are either full-time external agents or part-time embedded agents from outside the community. They represent a (perhaps unfortunate) break in the careful planting and growth of catechists as leaders from within. This new type of catechist, as envisaged by Father Alejandro Pinelo, the founder of the Legion of Christ's Fulltime Lay Missionary program, is part of a plan to mobilize catechists like an army. Pinelo started his program in 1994, and it is targeted toward indigenous as well as non-indigenous sectors of the population.

Pinelo sought to recruit, educate, and utilize pastoral agents, most of them committed full-time to evangelization in Mexico, Central America, and Venezuela. These pastoral agents receive financial support from the program, not from the community. An intensive five-week period of study and prayer serves as an initial program of formation for these agents, followed by one-week study updates on a regular basis. Pinelo observed the vast territorial expanse of parishes in Mexico and elsewhere, many with twenty to thirty chapels (way stations that priests could only occasionally visit) and gaps in the territories being filled in by Evangelical churches. "One can only respond with the laity to the great demand for formation, liturgical services, pre-sacramental courses, and preparation of catechists," he said.[22]

The full-time catechists are paid and are under the care and supervision of the Legionnaires, lay and clerical. They number 1,000 Indians dedicated full-time to evangelization. In turn, they have trained 35,000 part-time evangelizers among the indigenous.

If this sounds like a business model, Pinelo acknowledges that influence and believes that what is characteristic of his program is "apostolic effectiveness, reaching the greatest number of brothers and sisters in the least time possible." The model for the activity is largely an elite, professional one. "The program," Pinelo says, "is carried out by the laity, many of whom are professionals [among the non-indigenous] … and who wanted to put the best methodology at the service of the church."

Second Wave: Turbo-Charged Efforts

There is a strong sense of urgency not only in what the Legionnaires are doing about evangelization but also about what some other groups within the church are doing to employ lay persons in evangelization. Many of the persons that are becoming active in the third millennium of the church are, in fact, "turbo-charged" (to use John Allen's characterization)[23] by the need to meet the evangelical challenge that led to the defection of millions of poorly educated Catholics.

One may question—as does the author, based on years of closely following educational research—whether short-term (weeklong) adult learning projects such as those employed by Pinelo produce more than a shallow understanding of religious truths or deepen convictions sufficiently to withstand the challenges posed by Evangelicals. But the main point here is that even ultraconservatives, as the Legionnaires are commonly depicted, see that laypeople must be on the center stage as catechists.

This deployment of the laity was also the main emphasis in another contemporary evangelization enterprise, again in Mexico. Luis Butera, an older Italian missionary working in Mexico but with dreams of providing missionary help for Africa, became caught up in trying to improve the level of religious knowledge and commitment among non-indigenous Mexicans. He saw that many Mexicans were in danger of leaving the church. Many Mexican Catholics had a strong attachment to the church, reinforced by their family's choosing the side of the church in the church-state conflicts during the long Mexican Revolution period. But most people of the middle and lower classes were educated in highly secular public schools and thus had a weak intellectual appreciation of the church's teachings, were challenged by conflicting viewpoints, and were being attracted by Evangelical churches.

The religious environment in many areas of Mexico became overheated. After decades of fighting the state over the place of religion in a lay state, loyal Mexican Catholics felt they had reached a peaceful stasis in this relationship in the 1990s, when they perceived that they were being aggressively challenged by Pentecostals and other Evangelicals. The cardinal archbishop of Guadalajara, a major regional capital, was faced every day with a rabid Evangelical who shouted anti-Catholic slogans at him as he entered the cathedral for daily Mass. This was especially jarring in a region that was considered a conservative Catholic bastion. More serious than a single anti-clerical fanatic were reports of Mexicans joining the myriad small churches that were springing up in remote areas. Census figures showed very low real Evangelical growth between 1990 and 2000 because the dropout rate was high. But who knew for sure? Mexican Catholics and their leaders were alarmed. At the very least, Evangelicals were spurring Catholics on: Alarm had reached into the lay ranks. The laity had been mobilized before; thus, they could be mobilized again. Only this time, as Father Butera saw it, the laity would be fully employed in teaching other laity and not only as helpers to the clergy.

Butera had a vision independent of but similar to Pinelo's. Both wanted laypeople to catechize laypeople. As his plan took shape over some thirty years, a core of lay catechists evolved into a lay community that in turn became a religious congregation, with vows and community living. Members of this core group trained full-time lay catechists who, in turn, trained part-time laity to teach other laity. This was like throwing a stone into the water and seeing the ripple effect.

Three major themes of the contemporary Latin American church are captured by both Pinelo and Butera: first, the employment of laity; second, emphasis on the option for the poor; and third, the marriage of evangelization and mission, as will be seen in the following chapter. Both men stood at the historical point of transition from focusing on indigenous evangelization to amplifying evangelization for the majority population.

The second impetus for recruiting men and women as catechists centered in church renewal efforts that swept through the Latin American church in the last third of the twentieth century. Evangelization efforts in

Latin America have produced the 800,000 lay catechists who work with the majority non-indigenous populations. Their number was still growing in the later years of the first decade of the third millennium.

The goal of evangelization had been clearly stated by the Latin American church at the Third General Conference of Bishops at Puebla in 1979.[24] In the 1980s, persons in lay renewal movements in the Latin American church—movements already described—reached a level of maturity at which they wished to share their intensified faith and spirituality with other Catholics. Members of the Catholic Charismatic Renewal, especially their clerical advisers, were in the forefront of this impetus. One of the first great signs of this thrust was Evangelization 2000, headed by Father Tom Forrest, a Redemptorist missionary who had achieved admirable results working in Aguas Buenas, Puerto Rico. The project was started in 1986 as a very ambitious project, "promoting a Decade of Evangelization in Anticipation of the Great Jubilee Year 2000." By the following year, *Christianity Today* was reporting that the project hoped to raise one billion dollars and that the ten-year project would culminate with a worldwide satellite telecast on Christmas Day 2000, when the Pope would speak to a potential audience of at least five billion people. The project, said Forrest, looked forward "to giving Jesus Christ a 2000 birthday gift of a world more Christian than not."[25]

At the same time in the late 1980s, the Latin American church had its attention focused more immediately on two events that would occur in 1992: the fifth centenary of Columbus's arrival in Hispaniola (present-day Dominican Republic and Haiti) and the Fourth General Conference of Latin American Bishops (CELAM) that would take place at Santo Domingo, the capital of the Dominican Republic, in October 1992. The juxtaposition of 1492 and 1992 suggested a contrast between the first evangelization, considered a providential event but incomplete, and the need for a new evangelization; that is, presenting the Christian message with greater intensity than was typical of Latin American Catholics and with attention to the evangelization of cultures. General Conferences of the church in Latin America are preceded by months of preparation and include preparation of conference documents by theologians and pastoral experts, consultation about these documents with laity and clergy, followed by discussions of the vetted documents among bishops at meetings within national bishops' conferences.[26] The results of these consultations between 1990 and 1992 were then passed on to participants of the Santo Domingo Conference. There

Pope John Paul II, presiding over the meeting, further highlighted evangelization. The Santo Domingo document reflected this priority.[27]

General Conference documents are taken seriously in Latin America. The national episcopal conferences use General Conference statements as starting points in their strategic planning. Many conferences use such formats as three-year or five-year plans, readjusting their priorities and evaluating their progress against these plans. Thus, evangelization further enveloped the pastoral activity.

John Paul II reinforced evangelization through his frequent and widely noticed visits to Latin America, during which he further elaborated his ideas to reinforce his strong concern that Catholics use modern media technologies for their message (and not allow Evangelical and Pentecostal competitors to dominate this field). He was most effective in conveying this message in Brazil, where he met with seminarians and other audiences to persuade them to use radio and television as media for the Christian message. The young, priests and lay alike but most notably the priests, took the message to heart, became television personalities, and built small radio and television empires—all with the goal, they said, of evangelization.

Since evangelization in all its aspects was the main topic on the table within the Latin American church, it was hotly debated but eventually accepted as the first priority for the Latin American church. The topic was contested because a number of progressives considered poverty and development more urgent than evangelization at that time. In the 1980s Latin America was going through what was called the lost decade (one that continued until at least 1992).[28] Millions were throw into subsistence living by Latin America's change from state-sponsored capitalism to free-market capitalism. The option for the poor had become the signature of the Latin American church but now, critics said, this characteristic was being set aside. Putting evangelization at the top of the agenda in place of development implied more than words but a plan of action for a generation—that is, the twenty years between 1992 and 2012—within the church.

The tracing of this debate and its consequences is beyond the focus of this volume, except to note that arguments continued about the new evangelization in the wake of the Santo Domingo meeting. Evangelization 2000 and Lumen 2000, a companion project to Evangelization 2000, were heartily condemned by Brazilian activists and at least one North American academic as part of a Euro–Latin American alliance to kill whatever remained of the influence of liberation theology and its emphasis on the poor and vulnerable.[29] The progressive losers in this debate largely stepped aside to allow evangelization to be the stated goal of the church in its planning and implementation.[30]

Catholic Charismatics and Evangelization

Many of the groups that stepped forward to take the lead in evangelization in Brazil were from the Catholic Charismatic sector. These groups were diverse in their founding, their dates of entry into evangelization, and their methods of evangelization.

Two notable countries in which the Catholic Charismatic Renewal flourished in Latin America are Brazil and the Dominican Republic. The three principal figures in the founding of the Brazilian Catholic Charismatic Renewal were Father Marcelo Rossi, Father (later Monsignor) Jonas Abib, and Father Edward Dougherty. Rossi became the face of Brazilian Charismatics as a singing priest-performer and television personality, a Brazilian superstar. Abib and Dougherty built relatively large radio and television production companies and networks.[31]

Of the three priests, Jonas Abib is the least well known outside of Brazil but is most typical of those who encourage wide and deep involvement of lay Catholics in evangelization. Earlier than many others in Brazil, Father Abib created a covenant community of lay and clerical Catholic Charismatics. Sociologists call these groups intentional communities, and two levels of membership are typically available: the core group pledge themselves to a shared prayer life and ministry and a common purse, while the affiliates do not give up their family lives or jobs but contribute financial and whatever other kind of support they can to the ministry of core groups. Abib's lay communities and widespread evangelizing ministry are known as Nova Canção (New Song).[32] The geographical center was established at a large campus between São Paulo and Rio de Janeiro, Brazil's two principal cities, where Nova Canção has built the largest church structure in Latin America, the Bishop Hipólito Moraes Center of Evangelization, along with housing and civic structures needed for its core members, radio and television facilities, and the buildings needed for a flood of visitors.

Abib and his followers emphasize the creation and performance of Christian music. For Brazilians and some other Latin Americans, Christian music is an especially attractive medium for carrying messages of evangelization. While Nova Canção members do well in drawing people to musical performances and CD sales, none exceeds Father Rossi in record sales or TV audience numbers. He has topped the popular music charts with CD sales and draws immense crowds to outdoor events. He has been compared to Pope John Paul II in the size of the crowds he has been able to attract. One of his Missa-Shows (Mass and Music Show), staged at a racetrack, drew some two and a half million people. Other young priest-singers also attract large audiences. Rossi and the others credit John Paul II for inspiring them to take the stage to evangelize. Rossi also produced and starred in commercial films with biblical themes. He believes he is evangelizing popular culture as well as persons.

The countercultural element is a centerpiece for the Catholic Charismatic movement in Latin America. Although highly critical of the Charismatic movement, Ralph Della Cava, professor emeritus of history at Queens College and a longtime expert on religion in Brazil, noted that Charismatics like Father Rossi differ from other notable charismatic figures in Brazil's long religious history: "[Rossi] addresses a largely urban audience of young people in a world permeated by secular values, proposing a set of alternative values through the medium that has always been the most important in Brazil, the popular music of the day."[33]

Rossi, Abib, and other Catholic Charismatics became direct competitors with neo-Pentecostal and Pentecostal challengers in television. In Brazil, the Universal Church of the Kingdom of God (IURD), a health-and-wealth neo-Pentecostal church,[34] was a very fast-growing challenger to Catholicism.[35] This church, created by self-proclaimed Bishop Edir Macedo, acquired so much money so quickly through demanding money of members in return for promises of economic blessings from God that it purchased a major television network, TV Record. Anti-Catholic tirades on the network that included the kicking of a statue of the Virgin of Aparecida, Catholic Patroness of Brazil, increased Catholic desires to have their own TV outlets. Over a period of a few years in the 2000s, four Catholic networks came on air or increased their transmitting capability to attain more national coverage.[36]

While newsprint media portrayed this Charismatic response as a television war between religious challengers, Charismatics saw their television efforts in positive rather than reactive fashion. They wanted to evangelize on air by praying, proclaiming a biblical message, and instructing in Catholic faith and morals. Again, this was seen in countercultural terms, working against the drift to combat secular values.

Television programs and large public performances are the flashy elements of modern Catholic evangelization in Brazil. But the day-by-day fostering of deeper religious conversion and of reinforcing religious commitment in what Charismatics believe is a hedonist and consumerist society in much of Latin America is carried out by radio and Internet, schools and adult education centers.

Evangelicals have used radio effectively for decades in Latin America.[37] Catholics are doing so now. Nova Canção and other covenant communities that are dedicated to radio ministry employ radio not only for direct instruction on Bible, dogma, and doctrine but also for counseling, spiritual direction, and talk shows, with call-in questions and responses. The Internet offers a parallel effort with posted lessons and chat rooms. By both radio and Internet, intercessory prayer is encouraged. One of the goals of these radio and Internet efforts is to extend pastoral care in terms of individual attention; that is, responding to crises, doubts about faith, questions about personal vocation, loneliness, and individual questions about advancing in the spiritual life.

Many of the covenant communities dedicated themselves to a ministry of presence within a neighborhood. They rented or purchased a house or condominium in a neighborhood, held classes, prayed with neighbors, and attempted to influence behavior through the example of their own lives and values (such as sharing a common purse and doing effective work in their ministerial commitments). One of the largest covenant communities, Toca de Assis, which evolved into a religious congregation, deployed its 1,000 vowed members to living on the street as good neighbors (and evangelizers) among homeless and others hanging out on the streets in Brazil. This ministry of presence was also fostered by the covenant community founded by Father Emiliano Tardif, the Canadian missionary to the Dominican Republic and, through his worldwide travels, perhaps the best-known Latin American Catholic Charismatic.

While Tardif is further credited as one of the original founders of schools of evangelization, his efforts in the Dominican Republic pale in comparison to the efforts of a Mexican Catholic lay evangelist and preacher, Pepe Prado Flores, who established the San Andres Schools of Evangelization. Two thousand of these schools operate in sixty countries on five continents, all over Mexico, and are advancing in the United States in places as far-flung as Santa Rosa, California, San Antonio, and New Orleans. The number of his schools is believed to have doubled in ten years.

Catechists, Status, and Shared Responsibility

Appointing persons as catechists—that is, investing them with a formal office in the church—creates a role, brings forth a commitment and recognition, and establishes responsibility. Official roles anchor an institution. Persons view themselves differently, as do others who view them as having a new capacity. Further, status within an institution matters within most societies, certainly within Latin American societies.

Status helps to ensure incorporation within an institution. A commitment to a duty or responsibility on the part of the layperson who becomes a catechist is required, increasing loyalty and decreasing the likelihood of being drawn off by competitors. Indeed, one of the chief characteristics of the Pentecostal and Evangelical competitors to Latin American Catholicism has been assumption of organizational duties. These competitors have a low threshold of entrance requirements and a regular progression of duties within the churches, from tidying up after worship services to public-worship reader to street apostle. Most of the rapidly expanding churches in Latin America bestow increasing levels of responsibility upon new members. This, in turn, reinforces affiliation. Thus, one can trace a discernible conversion career pattern (here thinking of deepening commitment), including increased responsibilities within the institution, as Henri Gooren and others have shown in *Conversion of a Continent* (2007).[38]

The need for the office of catechist flows from the nature of modern organizations. Max Weber argued at the dawn of the last century that modern institutions accomplish their goals through making the goals the responsibility of designated, specialized officials. Catechists have come forward to become designated, specialized officials for education in the church. (Again, these are goals and responsibilities shared with priests and other officials.) Most catechists are unpaid but understand that they fulfill a vital function in the church. In the process of being catechists, they acquire a sense of ownership. They are the ultimate fulfillment of that policy choice of *pastoral de conjunto* made at the time of the bishops' return from Vatican II.

The office of catechist could be a key element in the drama of migrant religion now unfolding in the United States. This precious office could be taken into consideration in the large migration of Hispanics, including catechists, to the United States. The lapsing from church affiliation or church attendance that occurs in this migration-transition could be reduced if Hispanic catechists, for example from Guatemala, were incorporated with official recognition of their status within parishes in Jupiter, Florida; Richmond, Virginia; or wherever they migrate.

New Milestone: The Aparecida Conference

Thus, through the late twentieth and early twenty-first centuries an energized sector of the Latin American church engaged in evangelization. (This effort also lagged in much of Central America, a traditional backwater area.) The next General Conference of the Latin American church after the Santo Domingo meeting was delayed by the prolonged illness of John Paul II and the transition to the new pope, Benedict XVI. CELAM V was held at the Brazilian National Shrine of Aparecida in May 2007. By then a very large group of laity and clergy were engaged in evangelization. Further, Pope Benedict had crystal-clear ideas about New Evangelization and enthusiasm for it.[39]

A two-year process of consultations of laity and clergy, meetings of national councils of bishops, and preparing pre-conference documents took place within countries beginning in 2005. The church at the Aparecida CELAM Conference gathered the insights and sentiments of great numbers of lay and clerical leaders into the synthesis document, important here for summarizing those views.[40] The conclusion drawn from this consultation was: "Catechesis is the key formation in the missionary disciple."[41] In this view, the missionary disciple holds the future of the church in his or her hands and this primarily means renewed catechesis, recovering the experience of Christian initiation. The re-evangelizing of Catholics was the overriding concern of the Latin American bishops at their fifth General Conference. (The conference is generally known as CELAM V, or simply as Aparecida.)

Neither the media nor the church fathers at Aparecida comprehended the tremendous growth that has taken place in the ranks of the catechists; they spoke of thousands of catechists when in fact there were hundreds of thousands of them. When a very large institution like the Catholic Church decides to turn itself around, to reform itself, it takes decades for the reforms to begin to take effect. Time passes before fundamental changes are observed, since changes are not immediately discernible by most observers who are focused on local or national realities rather than on how the whole social institution had grown like a great glacier. The number of lay catechists grew to 1.2 million by the end of 2006, just months before the Conference.

Stemming Losses to Pentecostals in Brazil

At the time of the historic visit of Pope Benedict XVI to Brazil for the opening sessions of the Fifth Latin American Bishops General Conference in 2007, only a few reporters, including Andrew Downie of *Time* magazine, called attention to the notable success of the largest Catholic Church in the world. Downie wrote that the Brazilian church not only stemmed the incredible growth of Pentecostals but was thriving within its own church walls.[42]

The vitality of the church in Brazil was confirmed in the most recent figures then available from the Vatican.[43] A number of indicators are typically used by social scientists to mark the well-being of an institution. Key, of course, is the strength of its workforce. The number of Brazilian priests has continued to rise through the years, despite the death or return of many missionary priests to their home countries. The number of priests stood at 18,087 in 2006, up 9 percent in five years.

Seminarians are a useful barometer of the future, even if there will be dropouts from the seminary. Students in the last years of philosophy and theology have grown 907 percent since 1972 when their numbers were 939. The increases have held steady and rose to 8,215 in 2001 and to 9,450 in 2006.

While present and future priests are crucial to the functioning of a sacramental church, the numbers of laypeople who participate actively in the functioning of the church have also impressively expanded. Brazilian lay catechists increased to 482,370 in 2006. As instruments of evangelization, they have been key in retaining Catholics within the church. Andrew Walls, the Scottish scholar of world Christianity, believed that few educated and convinced Christians convert to other religions.[44] Studies in Latin America confirmed that the vast majority of Catholics who affiliate themselves with Pentecostal groups were nominal Catholics.[45]

In Brazil, the tide of defections to Pentecostal groups has been stemmed in the present decade. The national census showed the Catholic population in 2003 to be 73.8 percent of the nation and figures compiled by the respected Gertulio Vargas Foundation in 2006 showed 73.9 percent. Two factors were cited by Marcelo Neri, a Foundation researcher, for this new religious stability: greater economic stability and the adoption of Charismatic practices by Catholics.[46] One might add that one of the main Catholic Charismatic practices is engaging in evangelization.

Brazil may be the Catholic Church in Latin America with the greatest Charismatic influence. More than half of Brazilian Catholics identify themselves as Charismatics.[47] Some 6,000 of Brazil's 8,200 parishes have Charismatic prayer groups.[48] While most of the media attention has gone to curious facets of the Charismatic Renewal, such as Father Marcelo Rossi and other singing priests, solid growth in prayer and spirituality has been taking place, as is evident in the wide expansion of prayer groups throughout the country.

Moreover, the Charismatic movement has clearly matured through the formation of covenant communities, intentional communities in which lay members chose to live, pray, and work in common. The numbers of laypeople in Brazil vowed to living in these communities is unknown but membership reaches into the thousands.[49]

Since the 1990s, these covenant community members and Brazilian church leaders have emphasized evangelization and mission. Their evangelizing efforts range from television production and Christian musical production to the teaching of catechism to people who are semi-illiterate. These efforts have paid off in both keeping Catholics in the fold and in energizing large numbers of Catholics to take their place in the church as evangelizers. This extroverted quality of Brazilian Catholics is relatively new. Before the late 1990s, Brazilian Catholics did not typically go door to door to invite the unchurched to prayer or to Mass; nor did Catholics, lay or clerical, routinely preach in the streets, as they have done in the most recent decade.

A further view of this fervor can be seen in the number of Brazilians who became lay missionaries: 30,895 in 2000. Most of them served within Brazil. But large numbers—no one knows how many—have volunteered or been assigned overseas. One can find them in Europe, Canada, the United States, and Africa, with credentials from Nova Canção and other covenant communities. They will probably want you to pray and sing along with them. Their vitality is contagious.

In sum, throughout Latin America, virtually all the known Catholic Charismatic centers, broadcasting stations, and publishing houses emphasize evangelization. A number of older centers, such as Minuto de Dios in Bogotá and La Mansión in Santa Cruz, Bolivia, added *centro de evangelización* to their formal title to make clear their dedication to this purpose.

Many of the communities also impelled their members to missionary activity away from home but in their own countries as lay missionaries or outside of Latin America, especially to the United States, Canada, and Europe. Evangelization has become a missionary vocation for many Latin American Catholics.

CHAPTER 8

Choosing Human Rights and Dying for Them

Emergencies and tragic events bring out the best and worst qualities in persons and institutions. We remember Winston Churchill and Rudolph Giuliani for their capable leadership in responding to world-shaking crises. So, too, major sectors of the Catholic Church in Latin America reacted to the shock of military repression and are remembered for their heroic stand. But the church did not pause after the military left presidential palaces: it followed the military era with a succession of further initiatives in human rights.

In the twentieth century, before the 1970s, human rights as a contemporary issue was barely acknowledged or discussed in Latin America. Two decades later most of the Latin American church, except Argentina, was known worldwide as a champion of human rights advocacy. Many clerics, including three bishops, and thousands of lay catechists were killed in its cause.

The church itself revised the way it saw itself in relation to society. As a "Church in the Modern World"—the English title of Vatican II's final document, *Gaudium et Spes*—it had to face the great moral issues of the day, including social justice, and to go beyond a narrow focus on personal morality. To do so it drew on a wellspring of one hundred years of social teaching. Pope John Paul II's most repeated message in his travels throughout the world over two decades was human rights.

The Fight for Human Rights Begins

Chile was considered one of the true democracies in Latin Americas in the 1970s. The country had a long democratic tradition, with only one or two short instances of military intervention. Chileans had a high regard for the rule of law and, like most Latin Americans, considered themselves citizens and not mere inhabitants of their country. President John Kennedy made Chile a showcase for democracy in his Alliance for Progress in the 1960s. Therefore, the military takeover of government came as a great shock to both Chileans and North Americans.

The fight for human rights began in Chile and in Latin America with explosive force.[1] On September 11, 1973, in Santiago, rockets and bullets flew from Hawker Hunter planes, tanks with heavy automatic weapons, and small arms, all aimed at the presidential palace with the goal of doing away with President Salvador Allende Gossens and his elected government. Allende brought about his own end, turning a carbine on himself. A cloud of military governance now covered Chile.

The coup came with the trappings of constitutional provisions and approval of many political and church leaders because of the chaos into which Chile had fallen under Salvador Allende. However, the armed forces used unnecessary force in the takeover and, though their regime was initially thought to be temporary, they set no time limit on their rule. The military also did away with political parties and democratic political processes. None of this was acceptable to the Chilean Catholic church. Cardinal Raúl Silva and many clerical and lay leaders made clear their opposition.

The military ruled all but two countries in South America and all but one country in Central America. Brazil, the largest Latin American country, and Bolivia, among the smallest, suffered military takeovers in 1964. Other countries followed in the 1960s and 1970s. The regimes of the 1960s were considered "soft" dictatorships (*dictablandas*). Later regimes became brutally harsh and created the urgency of the fight for human rights.

Uniformed men snatched Chileans and foreigners from streets, offices, and classrooms. No warrants for arrest or explanations were needed. Military men and police gave commands and did not answer questions. Security forces herded thousands into vans and cars and drove their prisoners to unknown destinations. Relatives and friends would spend years looking for, often not finding, many detainees.

Chile not only offers a clear example of the human rights violations that occurred in many countries; it is also salient for the path and strength of its organized response to human rights violations, a response that brought the churches, especially the Catholic church, to the forefront of the fight for human rights. The church became "the voice of the voiceless."

Organizing against Repression

The magnitude of repression and shock experienced by Chileans was matched by exceptional response. No country generated a human rights movement more quickly or more appropriately than Chile. Within days, Chileans began pulling together. While military strategists in late twentieth-century Latin America designed takeovers to atomize society, the strength of Chile's civil society began to work quickly to counter them. Along with many other actors, the church in Chile and elsewhere became a major factor in the turn to democracy that flooded through Latin America beginning in the 1970s. Samuel Huntington called this the "third wave" of democratization. (The first and second waves occurred from 1828–1926 and 1943–1962, respectively, and each was followed by reversals.[2]) Unlike other countries, where the initial response to military repression was more fragmented, in Chile, citizens organized themselves rapidly through churches, the only institutions left standing with their civil rights largely intact. Within days, Catholics and some Protestants organized themselves into two groups. Committee One looked after foreigners who had come to the country to work for the Frei (1964–1970) or Allende (1970-1973) governments. Committee Two members worked for the protection and care of Chileans. Both committees sought as their first priority safe passage to exile, rather than detention or death, of persons threatened with incarceration.

A larger organizational force emerged from these efforts. Within three weeks of the takeover Chileans created the pivotal organization, the Committee for Cooperation for Peace in Chile (COPACHI). The Catholic Church, Methodist, Evangelical Lutheran, and Methodist Pentecostal churches, Rabbinical College, and World Council of Churches were the founding members. Catholic bishop Fernando Ariztía and Lutheran Bishop Helmut Frenz stood as the strong copresidents.[3]

The work of this Committee for Peace challenged the legitimacy of the government of Augusto Pinochet, leader of Chile's military government from 1973 to 1990. Pinochet attacked the Committee directly. Cardinal Silva quickly put the main thrust of human rights work under the protection of the Catholic Church. Thus was formed probably the most famous human rights organization of this era, the Vicariate of Solidarity. Beyond direct legal protection and work with survivors, it stressed the themes of democracy and human rights in contrast to authoritarian rule.[4] The Vicariate continued its work through the sixteen years of military dictatorship. With the return of civilian rule, the Vicariate closed its doors. This, however, was not the end of its work. The church created the Archives and Museum of the Vicariate of Solidarity with files and legal briefs from 45,000 cases of alleged victims of military abuse.

Latecomer: Mexico

Compared with most of Latin America, where human rights movements began in the 1960s and 1970s and greatly expanded in the 1980s,[5] Mexico was a latecomer in human rights organization. Human rights violations in Mexico went largely unchallenged until the mid-1980s. Abundant evidence existed of electoral irregularities, fraud, and corruption by the governing party. International organizations accused the police and security forces of committing widespread human rights crimes. Extrajudicial killings, disappearances, torture, and arbitrary detentions took place over most of the country. Among the victims were peasants in dispute with landowners, political militants, and many reporters.[6]

The Catholic Church in Mexico was more subordinate to the state than in most Latin American countries.[7] After the state's active persecution, which extended into the 1930s, the church gained a measure of freedom for activity in religion and education, but not politics.[8] The church continued in what J. Lloyd Mecham describes as "a precarious position,"[9] relatively weak, without juridical status or the right to own property in its name. It was prohibited from political activity and its priests denied the right to vote.[10]

While the church gained greater freedom in the 1980s and 1990s, most bishops felt constrained not to enter the public sphere. Instead, the impetus to human rights advocacy came from the middle sector of the church, from activist priests and lay leaders. Many of the new human rights organizations in Mexico were church-related. Several of the more prominent ones were started and maintained by Dominicans (the Fray Bartolomé de las Casas Center for Human Rights, for example) and Jesuits (for example, the Miguel Agustín Pro Center for Human Rights). The vast majority of the members of these organizations, however, were lay leaders, most of them formed in the lay movements described earlier.

Human rights organizations are part of a larger phenomenon. In Mexico, as in Latin America generally, the numbers of nongovernmental organizations have reached major proportions.[11] They contributed to establishing civil society as the basis for functioning democracies in Latin America.[12] These movements emerge only when opportunities for their activities arise. In more accurately characterizing their role in Mexico, Joe Foweraker eschews the idyllic depiction of "the birth of civil society" and points out that popular movements created active political subjects in civil society.[13] These are the kinds of persons hoped for by Paulo Freire and others who saw informal education within Catholic lay movements as empowerment for agency in society. In Mexico, they were the response to the over-bearing authoritarianism of one party-rule by the PRI (*Partido Revolucionario Institucional* or Institutional Revolutionary Party).

Central America: Peace-Making as Human Rights Activity

What appeared to be a hopeless situation of civil war and government-sponsored repression ended in late December 1996 with the signing of the Central American Peace Accords for Guatemala, Nicaragua, and El Salvador, with the help of the other Central American countries and Panama. The Accords would not have taken place without three key church agents: external global church groups, internal peace movements, especially in Guatemala, and persevering and effective bishops. All were important in a complex process that included the unusually successful work of UN commissions. Global agencies included the Vatican, Lutheran World Service, and the World Council of Churches. The peace movements included priests and sisters but the vast majority of members were catechists and other laity from small Christian communities and other lay movements who heroically stepped forward. In Guatemala, several bishops served on national reconciliation, peace, and mediation commissions. As mentioned, one bishop, Juan Gerardi, was killed for his efforts for a truth commission.

Transitional Justice

Civilian rule returned in Latin America at various times, mostly in the 1980s and 1990s. The last South American country under a dictatorship, Chile, saw its military rulers leave office in 1990. In Central America, the Peace Accords that ended direct military rule took hold at the end of 1996.

Two great tasks remained and the church was a vital part of both. The first was truth and reconciliation, more commonly referred to as transitional justice.[14] Latin Americans believed that a historical record had to be established of the human rights violations.[15] Most Latin American countries, with the exception of Uruguay, established truth commissions. In virtually all these cases, the church took an active part. Chile, in effect, had two truth commissions. The first, the Rettig Commission, was aided by records from the Vicariate of Solidarity. While the Rettig Report (1991) on those killed under military dictatorship was hailed as an accomplishment, its limitations became clear as time passed. When former dictator Augusto Pinochet was arrested in London in 1998 on a warrant issued through the European Union, a flood of repressed memories among citizens stirred the Chilean government to create a second commission concerned with the torture of political prisoners. This commission was headed by Bishop Sergio Valech, former head of the Vicariate of Solidarity, and included lay members who had served at the Vicariate. It issued the first part of its report in 2004. The impetus to bring torture forward so that it would not be forgotten was due in part to the unrelenting efforts of Father José Aldunate, SJ, and other priests and lay collaborators.

The most dramatic example of establishing a historical record occurred in Brazil and demonstrated the splendid cooperation among different Christian denominations that occurred in that period. Brazilians made their first step in the most dramatic way possible and they did it as no other Latin American country, or perhaps any country in the world, would: They established the past record *out of military files.*

In a tale of intrigue worthy of the best thrillers, a small group of Brazilians borrowed files from the military, photographed, and published them. They maintained absolute secrecy for five years while the project was being carried on and for another year and a half about the authors of the project.[16]

A cultural legacy of the Portuguese and Spaniards who helped establish the "Latin American way" is bureaucratic record keeping. Any visitor to Latin America twenty years ago or anyone dealing with customs officials has experienced the need to have official stationery, seals affixed, copies signed by many officials, and papers filed. Record keeping acquired a life of its own in Latin America. To this tendency, add Brazilian ambitions of technological advancement as a military power. Since most trials took place under military jurisdiction, this meant careful records of charges, imprisonment, confessions, appeals, and reasons for judgments noted. Records made in various parts of the vast country went to the national capital, Brasília, where they were sorted, filed, and stored carefully. "Records were better kept than prisoners," was a common complaint heard in Latin America during military dictatorships.

One can then imagine the storehouse of materials built from 1964 to 1979 in Brasília.[17] As the generals extricated themselves from governing Brazil, the military began in 1979 to permit lawyers restricted use of its archive, allowing lawyers to take out files on individual cases for twenty-four hours.

Astute lawyers, sympathetic to human rights causes, approached Jaime Wright, a Brazilian whose parents were from the United States. Wright was moderator of the Presbyterian church/USA in Brazil and had lost a brother to military repression. Lawyers proposed to him the idea of photocopying large batches of records from the military archives. This would provide a view of what had been going on in secret for many years. Wright explained:

> We sat in the car mulling over the existence of that archive, and the chances of our having access to it. One of the passengers of the car was a member of the staff of the World Council of Churches, visiting Brazil from WCC's headquarters in Geneva, and he became enthusiastic about the idea.
>
> We hatched the whole plan right there in the car.... We realized, of course, that everything had to be handled with the utmost secrecy. The next day I went into the Cardinal's [Arns] office and presented the plan to him. He immediately endorsed it, and volunteered his personal sponsorship.[18]

The World Council of Churches granted over $350,000 over time. The Catholic archdiocese of São Paulo, 1,000 kilometers from Brasília, furnished safe storage. After three years of borrowing files, photocopying them, and transporting them to São Paulo, the small band had put together a million-page record.

The next, more difficult, task was to collate the pages and print a report. The group accomplished this, still with no leak, until the publication date grew near, and they informed reporters about what was to happen. The report appeared first in Portuguese as *Brasil: Nunca Mais* (Brazil, Never

Again). The publication of the most unusual of all Latin American records made a strong impression on the public. As Lawrence Weschler comments: "These accounts of torture were thus doubly astonishing: first in the indisputable authoritativeness—the undeniability—of the testimony; and secondly, in the very fact, the virtual scandal, that such testimony existed at all."[19]

As far as is known, none of the persons involved in the assembly of facts and in the publication of *Nunca Mais* was harmed. In contrast, Bishop Juan Gerardi of Guatemala was bludgeoned to death two days after he promulgated the report of the Archdiocesan Commission on Historical Truth, commonly referred to as REHMI (Recovery of Historical Memory Project).

Peru, like Guatemala, experienced a civil war in which the indigenous population was the main victim. The Peruvian government under President Valentín Paniagua created the Commission of Truth and Reconciliation. Church leaders, lay and clerical, played crucial roles in carrying out the work of establishing an historical record and in creating suitable ceremonies to honor the dead. Peru's human rights leaders were adamant in their determination *qué no se repita* (that this never be repeated).

Even in Uruguay, the small human rights sector kept alive the goal of having an historical record of military misdeeds for more than twenty-five years. One of the most prominent of these activists was Luis Pérez Aguirre, a Jesuit who had been imprisoned and tortured. Finally, in 2006 Uruguayan president Tabaré Vázquez promised justice for victims of abuse and murder by a military dictatorship that had held power decades earlier.

The Role of the Church: Education in Human Rights

The other great task for societies after military rule was educating citizens in the wide range of rights that need to exist in order to consolidate democracy. The Brazilian bishops saw an opportunity to collaborate with the state, which was struggling to inculcate democratic values in inhabitants who had no such experience.

In approaching the millennium that was to be celebrated with reflections on society, the Brazilian church took a leadership role in Latin America in church-state relations. In April 1996 the Brazilian National Bishops

Conference (CNBB) unveiled a four-year plan in which they addressed social issues, *Rumo ao Novo Milênio* (Way to the New Millennium).[20] Human rights was a core concern of the new plan.

Extensive activities supported this plan. The church at many levels has been shaping contemporary Brazilian politics. This new phase followed twenty-one years of increasingly repressive military rule (1964–1985). The Brazilian church was a major factor in fostering a return to democracy.[21]

Most Brazilians did not remember living in a democracy. Nor did all believe democracy to be worth the effort. Nonetheless, large numbers of Brazilians, many of them with close ties to the church, had been prodding the government to stimulate the processes and resources democracy is presumed to provide.

Their efforts met strong resistance. Democracy proved to be almost as conflictive as military rule. One of the first contests to occur under civilian rule began at the top. Fernando Collor's presidency (1990–1992) made democracy seem like a license to steal for the president and a small cabal around him. However, ordinary Brazilians, strengthened by their struggles with the military, proved intolerant of presidential misbehavior. The press, with new freedom, computer technologies to trace financial dealings, and the example of Watergate-era investigative journalism, helped bring Collor down. Despite the reluctance of legislators to police their own, public pressures prevailed. Collor resigned and Congress annulled his political rights for the near future. Collor became the first president in Latin American history forced to step down because of corruption.[22]

Since the military left the Planalto Palace in 1985, day-to-day violence, including that of security forces on civilians, has hardly abated. The massacre of street children and adolescents in the Candelaria area of Rio brought worldwide concern. Nevertheless, the killing of children and adolescents has continued. In 1996, a Franciscan priest-activist reluctantly admitted: "Frankly I prefer military rule to what we have now. The military was largely predictable. Now one does not know when or why violence will strike."[23] Violence has intensified as a social and cultural issue. Paulo Sergio Pinheiro, head of the highly regarded Nucleus for the Study of Violence at the University of São Paulo, became a major figure in Brazil for bringing attention to the problem. "The Brazilian way of dealing with child criminal behavior is killing," he said to Steve Kroft on *Sixty Minutes*.[24] Nonetheless, growing public intolerance for state violence is beginning to bring effective pressure. Two policemen were sentenced to 309 years in prison for the Candelaria slaughter.[25]

Frequent targets for violence by security forces or rural gunslingers have been not only street children and adolescents but also the homeless, and especially the *sem-terra* (the landless). Several million Brazilian farmers own no land in a country with millions of hectares lying untilled but promised them by various governments. In the struggle to obtain land titles, hundreds of the landless or their advocates have been killed in the last ten years. These deaths include the prominent cases of the Eldorado massacre and Father Josimo.[26] Violence thus surrounds key issues for the church and Brazilian society, land, and the homeless.

The clearest indication that the social justice, participatory pastoral approach was still alive for the Brazilian church is in the three-year plan for service in *Way to the New Millennium*, issued in 1997. Human rights received exceptional attention. The church concentrated on one or another area of human rights for each of the three years leading up to the millennium. As far as is known, no other church has proposed as wide a program of promotion of human rights as the Brazilian church.

During 1997, the church concentrated on civil rights, including: integrity of life, liberty, equality under the law, and, above all, freedom from the "coercion of violence," the evil that so bedevils daily life in Brazil. The following year, 1998, concentrated attention on social rights, as education, health, and the environment. The third year, 1999, emphasized economic rights, as the basic means of life (food, work, and housing.)

Since these themes were too general to be communicated effectively, each year a more compelling specific theme was chosen. For 1997, the theme was the condition of persons in prisons, and it was explored through the lens of scripture. Many Brazilians were aware of bestial conditions of prisons since the appearance of numerous stories of slaughter of prisoners by police and of overcrowding and sickness in prisons.

The Campaign for Brotherhood has been at the heart of the emphasis on service. During each Lent, this campaign has been mounted nationally to call attention to a single theme. In 1995, the *excluídos* (those excluded from the benefits of society) were emphasized; in 1996, *política* (politics). During the six weeks of Lent, parishes are expected, at a minimum, to preach on the theme chosen for that year, emphasizing one particular Gospel (Matthew, for example), and to raise money to benefit national and local agencies. As Lent approaches, a campaign poster appears around the country on bus stops, billboards, and parish church and school walls. Politics, the 1996 theme, posed a special problem for the team of biblical, liturgical, and educational experts who were designing materials for the campaign. The group needed a strong biblical motif and chose the Old Testament phrase "Justice and Peace Will Embrace." The poster shows two arms gripping one another in a gesture of survival.

Since church attendance increases during Lent, the national bishops' conference has regarded the Campaign for Brotherhood as an occasion to educate Catholics in sacrificial giving. This draws them closer to the practices of the Pentecostals, many of whom give a *dizimo*, a tenth of their income, to their churches. Lent is also an opportunity to evangelize. In many parishes, the yearly Lenten theme becomes a way to instruct large numbers in adult education classes.[27]

Human Rights Commitments

The Brazilian church's human rights campaign grows out of its existing human rights commitments. It builds on these commitments and raises hopes for new initiatives, such as in the urgent cause of prison reform.[28] As mentioned, the designers of the campaign also created it as way to educate members in the religious reasons for human rights protection.[29]

The church's past efforts have been impressive. Murray Kempton, writing in *The New York Review of Books*, said: "Even unbelievers like myself have to conclude that the Catholic church has become the steadiest, and in many places, the only defender of human rights the wide world can show."[30] In his extensive travels for Oxfam, Neil MacDonald found: "The vast majority of today's citizen activists had their first experience taking control of their lives through the church's grassroots Christian communities in the 1960s and 1970s."[31] Rowan Ireland, another longtime observer, studied participants in contestatory social movements: "I have yet to meet a person who did not have some small Christian community experience."[32] In a word, veterans of basic Christian communities serve as backbone for the expanding human rights movement.

Further, the majority (more than 60 percent) of the more than three hundred groups that comprise Brazil's National Movement for Human Rights (MNDH) were tied to the (mainly Catholic) churches.[33] A sense of the strong religious influence within the movement could be seen on the

MNDH's tenth anniversary in 1991. At the national meeting that year, Father Francisco Cavazutti, who had been blinded by landowners' gunmen in his struggle for Brazilian landless, was introduced and received a standing ovation. Father Virgílio Leite Uchoa, from the Brazilian Bishops Conference; Catholic Bishop Matthias Schmidt; and Bishop Alimr dos Santos, of the National Council of Christian Churches (CONIC), joined him at the same prominent table. The formalities culminated when then-Franciscan Father Leonardo Boff received the National Human Rights Award.

The church's activities closely parallel the goals of the MNDH (land, labor rights, and the struggle against violence). The church's institutional commitment to the landless has been expressed since 1975 by an extraordinary corps of persons making up the Pastoral Land Commission (CPT).[34] In her study of Amazonian farmworkers, Madeleine Cousineau Adriance found that Pastoral Land Commission "appears to be the single agency that is doing the most to help rural poor people gain and hold on to land and to organize efforts toward agrarian reform."[35]

CPT members have been in the forefront of the national Movement for the Landless (MST). The Movement for the Landless "cannot be easily shrugged off," says Brazilian social scientist Fábio Petrarolha. "Hundred of thousands of [rural] workers have become involved."[36] The seamless bonding among active Catholic laypeople and priests and the landless movement is evident in the national assemblies of grassroots Christian communities (CEBs). The assembly each year displays a large cross. Participants attach small placards with names of those killed in the struggle for land. The names are now crowded on the cross—more than five hundred—with Father Josimo best remembered.

Margaret Keck, the recorder of the Brazilian labor movement, marks the general influence of the church: "It is impossible to overstate the importance of the Catholic church's role in providing space … communications network, and human rights advocacy" during military rule.[37] CEB members headed opposition slates in the key metalworkers unions. In the progression of events, they spearheaded the formation of the Labor Party (PT) that won the Brazilian presidential campaigns of 2002. Moreover, the church's support for these movements and their efforts continues. Paulo Sergio Pinheiro, the leading figure in Brazilian human rights, believes: "The Catholic church continues as a strong force in human rights protection. Its activity at many levels is crucial."[38]

The same cannot be said of the government's credibility. In April 1996, Brazilian military police killed nineteen landless workers, shooting many of them in the back at close range.[39] The dead from this massacre at Eldorado de Carajas were being commemorated in Brazilian churches as President Cardoso left for Paris. There, with Pinheiro and the National Plan for Human Rights proposal at his side, Cardoso attempted to woo French supporters and investors.[40] Back home, in the debate about Eldorado, Pinheiro publicly stated that the most important protection of human rights and the best possible response to the massacre would be transfer of cases against the military police to civilian courts. However, congress rejected civilianization near the eve of the publication of the National Human Rights Program.[41]

Why do Brazilian Catholic bishops and activists continue in the face of such intransigence? Keck explains:

> Grassroots Catholic organizing promoted an ethos whose key values were autonomy (from state and party) and self-organization, and whose prototypical image was the *caminhada*, or long march of the people of God toward a just society, or the kingdom of God. The significance lay in the process itself more than its ends.[42]

More than process is involved. Several social scientists interviewed agreed that the human rights situation has improved significantly.[43] One outstanding achievement has been the formation of a Brazilian coalition to defend street children and adolescents, the kind that are slaughtered at the rate of about one a day in Rio and São Paulo.

The Street Children and Adolescents Movement (MNMMR) grew from pioneering groups formed under military dictatorship. Since then, the National Conference of Catholic Bishops joined with MNMMR, the National Front for the Defense of Child and Adolescent Rights, the National Order of Attorneys, and others groups to form a loose coalition. In a monumental effort, including 3,000 print articles and 72 television programs, the coalition saturated the country and mounted a massive mobilization. The process culminated in the passage of Article 227 of the Constitution and, more importantly, the Child and Adolescent Statute, in July 1990. The change of perspective between the old Minor's Code and the new statute was radical.[44] The latter now emphasized "child" and "adolescent" as categories that referred to all Brazilians in certain age categories. Previously, the offspring of the Brazilian wealthy had been called children and adolescents, while the offspring of the poor were called *meninos* (minors). Paul Jeffrey recalls a headline in Belém: "Minor Attacks Child" (meaning a poor child attacked a rich child).[45] The statute's abolition of *menino* allowed emphasis on the basic rights of children and youth as human beings.

Cynical observers could point out that what was granted by legislators were words, printed laws. Neither Presidents Fernando Collor (1990–1992) nor Itamar Franco (1992–1994) nor national legislators granted monies needed to make the program effective. Further, power holders within the political-bureaucratic apparatus carried on the authoritarian past. Eli Diniz and Renato Boschi point to features that persist: closed style, low transparency, little accountability, strong clientelistic ties, and low capacity for implementation and enforcement.[46] Thus patronage and cronyism act as obstacles to implementation of the Child and Adolescent Statute.

Numerous small steps at the municipal governmental level have taken effect in Brazil. At this level, the interplay between nongovernmental and governmental actors continues as a political battleground. Nongovernmental organizations (NGOs) dealing with children and adolescents have wrested a measure of power in newly created municipal councils in some cities. In many others, NGOs are ignored or held at arm's length, or their initiatives incorporated into local government programs for children where benign aspects of the program die.

Nonetheless, human rights activists point to a fundamental achievement: change in the law by which they are willing to live. If a law is on the books, a good chance exists that public prosecutors will enforce it. As Anthony Dewees and Steven Klees remark, they do so "in part simply because the new law exists and their responsibility and personal orientation is to enforce laws."[47] Human rights activist lawyers march on, presenting case after case, seeking justice for the killers of children. They helped to bring down a celebrated *justiciero* (vigilante), Cabo Bruno, a former policeman who had bragged to the media about getting away with more than fifty killings.

With a National Plan for Human Rights approved, the church had further reason to pressure the government for action. Laws increasingly have consequences in Brazil. Willingness to pursue the rule of law continues to drive human rights activists and the church and marks a sea change in Brazilian and many Latin American societies.[48]

Contemporary Themes

The focus of observers of Latin America on how Latin Americans and the church have dealt with the past obscures the contemporary activity that has branched off into new areas with considerable vitality involving millions of church members.[49] Notable achievements have been made in terms of women's rights, street children, landless, policing, and torture. Some of the struggles have been noted in the case of Brazil. Indigenous rights and corruption are further significant issues.

With regard to indigenous rights, Latin America's forty million indigenous have recently made major strides in gaining political recognition and civil rights after more than five hundred years of marginalization. The church played important roles in indigenous activism, helping to strengthen indigenous identity and contributing intellectual and physical resources for the struggle to obtain educational, occupational, and heath benefits in racist societies.

The most prominent example of indigenous activism occurred in Chiapas, Mexico, where Bishop Samuel Ruiz Garcia became known as the Father of the Indians. Similar indigenous resurgences took place in Guatemala, Bolivia, and elsewhere. This occurred especially through a cooperative effort of bishops, missionary priests from the United States, Canada, and Europe, and lay catechists. The catechists were crucial in the roles as community leaders and brokers in the cultural assimilation of the Christian message. The effort also resulted in the production of native intellectuals and the beginnings of indigenous theology.

The second human rights issue, corruption, has been present for centuries. Now in Latin America, along with some other regions of the world, human rights groups have made corruption a special target. Corruption has increased in scale due to new opportunities and so, too, have efforts to combat corruption. The globalization of national economies in the last fifteen years offered new opportunities for enrichment. Not only did a globalized economy in general bring large opportunities for illicit enrichment, national institutional sources of corruption increased in post-authoritarian situations. Transnational sources of investment money and "incentives" add new and often secret sources of enrichment. The size of development projects mean billions of dollars available.

The Catholic Church, especially in the person of one of its main leaders, Cardinal Oscar Rodríguez, archbishop of Honduras, has thrown its weight into this struggle since the mid-1990s. The church, especially Cardinal Rodríguez, has forcibly echoed the argument voiced by human rights activists that corruption in government steals from the poor the resources that should provide for their health, education, and other services. The Latin American Bishops Conference (CELAM) began in the late 1990s to lay a foundation for what would become a major thrust of the church. In its 1997 *Declaración ética contra la corrupción*, the church analyzed the situation of public and private corruption. National bishops' conferences followed this lead. The Central American bishops were soon described by the Honduras newspaper *La Prensa* as making anticorruption efforts "the new war horse of the Catholic Church."

The Ecuadoran bishops in 1998 made a strong appeal from scripture and the social teaching of the church. The Argentine bishops took a sharp stand in 2001, calling corruption the evil that undermines the country. In 2004, the Mexican bishops proposed a five-point plan to combat corruption in the country. While some may view these as heady discussions, others see church efforts as useful in stimulating a national discussion about corruption. One Rome participant, a European based in Tokyo and a corporate vice-president in charge of risk assessment, told me that he had been attending conferences on corruption for ten years and almost never encountered a church person. "It is essential that the churches be an active voice in national discussions," he said.

After Cardinal Rodríguez left the presidency of CELAM, he continued in a key leadership position in CELAM as chair of the Commission on Justice and Peace. However, it was primarily in his role as the ranking cleric in Honduras that he carried on a public campaign to call attention to the national evil of governmental corruption and the need to combat it. As always, reform depends on opportunity. One presented itself when hurricane Mitch devastated sections of the country and citizens wondered what happened to the large funds generated for disaster assistance. A fair percentage of Hondurans felt that government officials had pocketed some of the money. This suspicion thus fueled discussion of corruption as a major national issue.

The government responded to Rodríguez's lobbying by forming a National Commission on Corruption but could not find anyone willing to chair the commission. By default, Rodríguez took over the chairmanship. He is much admired by most Hondurans, although esteem offers him no personal shield against attack on his person. When the author went to interview Rodríguez at his office, the archbishop arrived in a jeep-style vehicle with two alert SWAT team policemen with automatic weapons. Rodríguez had been receiving death threats. While he could point to no measurable success of his commission, he did say that he would have been content to increase awareness of the problem. That was in 2004. Two years later, a half million Hondurans had taken part in programs sponsored by the commission.

Corruption has been engaged as a human rights issue and will be on the table for a long time. Human rights has been an issue since the 1600s and will continue to engage lay and clerical leaders as part of the implications of their discipleship.

CHAPTER 9

Peace-Keeping
and Mediating

During the 1970s and 1980s, several church leaders and many ordinary Catholic faithful in Latin America put their lives on the line, were killed, and are hailed as spiritual models for the contemporary church. The two major roles played by these heroic witnesses—promoting peace and acting as mediators in conflicts—fostered deep confidence in the church.

The peacemaking role came to the fore in the 1980s and 1990s, but peacemakers continue to this day to promote transitional justice, which entails, at a minimum, establishing a historical record of the injustices committed during armed conflict. These peacemaking activities are among the contributions to the promotion of democracy and the rule of law as its cornerstone.

The Catholic Church was a major player in advancing democracy in Latin America, after decades of authoritarian rule by military or one-party totalitarian regimes. Harvard historian Samuel Huntington, who delineated waves of democratization in the modern world in his groundbreaking work, *The Third Wave: Democratization in the Late Twentieth Century*,[1] identified the Catholic Church, especially in Latin America, as the second strongest factor after socioeconomic development that contributed to the remarkable turn to democracy.

Civil wars, real and threatened,[2] occupied the energies of many Latin Americans during the latter third of the twentieth century. Latin American Catholics were also occupied with peace and justice issues that accompanied the transition to democracy from military rule in the Cold War period to civil governance. One facet of the transition was commonly described as transitional justice, or the accounting for abuses that occurred, including the establishment of a public record. The church found a special niche there. It also revived a longstanding tradition in Latin American societies of acting in public as mediator, a role it seldom exercises in Anglo-Saxon countries such as the United States or Canada.

The Central American Internal Wars and Fostering Peace

Nowhere were contemporary Latin American peacemaking efforts more difficult—and dangerous—than in Central America. Bishop Juan Gerardi, one of several martyrs of the period, was murdered two days after he reported the findings of the Interdiocesan Truth Commission in Guatemala City. The peacemaking effort was notable here also because it was widely transnational, involving the five Central American countries along with Panama, the United Nations, and transnational nongovernmental organizations. While the Catholic Church employed a range of agencies in the peace effort—including the Conference of Bishops of Central America and Panama, the national bishops' conferences of these countries, and individual bishops—such upper-level public efforts were backed by grassroots peace movements that involved many believers, both Catholic and Protestant. Ecumenical efforts toward peace were especially strong in Central America.[3] The World Council of Churches and the Lutheran World Federation played crucial roles in the process. Persons from both Catholic and Lutheran traditions filled the ranks of the peace movements.

Guatemala

In terms of numbers of those killed or otherwise personally affected by armed conflict, Guatemala exceeded all other countries in Latin America. Here the UN Truth Commission found that more than 200,000 persons were killed, 93 percent of them by state armed forces.[4] Moreover, because the majority of victims were indigenous, the conflict was regarded as ethnocide.[5] Beginning in 1954 Guatemala was increasingly torn apart by its armed forces and by leftist militants. Although the struggle was confined within national borders, it involved many outside forces, including covert operations carried out by the CIA and other agencies of the United States.[6] The conflict was enshrouded in secrecy in Guatemala itself, where the government denied or downplayed its antisubversive activities, as well as in the United States, where the government continued to deny its role in fueling the conflict until President Bill Clinton offered an apology in March 1999 for United States involvement.[7]

Guatemalan governments, closely allied with wealthy elites and the military high command,[8] concealed the existence of armed militants in the country in order to avoid loss of foreign investments and, to avoid scrutiny by transnational human rights advocates, hid the indiscriminate anti-guerrilla tactics of its military. Thanks to the work of three Truth Commissions, the release of archival materials, and the diligence of trustworthy historians, a reliable narrative of the conflict can be constructed.[9]

Among the various causes of the violence in Guatemala were the thwarting of the democratic processes by the ruling elites, the need for land reform, and the militarization of conflicts[10] rather than resorting to political processes.[11] Large numbers of those murdered in Guatemala between 1960 and 1996 were innocent people killed by the military without judicial process. Many victims were community leaders in indigenous areas, the Catholic catechists mentioned in a previous chapter. Not only lay leaders, but also fourteen priests, two religious brothers, and a nun were among the slain Catholic leaders.[12]

While violence raged in Guatemala, Nicaragua, and El Salvador, heads of the Central American states forged the Esquipulas I and II Accords in the 1980s. Neither brought immediate peace. Catholics and Lutherans formed an international ecumenical peace delegation that persuaded an influential sector of the Guatemalan army to allow the Comisión Nacional de Reconciliación (CNR) to hold talks with the united guerrilla group, the Unidad Revolucionaria Nacional Guatemalteca (UNRG), in an Oslo church in March 1990. In the next step sponsored by these religious actors, the UNRG met with five sectors of Guatemalan society. The meeting with the religious sector in Quito in September 1990 established an agenda of political and other issues that were to be resolved in a peace settlement.

Contentious factions among the insurgents and the military made the peace process from 1990 to late 1996 arduous and convoluted. The step taken by the Oslo initiative, however, demonstrated the ability of many transnational actors to facilitate the process. Lutheran pastors in the United States and Scandinavia persuaded the Lutheran World Federation to form a peace team and sponsor behind-the-scenes efforts. The Vatican's Pontifical Council for Promoting Christian Unity, the Guatemalan Catholic bishops, the Catholic Episcopal Secretariat for Central America, and the U.S. Conference of Catholic Bishops all joined in the cooperative effort. This venture was later expanded.

Bishop Rodolfo Quezada Toroño of Zacapa, the future cardinal archbishop of Guatemala, became the Catholic Church's chief delegate to the Comisión Nacional de Reconciliación (CNR) and its president as well. Bishop Juan Gerardi Conedara, auxiliary bishop of Guatemala City, became Quezada's back up. This commission promoted an unusual initiative (for the time) of sponsoring a National Dialogue that paved the way for Guatemalan civil society to enter the national discussion. Some sixty organizations took part, with many participants from six church groups.[13]

When the National Dialogue collapsed after two years, the vibrant civil sector stepped forward with a new peace initiative in 1994. Religious groups and popular organizations, now numbering in the hundreds, formed the Assembly of Civil Society (Asamblea de Sectores Civiles, or ASC). This grassroots group proposed consensus positions on peace issues and decided whether to ratify accords completed in high-level negotiations. This represented a consolidation of the peace movement fueled by Catholic and other religious activists.

Many leaders of and participants in the peace movement came from the religious sector. Movement members struggled to create a national constituency for peace that would be actively aware of the peace negotiations. In a society whose media had no experience in open reporting, peace movement members pressured press and radio directors to report peace negotiations; they marched in demonstrations, held ecumenical services, and discussed refugee concerns, resettlement, and human rights.

Once armed conflict between the URNG and the Guatemalan army had ceased in late 1996, members of the peace movement were adamant that the gross human rights violations of the previous thirty years be publicly investigated and documented. Latin American Catholics and many other members of human rights organizations were determined to establish investigations and reports into the gross human rights violations that had occurred, especially in Guatemala, where many offenses, including mass slaughter, took place clandestinely and with slanderous rumors spread by government forces about alleged subversive activity carried on by Catholic catechists and other leaders.

The church in Latin America believed that their societies needed to confront the burden of the past to restore a sense of justice for all citizens, especially the numerous victims, to engender trust in state institutions that had been lost, to bring about reconciliation of perpetrators and victims, and to prevent future abuses.

The Catholic Church in Guatemala seized the initiative by establishing the Interdiocesan Project for the Recovery of Historical Memory (Recuperación de Memoria Histórica Interdiocesana, or REMHI). The effort to compile the report—entitled *Guatemala: Never Again*—was enormous and painstaking. Two days after it was issued, on April 26, 1998, the chief spokesman for the project, Bishop Juan Gerardi, was beaten to death.[14] Intimidation of other project leaders also occurred.[15] However, the internationally sponsored Commission for Historical Clarification's *Guatemala: Memory of Silence* (1999) confirmed the church's report.

Bishop Gerardi's efforts toward national peace and reconciliation followed a long and arduous path. A son of Italian immigrant parents growing up in the capital and partly educated in the United States, he was fortunate in his early priestly life to be assigned parochial care of Guatemala's majority indigenous. They were from a culture and class that Gerardi, as a white European, did not know well. For some twenty years, he allowed himself to be open to, rather than dictate to, a sector of society that was typically lower class, unlettered, and poor, with a culture foreign to his own. Further, this prolonged contact and the cultural learning that took place during Gerardi's first decades as a pastor raised the issues for him that would motivate him for the rest of his life. A central issue, as he saw it, was the exclusion of talented and religious persons from full participation in Guatemalan society and from the enjoyment of human rights. He came to see that the Mayan peoples had a high civilization, but had lost their cultural hegemony to Europeans and were held in check by repressive means employed by Guatemala's ruling elites in union with the United Fruit Company and other U.S. agencies.

As an active and trusted priest, he was promoted to bishop. As bishop of El Quiché in the heartland of Mayan civilization, where the Guatemalan army was battling guerrilla forces, he became acutely aware of the indiscriminate murders, between 1980 and 1983, of many catechists and Delegates of the Word.[16] Gerardi protested these killings. He began then to pay a price for his protests and was exiled by the Guatemalan government first to El Salvador and then to Costa Rica, where he led the unsettled life of the exiled.

Unable to return to El Quiché, he accepted assignment as auxiliary bishop of Guatemala City. Having gained a toehold back in his own country, he set about organizing a team of lay professionals and obtaining foreign church support in order to establish the Archdiocesan Human Rights Center of Guatemala City (Organización de Derechos Humanos Arquidiocesana, or ODHA) in 1983. The ODHA investigated the victims of "the violence," as the ethnocide and the systematic violation of human rights were called at the time. His efforts came to be supported by other dioceses. ODHA grew in size and became well known internationally. Its staff included lawyers, forensic specialists, and an inner core known as the Untouchables because of their good fortune in not being assassinated for their careful investigations into crime scenes that were mostly caused by government forces.

A new archbishop, Próspero Penados del Barrio, gave unswerving backing to Gerardi and ODHA. This gave Gerardi a measure of protection in his increasingly important role as one of the church's voices in the peace process. The Peace Accords that were patched together over some years went into effect in December 1996. They included provision for a truth commission sponsored by the United Nations. The UN Historical Clarification Commission was intended to establish the history of the crimes of the previous years. Gerardi and many other human rights activists who had participated in the peace negotiations had good reason to doubt that the UN Commission would have enough cooperation within the country to obtain a trustworthy account of the events. The UN Commission was also limited because it agreed not to identify human rights violators by name and not to assign responsibility for the killings. Nor could testimony given the Commission be used for future prosecutions. Most observers agreed with author Francisco Goldman's assessment that Gerardi pushed ahead with ODHA's own investigations and report as a "counterweight" to the UN's efforts through REHMI a parallel and supportive investigation established by ODHA.[17] "For half a century," wrote Goldman, "the military's clandestine world seemed impregnable.[18] The Gerardi case opened a path into that darkness."[19] In other words, Gerardi's work was necessary for the future UN Commission that received a sufficient measure of acceptance within the country to carry on its work.

Peacemaking Beyond Guatemala

The church's report ran to four volumes and 1,400 pages and assumed the same name and purpose of Truth Commissions sponsored largely by church groups elsewhere in Latin America: *Guatemala: Never Again*. The best-known and most dramatic case was Brazil. Through protection offered by the archbishop of São Paulo and financing largely from the Protestant World Council of Churches, a million pages of military records were quietly photocopied and compiled into a lasting record of military government abuses in the country.[20]

As the Brazilian church formed a safe citadel for historical records, so too the Chilean church took into its safekeeping the records of military abuses in that country. (Records of contested cases in Latin America have a history of being burned under suspicious circumstances.)[21] The famous advocate of human rights in Chile, the Vicariate of Solidarity, went out of existence after democracy returned to Chile, but its 40,000 dossiers on individual victims of human rights were well protected at the Archives of the Vicariate on church property in Santiago.

In all these efforts to establish truth commissions or a process of some sort after massive human rights violations, the church made clear that justice and peace are inseparable. Some sort of accounting along the lines of Brazil took place in Argentina, Uruguay, Paraguay, and Honduras.[22] Since Vatican II, from the Vatican down to national-level bishops' conferences to individual dioceses, almost all offices dealing with religion and society are called justice and peace, often understood simply as human rights. Nowhere, I would contend, has the human rights tradition been more evident (and more appreciated by common people) than in Latin America. In this I follow Harvard Law School's Mary Ann Glendon and Notre Dame Law School's Paolo Carrozzo, who argued that Latin America has a distinctive human rights tradition beginning in the sixteenth century with the Dominican missionary Bartolomé de las Casas.[23] The most recent evidence of this tradition was the preponderant Latin American contribution to the Universal Declaration of Human Rights (1945), in contrast to the inertia or open opposition of the European nations and the United States to the Human Rights Declaration.[24] Those countries, still caught up in colonialism or racism, were cautious about accepting the full extension of human rights to all citizens.

Gerardi and others thus staked their lives on implanting a strong measure of justice into the peace process. He and many others believed it would not suffice simply to put aside arms and begin living peacefully. Injustice had to be recognized; then reconciliation could follow. Peace, in other words, was actively achieved by the restoration of justice or, in the long-standing Christian phrasing, by repairing the fabric of society.

The costs to the church in terms of personnel lost through assassination were high and were still being felt in 2008 in places like Rabinal, Guatemala. Father Tim Conlan, OP, writing from that area, observed: "The struggle to resurrect the church after the deaths of so many priests, catechists, and simple faithful goes on at many levels."[25]

The blood of martyrs brings forth new life in the church, concluded Brian Pearce, another Dominican priest who spent years in Honduras and Guatemala.[26] Increases in vocations to the priesthood and religious life are indicators of that new life. In both Guatemala and El Salvador, where state-sponsored terrorism was the greatest in Central America, the number of priests increased notably, despite death, exile, and departure of foreign missionaries. In Guatemala, the percentage of priests increased 301 percent between 1956 and 2006; in El Salvador, the increase in the same period was 201 percent. The percentages of seminarians—signs of the future—increased 169 percent in Guatemala and 130 percent in El Salvador between 1972 and 2006. The numbers of seminarians had been dismal in both countries before the internal wars.

The numbers of women in religious life increased from 1,018 in 1972 to 2,743 in 2006 in Guatemala and from 705 in 1972 to 1,625 in 2006 in El Salvador. The latter country suffered the well-publicized and horrific murders of three religious sisters[27] and the lay volunteer Jean Donovan, whose life was commemorated in best-selling nonfiction and film.[28] In contrast to the United States and Europe, where numbers of women religious are experiencing a great decline, the women religious of these countries are thriving. They are also actively engaged in civic and religious organizations to rebuild the church and society.

Lay catechists, who were the targets of thousands of political murders in both countries, have increased phenomenally to 50,267 in Guatemala and to 16,593 in El Salvador. As noted previously, virtually all are dedicated to evangelization. Among them are a number of lay preachers who participate in the Catholic Charismatic Renewal. The church that was persecuted and lost thousands of members by death in the internal war has come alive with thousands of active lay ministers, evangelists, and communicators bent on spreading a Catholic evangelical message in ways that were not common before the thirty years of war. Members of the Charismatic Renewal have emphasized both prayer (often in ecumenical settings) and activity (for example, a Guatemalan health clinic called the Peace Clinic and accessible to people of all faiths). At the end of October 2006, the movement sponsored the Central American Vigil for Peace. Some 30,000 attended, even though traveling within Guatemala City, especially in the evening, is dangerous because of violent crime.

Having been through an era of martyrdom, Catholic leaders and faithful together created memorials that serve as way markers for pilgrims to Central America. These memorials were put up primarily to remind Central Americans of what had occurred and to prevent such killings from happening again. The centerpiece of all the memorials, and one visited by Salvadorans and foreigners with equal fervor, is that of Archbishop Oscar Romero. He is viewed as a saint and a popular icon has been created for him that many carry with them as a holy card or display on the walls of their homes.[29] Visitors stop at his tomb and attend Mass nearby at the altar of the Hospital of Divine Providence, where he was slain. Another significant memorial that draws some 40,000 persons yearly commemorates the Jesuits and Companion Martyrs at the Catholic University in San Salvador. There a Rose Garden and Museum help re-create a sense of the meaning of their deaths as a message of peace. On the tenth anniversary of their death in 1999, Ismael Moreno wrote, "By their death, the martyrs showed that dialogue and negotiation continue to be the privileged instruments for seeking profound responses to conflicts in society."[30]

These memorials became main stops on the annual weeklong pilgrimage sponsored by Maryknoll Fathers and Brothers. In January 2009 the pilgrimage, or retreat, for bishops, priests, and deacons from the United States, was in its tenth year. After visiting the resting places of Romero and the Jesuits, the pilgrims moved on to the nearby tombs of Father Alfonso Navarro and Father Rutilio Grande. They also spent time at the Martyrs' Wall at San Salvador's Cuscatlán Park. Among the 25,000 names engraved there in alphabetical order is Oscar Arnulfo Romero, without further distinction, indicating that he made himself part of the people and those who died violently. His name has been rubbed so frequently that a sheen has developed.[31] He is referred to by the ordinary people visiting there as "San Romero," a curious but affectionate use of last rather than first name. The pilgrims then pushed on to Santiago Nonualco, where the four churchwomen from the United States were slain.

The pilgrims crossed into Guatemala to trace the life of another North American, Father Stan Rother, a priest from Oklahoma City, who stayed as pastor in Santiago Atitlán despite certain death. Fr. Rother captured that sense of foreboding in his letters, which were published as *The Shepherd*

Cannot Run.[32] Two films were also made about his life.[33] The villagers petitioned successfully to have his heart interred beneath the altar of his parish church in Atitlán, although his body was buried in Oklahoma. The Oklahoma City archdiocese initiated his canonization process in 2006.

Nine years after Rother's death, the Guatemalan army massacred eleven villagers at Santiago. A Peace Park has been created at that killing ground. Each year the people of Santiago celebrate eleven days of ceremony, to keep the memory alive and to foster attitudes of peace and reconciliation. (Their optimism, also a reflection of Rother's joyfulness, was captured years ago on the *MacNeil-Lehrer Report*).[34]

The Maryknoll pilgrimage ends at Guatemala City, with reflections on the life of Bishop Gerardi and a visit to Cardinal Rodolfo Quezada Toruño and to the Archdiocesan Office of Human Rights. The very large Tenth Anniversary Commemoration of the death of Gerardi and the steady stream of visitors showed the lasting effect of linking memory and justice to peace and godliness.

In the United States, memorials to Archbishop Romero continued long after his death in 1980. Father Robert Pelton, CSC, made a determined effort to bring Romero to the attention of wave after wave of University of Notre Dame students and to a wider audience. He has used a variety of means to do so but none is better known than the annual campus commemorations with keynote lecture, discussion, and Mass. A selection from the yearly series of lectures resulted in the publication of *Monsignor Romero: A Bishop for the Third Millennium.*[35]

Father Pelton was acting as producer of a new film on Romero, two decades after the film *Romero* (1989) that starred Raúl Julia. The new movie would incorporate the Fresno, California, trial of the person liable for organizing Romero's murder, former Salvadoran Air Force Captain Álvaro Rafael Saravia. He was brought to trial and convicted in the United States through the San Francisco–based Center for Justice and Accountability because Salvadoran governments had granted blanket amnesty to its armed forces.[36] While the legal details of trying a foreigner on American soil are of curiosity to legal practitioners,[37] more important here was the spreading of the vision of ensuring that justice and peace in another country could be promoted across national lines.

While a measure of justice was obtained by the U.S. court case in Fresno, the church in El Salvador renewed its campaign urging the Salvadoran government to reopen the case. An editorial of the weekly

Catholic magazine *Orientación* argued: "We have to recognize that to establish the truth through judicial sentence contributes to the character of our society and can help to heal it."[38]

The president of El Salvador, Antonio Saca, rejected the argument, claiming that maintaining amnesty avoids opening the wounds of the past. The church's legal office responded, "the wounds of the past have never been closed, because justice has never been done." International opinion favored the church's position. The Consortium of Human Rights Organizations proposed that El Salvador overturn its amnesty law, asserting that amnesty violates several international conventions and treaties, as well as El Salvador's own Constitution. María Silvia Guillén, director of the Foundation for Studies in the Application of Law, agreed that there would be no healing without justice.[39]

Among other groups in the United States that revered Romero, few can compare with Catholics in Camden, New Jersey, one of the poorest urban areas of the country. There a largely lay group has backed a yearly lecture by notable persons on the date of Romero's death (March 24). Romero is honored as a prophet and saint who calls the people to favor the poor and to work for peace and justice.[40] Not long before his death, Archbishop Romero wrote to President Jimmy Carter, pleading for assistance in building peace. He was ignored by Carter but heard by the poor of the United States.

Church as Mediator

The prophetic stance for peace is far from the only major public role of the Latin American church. In fact, one can argue that mediation has been as common as prophecy and perhaps, in many contexts, a preferable alternative. The dilemma of whether to continue as prophet arose early in the career of Arturo Rivera y Damas as he succeeded Romero as archbishop of San Salvador. Rivera's councilors advised him to pursue the path of peace negotiation and mediation rather than continue on the prophetic path marked out by Romero. He did this, seizing every possible opportunity to bring rival groups to the bargaining table. This change from Romero's way of operating brought intense criticism inside and outside the country. Nevertheless, in the end, Rivera prevailed. With reinforcement from Central American leaders and transnational agencies, El Salvador signed peace accords with rebels in 1992. Rivera died peacefully in 1996, recognized as an honorable successor to Romero. In short, both functions served the church and society well in troubled El Salvador.

Of all the many roles churches play in politics in the United States, the role of mediator is notably missing. In thirty years, I was able to note only one instance of mediation, that of the auxiliary bishop of Miami who acted as mediator of a prison riot. In Latin America, by contrast, the Catholic Church mediates conflicts as a birthright, as one of its most accepted and important roles. Even when both sides to a conflict are avowedly secular, even anticlerical, the church has been called in by both sides as a broker to a possible agreement.

This role seems to be perceptible only to Latin Americans, especially those who discover their religion as adults, such as Emelio Betances, a scholar from the Dominican Republic who has written one of the first academic accounts of this role.[41] The role is so natural, so accepted as part of many Latin American societies, that it is often overlooked. Scholars have been slow to focus on the church's mediating role. It is almost never mentioned by major figures writing about politics and religion in Latin America, although journalists and historians have routinely reported on critical interventions in which the church played a crucial role. Jeffrey Klaiber, a Chicago Jesuit long resident in Peru, and Emelio Betances are believed to be the first to have published on the theme in contemporary times.[42] Betances and I have been attempting to trace this theme since 1994. The following account, then, results from long reflection on what is one of the least understood but most positive roles a church can perform.

Conflict mediation may seem a trivial pursuit when carried out as resolution of differences of minor conflicts in a city neighborhood. However, it has been carried out, as well, in the high drama of the brink of civil war, such as in Venezuela and Bolivia. The first notable mediation in contemporary times by the church occurred in Venezuela. In the mid-1950s, after a series of military presidents and social and economic crises, the country appeared to be on the brink of political disintegration. The major political actors recognized the gravity of the crisis and the possibility of civil war. Major players in society were called in to forge a National Accord. As a result, the major political parties agreed to cooperate by alternately ruling the country. At that time, the parties were deeply divided by ideological differences and did not trust one another. The Catholic Church acted as mediating guarantor of the agreement. The Venezuelan church was institutionally weak but nonetheless recognized as omnipresent and part of the moral fabric of the country. Without the church, there might not have been the long peace that followed. Venezuela had the longest running democracy in Latin America through 2007. That the democracy may be derailed by President Hugo Chávez in subsequent years is due in part to his rejection of the church's overtures toward national peace and reconciliation.

After the 1950s Accord, the Venezuelan church receded to the side-lines of public life until the late 1980s. With encouragement from the Vatican, the bishops and leading Catholic intellectuals played a prominent role in public life, stirred by events surrounding the uprisings in the barrios of Caracas. In 2002, as President Chávez had yet to put his full authoritarian stamp on national politics, bishops from the Venezuelan Bishops Conference (CEV) met with various foreign mediators from the UN, OAS, and the Carter Center. The bishops offered to sponsor mediation between the government and opposition groups, if a clear agenda could be put forward beforehand. As has been increasingly clear, this was a critical juncture in Venezuelan history. As the bishops and many others saw it, extremists on both sides must not be allowed "to set the rhythm that this country has to dance to."[43]

In the early 1980s, Bolivia experienced a situation somewhat similar to Venezuela's near breakdown in the 1950s. That perpetually fractious country (200 governments in 150 years) was on the verge of breakdown, with political actors unable to agree upon the selection of an interim president when the elected president admitted he could not govern. Bolivia's military left the presidential palace in 1982. Civilian governments struggled thereafter. By 1984, President Hernán Siles could not deal with the workers' union. Siles went on a hunger strike. The papal nuncio and three Bolivian bishops went to the president to plead with him to desist. Siles portrayed himself as powerless and the country was on the verge of unthinkable collapse.

The bishops, realizing the depths of the crisis of governance, planned a major summit meeting. They met first with political leaders, then with workers, and then with the Confederation of Private Businessmen (CEPB). The church divided the agenda in two: first, how to make the country governable, and second, how to deal with the economic crisis. Bolivia may have been at the lowest point in its history until agreement was reached on the electoral process. The church acted as guarantor of national elections and assured that the results of the elections would be respected. It acted as a kind of safe flotation gear toward the future. The Bolivian church continued in this role of mediator on a regular basis for five years.

This mediatorial process involved the church in hosting the discussions. The bishops proposed general principles to serve as the basis of negotiation, and the contending parties were supposed to work out the details of agreement. The bishops were third parties who intervened only to move the dialogue along. As Jeffrey Klaiber observed, "They encouraged one party to listen more carefully ... they nudged both sides toward consensus. Their signature on the compromise documents, although it had no legal or political authority, endowed the final agreements with what could best be described as moral legitimacy."[44]

Many Bolivians accepted the church as mediator because of the profound roots of popular Catholicism among the majority of the population, especially the indigenous. Further, the church supported the ideals of the 1952 Revolution. These ideals were, as Jeffrey Klaiber says, "the touchstone of a new social and political legitimacy" for middle-class elites and lower classes.[45]

However, negative aspects became clear about the church mediating the repeated Bolivian crises. First, mediation by the church was a sign of relative immaturity on the part of civil society; it revealed the insufficiency of political mechanisms that democracies should have functioning for disputes. Second, the church ended up in innumerable conflicts. Third, the bishops sometimes stepped in too quickly and aborted a process that, if allowed to play itself out, would have strengthened democracy.

In the end, however, a positive outcome prevailed. The very act of seeking out dialogue with a political adversary, even if through an intermediary, is a sign of civic maturity and responsible statecraft. The process of performing in public in the presence of the church as a witness forced politicians to back down from posturing and adopt a position of statesmen, taking positions with the common good in mind. The church was generally acclaimed by all sides. Thus, the church served as a stabilizing force and universally acceptable mediator in the midst of intensely polarized forces

Finally, sometime in the early 1990s the bishops made it clear that the period of transition to fully democratic functioning had passed and that it was time for political actors to settle conflicts themselves. The mechanisms of elections and of legislatures for negotiating issues were in place. Within a decade, relying on negotiations between parties and interests, Bolivia's political system consolidated into a functioning democracy, one of the four of the twenty-two nations in Latin America that Guillermo O'Donnell, one of the grand figures of Latin American political science, counted as consolidated democracies. This, in his view, was a huge achievement for Bolivia and the other countries.[46]

Contrary to the view that mediation typically occurs in countries like Bolivia and the Dominican Republic that are weak in political institutions, church leaders have offered useful mediation at various times in countries ranging from Argentina to Mexico. Argentina saw its bishops extend a mediating hand at a critical juncture when the country almost descended into political as well as economic collapse. In the 1990s, Argentina unwisely pegged its peso to the U.S. dollar and fell into an economic heap.[47] One in a series of temporary presidents, Eduardo Duhalde accepted the national bishops' conference's offer of Dialogue Roundtables (Mesas de Diálogo, somewhat similar to the Bolivian bishops' mediation efforts). These efforts contributed to the process of presidential elections that propelled Norberto Kirchner to power and eventually put Argentina on an even keel by 2005.

The Mexican Bishop Samuel Ruiz of Chiapas in southern Mexico drew the most attention of any church leader in the 1990s by his actions as mediator. The so called Zapatista Rebellion occurred on January 1, 1994, when the contentious North American Free Trade Agreement went into effect. In the years-long standoff between government armed forces and the Zapatista guerrillas, Ruiz expended considerable energy to position himself as mediator in the conflict.

He found the mediation extremely difficult because he supported the Zapatista issues (employment, health, and education, for example) but opposed their threatened use of violence. He had comparable problems with the government, which was used to hidden authoritarian ways, including its record of exterminating guerrillas in the state of Guerrero. As with other Mexican standoffs, this one concluded with no clear victors but no new fatalities either. Ruiz emerged as a hero, to be honored by large audiences at Stanford University, the University of Oregon, and elsewhere.

The Mexican Bishops Conference (CEM) began supporting Ruiz's initiatives. Whereas his previous initiatives in Chiapas were met with skepticism by other bishops in Mexico and Latin America generally, the strategy of mediation deeply appealed to the Conference leadership. They called for classical means, such as "becoming flexible in their demands" and "to hear with patience, respect, and great openness." The Conference leaders took many opportunities to keep public attention and pressure on the guerrillas and the government, calling this an "historic moment."

Attempts at mediation thus shifted from a remote and steamy province to the national stage. From then on, individual Mexican bishops appeared to accept the mediation role as an excellent way to enter more fully into public life after decades of being forced to the sidelines by the severely restrictive anticlerical Constitution of 1917. In 2006–2007, the teachers' strikes that severely convulsed Oaxaca brought new appeals for the local bishop to bring feuding parties to the bargaining table. The bishop resisted for a long time, perceiving lack of conditions for a suitable dialogue.

A fourth country, Chile, saw its bishops individually attempt to mend a wounded society by also sponsoring Dialogue Roundtables. These meetings brought the relatives of the disappeared (people dumped in the ocean or buried without markers by the military dictatorship) together with military leaders. At first very far apart in the attempt to account for the disappeared and to locate their bodies, the relatives of the disappeared and the military leaders reached a strong measure of understanding and reconciliation.

In Peru, the church has been well accepted as a mediator. The best-known case was the long siege of the Japanese embassy in Lima, where Marxist guerrillas held hostage a large number of foreigners and nationals. Archbishop Juan Luis Cipriani, then of Ayacucho, shuttled back and forth between government and terrorists in an attempt to secure a safe release of the hostages. This was only one of the conflicts mediated by the bishops. In 2003, Archbishop Luis Bambarén was identified routinely as the "government-appointed" mediator for a national teachers union strike that had brought on a declared "state of emergency."

The role as mediator has caught on in other countries as well. In Colombia, the bishops and priests regularly offer themselves as intermediaries in talks between parties in the armed conflicts of guerrillas, private armies, and the government. A bishop and several priests have been murdered in part because of their attempts to bring peace and reconciliation.

Informal Mediation

More frequently, church mediation has been informal. At the national level, the church—specifically bishops and bishops' conferences—visited the president or government officials to make their case for select issues or to arrange dialogue of government leaders with their counterparts in opposition parties. Chilean bishops at critical periods during the military dictatorship (1973–1990) invited government representatives and political party leaders to a working lunch, as they did to promote the holding of elections and the eventual ouster of the dictator. In a country like the Dominican Republic, bishops, individually or collectively, seem to be offering mediation services in one crisis after another. As Betances notes, this came to be called the Pastoral of Dialogue.[48]

At the regional and local levels, individual bishops and priests acted as mediators for a range of conflicts. While they did not receive much attention in the media, the issues mediated were (and are) important. They include land tenure, agricultural credit, natural disasters, migration from other countries, promised governmental support to farmers, use of water, the impact of tourism on the environment, and sanitation. While the effective control of the government barely reaches beyond cities, the church is typically present in open country areas. In political and social disputes, the church becomes a handy third party. Again, it is necessary to say that the church leaders at the lowest levels are most often those lay catechists and missionaries in their role as church and community leader. In a word, the church (the People of God) offered at various times and levels the glue to hold society together. The sense of these dialogues has been, "We're in this together; let's work things out." This is a communitarian spirit typical of Latin Catholicism.

Kenneth Serbin has called attention to a major unknown dialogue between church and state in Brazil. His book, *Secret Dialogues*, takes readers into the prolonged mediation of Brazilian bishops and the generals who ruled the country to find a compromise between the generals' hard line stands and the positions of political and church activists.[49] Serbin's apparent surprise that the church would adopt dialogue as a course of action may indicate a lack of perception of the embedded cultural position of the church that facilitated informal interactions. From many interviews that I conducted in Brazil in the 1970s and 1980s it was evident that bishops met with local military leaders at their garrisons on many occasions, attempting to conciliate land tenure, water rights and similar issues during the military dictatorship.

Analysis

The actions by Ruiz and the bishops' conference were untypical in Mexico at that time, when anticlerical governments had forbidden political action by clergy. Thus, differences in the countries' cultures and the strength or weakness of the political party system are factors that affect mediation. Mediation on the part of the church occurs more frequently where cultures are more favorable to clergy and where the political party system is relatively weak. Some countries, such as Mexico, Uruguay, and Venezuela, had a more anticlerical culture than did others, such as Bolivia or Colombia.

Two fundamental bases support the church in assuming mediatorship. First, as already noted, in most Latin American countries the church enjoys a higher level of trust than do other institutions in society—for example, the government, the media, the military, and schools. The second and most fundamental reason is the historical and cultural position of the church in Latin American society. In a word, the church is recognized in Latin America as an institution existing in society with rights anterior to the state. Historically the church preceded the formation of Spain as a nation and of the Latin American nations, which were founded between 1810 and 1832. This recognized status caused the church to be regarded almost as a fourth branch of government, especially during Iberian rule. This recognition of the prior existence of the church to the state also accounts for the status of the Vatican in world politics.[50]

A contrast in practice between California and Latin America provides a vivid example of the difference between English and Spanish America in this regard. In California, prison chaplains used to enjoy a certain status as members of an important social institution interacting with another institution, each with rights and obligations. Chaplains used to communicate with the warden as they do in Latin America. Now California state chaplains receive no special status. They are grouped together with numerous representatives of self-help groups, such as Alcoholics Anonymous and Narcotics Anonymous. Neither religion nor the church as an institution has any special recognition. So far as is known, nothing like that has occurred in Latin America.

Conclusion

The church came alive in twentieth-century politics as the first Voice of the Voiceless. This voice became articulate under the stress of authoritarian governmental abuses and of being the only institution in society not silenced by the government. In many countries, with the turn to democracy after military rule the church continued to be a voice for the poorest during the economically troubled transition to free-market capitalism in the late twentieth century, and again the church served as the voice of the poor through its campaign against the governmental corruption that stole from the poor.

The church also acted in the public square in political mediation— that is, the process of bringing contending interests to agreement. It served as a major facilitator in the all-important turn to democracy in the region.[51] This relatively new role made the church appear to be non-partisan in societies that were rife with social and political inequalities and hard-line stances. It is a function that benefits society and generally increases the perceived worth of the church without tarnishing its image. The role carries inherent risks for the maturity of the political order, and so its judicious use was called for and recognized in Bolivia.

The study of the mediator role of the church is far from complete. The truth (or otherwise) of Ivan Vallier's claim, in his summary of the nineteenth and early twentieth centuries,[52] that the Catholic Church was a weak actor in society, one that acted publicly through informal ties, needs to be evaluated. The details of how the Mexican church reached an accommodation with the ruling PRI party (1929–2000) through dialogue also merit further investigation. This chapter has uncovered the most direct indicator of what has been stressed throughout this book: During the last decade, the church has enjoyed the highest level of confidence of any social institution in Latin America. The choice of the church as mediator implies a high degree of trust. Thus, willingness to accept the church in this role confirms the Latinobarometro polls, mentioned in Chapter One, about trust in institutions.

Further, this volume has not attempted a systematic comparison with the Catholic Church in other countries, especially the United States. However, one should note that the theme of being voice of the voiceless, of acting on behalf of the poor, vulnerable, and marginal members of society has entered the consciousness of the universal church. In the United States, these themes are incorporated into the policies and statements of the U.S. Catholic Conference of Bishops and, perhaps, even more clearly in the attempts by the Catholic conferences of the individual states that heroically try to hold the poor up for consideration by the state legislators. To a degree seldom acknowledged, money and power have devolved from the national level to the states where the Catholic laity fights for the rights of the poor in the name of the church.[53]

Lastly, despite the warts that deface the Catholic Church in Latin America, the public face of the church expressed as peacemaker and mediator of conflicts and made manifest in the heroic stance of persons like Oscar Romero and the everyday courage of the Maryknoll sister-martyrs and thousands of ordinary persons shows forth an inner vitality and conviction that has divine roots. It is no accident that Penny Lernoux, who first made known to a wide North American audience that something extraordinary was happening in the Latin American church in the 1970s,[54] became Catholic as a result of viewing and reporting upon the church.[55] Similarly, two other writers, one Marxist and the other Jewish, either returned to the practice of the Catholic faith or became Catholic through observation of the church.[56] Acting as voice of the voiceless and carefully preserving justice as part of peacemaking are signs of the presence of God.

CHAPTER 10

Sending Missionaries with a Message of Solidarity

The most profound sign of vitality of the Latin American church, one beyond growth in priests and seminarians and commitment of hundreds of thousands of lay ministers, is the recent sending of missionaries. When a church switches from being a missionary-receiving church to a missionary-sending church (such as happened in the United States), this signals the final stage of coming to age. Thus the Latin American church, previously largely focused on itself, is reaching a key point in its maturity.

After five hundred years of Catholicism, Latin America was extremely slow in developing a missionary outreach. One major factor that perpetuated this deficiency came about in the nineteenth century when the church was decimated of its clergy by the independent Latin American republics that were formed out of the Iberian empire and whose governments forced Spanish priests to leave the continent. Further, the anticlerical governments in many of these countries severely restricted the church in terms of income, participation in public life, and education. Further, most of the ancient and respected Latin American universities were stripped from the religious orders and from the church and given over to state authorities who encouraged or allowed a secular and anticlerical faculty to inculcate students in an Enlightenment anti-church ideology for its future leaders.

In Guatemala, the clerical situation was so dire that no more than 110 priests served the needs of millions of Catholics in the country from the late 1800s to the mid-1940s. Vast areas of the Latin American church became priestless territories. Faced with this mammoth vacuum, in the 1950s, a large

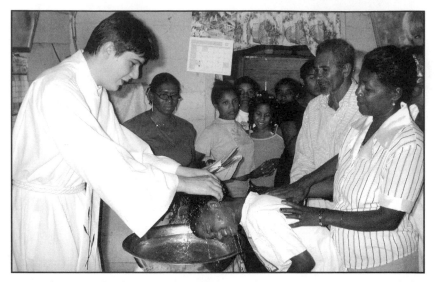

Evangelization of indigenous non-Christians has been an important task for the church in Latin America. Here a deacon baptizes a new Christian in a mountain village.

cohort of foreign missionaries poured into Latin America in what was called a Missionary Crusade.[1]

Latin America was desperate for priests and other personnel, such as trained teachers. Even the hundreds of missionaries who came to Latin America were not sufficient to fill all the pastoral needs of the people.

From Mission-Receiving to Mission-Sending

By 2000, most of the missionaries had died or left Latin America to return to the United States, Canada, or Europe. Unnoticed by many observers, however, especially Protestant or secular ones, seminaries in Latin America were filling up to a remarkable degree. In most countries, new seminary buildings had to be built to accommodate the increasing numbers. Mexico's Guadalajara seminary had some 1,000 students in the 1980s and had to refuse candidates because of lack of space. A number of these candidates made their way to other seminaries in Mexico or the United States.

The increases, while encouraging, were not able to keep up with the demands of Catholics for priests because of general population increases (this despite drastically falling birth rates) and because of the much heightened interest in spirituality. Therefore, despite *not* having a surplus of priests, Latin America came to a crucial point in it history: a critical number of missionaries, beyond a trickle, were going *from* Latin America to other regions in the world.

In the 1990s, the number of Latin American missionaries was still growing. The gathering of accurate numbers has been difficult for a variety of reasons, primarily the fragmentation of mission-sending groups and very loose communication among those groups. Nonetheless, since the 1990s the Mission Department (DEMIS) of the Latin American Bishops Conference has improved its ability to keep records of missionaries going from Latin America.

DEMIS's statistics make clear that: 1) most countries in Latin America send some missionaries; 2) numbers of missionaries from a country tend to reflect the size of the country's population so that one may say that this is a generalized phenomenon; and 3) Mexico leads the way with the largest number of foreign missionaries. Its numbers are disproportionately larger than Brazil's, the region's most populous nation.

One should note that for at least the last fifty years the Mexican church had a larger corps of priests and seminarians than most Latin American churches relative to its population. This surprises older Americans who heard tales of the Mexican persecution of its priests. Training priests in Mexico was either forbidden or severely restricted in the early twentieth century, depending on the political climate at a particular time. (Many Mexican seminarians made their way across the New Mexican border to attend Guadalupe seminary in the United States.) After President Lázaro Cárdenas granted a measure of peaceful coexistence to the church in the 1940s, Mexican seminaries, noticed by hardly anyone, began to flourish. Mexico's seminarians reached a relatively high baseline of some 2,200 in 1972.

One accepted test of authentic Christianity is mission. This is the willingness to share the gift of faith with others at some cost to oneself. Through centuries mission was defined as going to non-Christian people, *missio ad gentes*, generally in a distant region. By the twentieth century, this meaning of mission expanded to mean leaving one's home to go to another region of the world, even if the mission-receiving area was Christian. More recently, mission also meant leaving one's home for another part of the same country or for some other country in Latin America.

A central question for any diocese or parish, regardless of its geographical or economic situation, is: does it have a missionary consciousness? The church, local or national, is by its nature missionary. Every bishop and his subjects have responsibility for the whole church. The Latin American church recognized this responsibility in 1979 when it said that it "would have to produce missionaries out of our poverty." [2]

By the ancient criterion of going to another part of the world, how is Latin America doing? For at least ten years, Latin America has sent some 4,000 missionaries to foreign parts; in addition, a very large sector works as missionaries within Latin America. The substantial foreign missionary activity is a notable milestone in the Latin America church's journey to maturity. In addition, large numbers have left their homes to become internal missionaries, sometimes short-term but nonetheless at some sacrifice. Thus, 118,784 Catholics became lay missionaries in 2000, mostly in Latin America.[3] Lay missionaries are understood to be lay men and women (excluding men and women religious) who serve as missionaries at home or abroad.[4] They represent a solid achievement for the Latin American church rarely mentioned by superficial commentators who, fixated on reporting competing evangelical growth, are blind to the general religious revival that also affects Catholicism.

History

Little known but nonetheless significant are early twentieth-century attempts at missionary activity. In Mexico a new congregation of priests, the Guadalupe Missionaries, began in 1949[5] to send missionaries to foreign lands, including Japan and other countries, not long after their founding. In 2005, they celebrated their fortieth anniversary of being in Kenya. While the Guadalupe Missionaries remained relatively small, they contributed immeasurably to the Mexican church's sense of world mission as part of the Mexican church's vocation, unlike most other Latin American national churches at that time. As a further indication of the sign of the times, the Guadalupe Missionaries began recruiting and sending lay Mexicans as missionaries.

Missionaries from Guatemala began taking shape in the 1980s.[6] Other efforts, from Colombia and Brazil, likewise began at this time. These were largely missionary efforts mediated by foreign missionaries' societies, such as the Italian Comboni congregation.

Missionary Impulses

Two strong impulses for mission affected Latin America. First, foreign missionaries who took charge of most of the indigenous areas of Latin America from the mid-twentieth century found that religious practice had fallen into the control of native non-Christian religious hierarchy. In a word, the missionaries had to undertake a second evangelization. The new catechesis with its strongly biblical basis and with a new appreciation of the religious values of native cultures gave dynamism to the religious (and political) resurgence of the indigenous sector of the church. Latin American missionary impulses have their roots in this revival.

The second powerful influence was external and only slowly affected the Latin American church. The Second Vatican Council's Decree on the Church's Missionary Activity, *Ad Gentes* (1965), made it clear that the entire church is missionary, that mission was not just the concern of missionary orders, and, by implication, that the Latin American church was highly deficient in this regard.

Of all the regional churches, the Latin American church responded more wholeheartedly to Vatican II than the other churches. As already noted, no other church systematically applied the council's teaching to its region as happened at the Medellín Conference. However, the church lagged in implementing missionary activity. It had not internalized the mission vision and lacked the necessary organizational resources. Nonetheless, the Latin American Bishops Conference (CELAM) dutifully put in place in 1966, a year after the Council, el Departamento de Misiones (DEMIS). This department organized meetings in the two following years to identify the situations in Latin America that called for missionary activity. In doing so, they contributed to mission theory. Participants at the meetings rejected the traditional definitions of what was "mission territory," understood as a region where the majority of inhabitants were non-Christian, to emphasize instead "missionary situations." Some groups need missionary activity rather than just typical pastoral care because their cultures have not yet encountered what John Gorski calls the life-giving force of the Gospel.[7]

DEMIS, of course, found targets for missionary activity among Latin America's indigenous. Unfortunately, the organization thereby became known informally as the Department of Indian Affairs. Since most Latin American countries had small minorities of indigenous and since the president of DEMIS from 1969 to 1974 was Chiapas's Bishop Samuel Ruiz (considered untrustworthy in his implementation of reforms but eventually vindicated), most church leaders focused on what they considered more urgent questions. Typical of the times, these leaders considered the indigenous to be socially marginalized groups rather than as peoples with ancient cultures worthy of detailed attention.

That outmoded view was to change dramatically at the bishops' Third General Conference at Puebla (1979). Following their methodology of see-judge-act that required a wide and accurate description and analysis of the continent, the bishops acknowledged several missionary situations in the region: not only the indigenous (who, by then, had made great progress) but also the African–Latin Americans and the numerous out-of-place and often-unwanted migrants within Latin America. Further, the church recognized groups in difficult missionary situations—politicians, titans of business and industry, the military, and others—who were presumed to be in situations not merely indifferent to evangelization but resistant to or impeding of missionary efforts.

The Puebla Conference thus not only contributed something original in conveying a sense of mission to the regional church, it also opened the door to other initiatives for mission to persons and agencies outside of DEMIS. Momentum toward growth in missions shifted to groups outside the Mission Department. This was especially true in the indigenous mission sphere where organic intellectuals and leaders now were themselves indigenous.

The church had changed its policy from *pastoral indigenista* to *pastoral indígena*, from paternalistic to empowerment.[8] The notable growth of indigenous intellectuals and church leaders was the fruit of this policy change. The indigenous theologians' creative efforts have brought forth *teología india*, a major theological development that is distinct from liberation theology in its emphasis on culture but dependent on liberation theology's emphasis on context. Here then are indigenous people creating theology from the margins of Latin American society but adding to the general richness of universal theology through contributing insights into God as male and female and into the care of the earth as an ethical responsibility. Indigenous took the lead in their creation of an organization for ecumenical dialogue, the Latin American Articulation of the Indigenous Apostolate (AELAPI). The group has sponsored five continental encounter-workshops and several subregional meetings. This small but important movement brings together leaders from both Christian (Catholic and mainline

Protestant) and non-Christian indigenous sectors, especially from the more numerous highland groups of Mayan or Incan backgrounds. The dialogue has highly unequal partners, given the academic sophistication of the Catholic and Protestant partners in contrast to many native Non-Christian leaders, but has survived more than twenty years of ups and downs.[9]

Internal Mission to African Religions

The mission to African religions in Latin America is still at an early stage, but it has produced a solid theological footing for dialogue with these non-Christian or hybrid faiths. The main centers are in Brazil, where academic resources are available and where a whirlwind of belated activity in relation to the black religious experience has been taking place. This is in contrast to the mostly black nation of Haiti, where the almost collapsed state of its government precludes sustained and systematic dialogue with voodoo leaders. Talented young Afro-Brazilian intellectuals have taken up the deeper missionary issues. Josuel dos Santos Boaventura, for example, showed the need for a theological synthesis that takes into account the black (African) way of expressing faith in the God of Jesus Christ.[10] Other national churches, even those without significant numbers of blacks, have engaged in dialogue and theological reflection about the African diasporan religions.

World Mission Responsibility

The greatest change in the pastoral vision of the Latin American church in recent times has been its inclusion of foreign missions as one of its goals. The change also includes a surprise: lay people form the majority of persons with this movement.

If one can mark progress in the missionary outlook of the church by national and regional missionary congresses, then Mexico took the lead. National missionary congresses have been held in Mexico since the 1940s to awaken and focus a world mission spirit. This activity took place in a church aware of its own scarcity of resources. By 1997, the seventh congress took place at Torreón. This meeting marked the beginning of inclusion of persons from other Latin American countries and became the First Latin American Mission Congress, marking the historical take-off point for Latin America's turning toward the larger world and its needs.

Organizational structures had an impact on furthering the change in outlook and channeling zeal. By church law, every diocese, even the weakest, is expected to create and support a mission office. In addition, national churches that mostly pulled themselves together in the 1950s into more or less effective national bishops conferences had to appoint national directors of the Pontifical Mission Societies. Local and national structures were thus in place for what was to take place, even though resources and widespread motivation were lacking. Only a small number of non-Mexican bishops and national directors of the Pontifical Mission Society attended the first continental meeting at Torreón. From then on, sizable national delegations from all countries not only attended but also did so with prepared participation and follow-up programs in their own countries, using the newly installed structures.

These continental meetings, held every four years, reinforced the vision by which every diocese would be the basis of missionary activity in the church. By the Third Congress in Bogotá in 1987, a major step was taken in recognizing the missionary commitment of *lay people* and in establishing various Missionary Institutes. Alongside these initiatives, Pope John Paul II issued a comprehensive encyclical on world mission, *Redemptoris Missio*. This was taken to heart at the next congress in Lima in 1991 and fueled renewed discussion of New Evangelization, the main theme of the General Conference of CELAM, at Santo Domingo (1992). While it appeared to be taking a step backward, the next mission congress in Brazil paid special attention to indigenous and African cultures at home and the question of inculturation. Getting straight the church's approach to these cultures and to inculturation strengthened its hand in sending missionaries overseas.

One of the Latin American missionaries from this period, Nicanor Sarmiento, was already a promising theologian and student of inculturated religion. Father Sarmiento, a native healer in his own Quechua community, was assigned by his Oblate of Mary Immaculate superiors to work as a missionary in Labrador, Canada. His several years of pastoral work in Goose Bay gradually extended and deepened his views of effective mission work. He was forced to learn Inuit and to polish his English while dealing with other cultures as a missionary. He then moved in 2006 to Berkeley's Graduate Theological Union to pursue doctoral studies in theology, with the desire to teach missiology from a Latin American perspective and to be a bridge between the churches in the Americas.

As Sarmiento was moving to the far north, bishops and mission directors went south from Canada and the United States to attend the Latin American mission congresses. These meetings thus became also known as Congresos Americanos, in line with John Paul II's view of one America, North and South.

Latin American Missionary Initiatives

Hence, from the 1990s a large set of initiatives occurred in various parts of the region that took place as spontaneous irruptions of missionary initiatives in various places and with very different ideological colorings. Two of the notable efforts of that decade that continue strongly in the 2000s are those of Maryknoll and of the Legionnaires of Christ. The most organized approach was taken by the Foreign Mission Society of America, commonly known as Maryknoll. In the 1990s, society members began expressing opinions about fostering a formal recognition of organizational change from mission-receiving to mission-sending of the Latin American church. Frank McGurn, MM, one of the creators of the highly regarded Maryknoll Instituto de Idiomas in Cochabamba, bowed out and turned over the effort to Stephen Judd and Thomas Henehan. Thus in 2002 was born the Latin American Office of Mission Services (OLASEM) at the Maryknoll School at Cochabamba, Bolivia. For years, the school prepared foreigners for mission work in Latin America; now the school is primarily aimed at preparing Latin Americans for mission work. Some 200 Latin Americans have taken the basic missionary course and have moved on to mission work. In contrast to times past, most of the missionaries-in-training are *laypeople*.

Cochabamba also became the venue of an equally significant missionary effort in which Maryknoll cooperated. The Catholic University at Cochabamba, a branch of the main campus in La Paz and allied with Universidad Xaveriana in Bogotá, started a major missionary initiative, probably the first of its kind in Latin America: a fully academic unit devoted to mission studies. The faculty is made up of missionaries from North Atlantic countries, with degrees from prestigious institutions such as Rome's Gregorianum and Stanford, select students, and a research library funded from Holland. The institute is bolstered by a sister Institute of (applied) Anthropology, again with an excellent library, an uncommon feature among newer universities in Latin America.

In contrast to the planned mission enterprises in Bolivia, Mexico's most ambitious mission venture grew out the desire of a former Amazonian missionary resident in Mexico. Thomas Moylan, a Legionaries of Christ priest, started Catholic World Mission in 1998. His great success and that of his successor-directors of CWM has been the recruitment of laypeople as missionaries. He invited and received many candidates—now graduates—to a school to prepare fulltime lay missionaries. This is remarkable for two reasons: many Latin Americans thought being missionary meant being a priest or sister and the Legionnaires upon whom this effort is built are often depicted as the consummate clerical and controlling group in the church. Through his CWM project, Moylan made it clear that the situation in Latin America and elsewhere is dire from a pastoral point of view. There is clear need for all hands to be utilized. Even here, then, laypeople are employed not because there are not enough priests but because laypeople are called to ministry and mission. Priests accompany laypeople's work, not vice versa.

These laypeople are known in Spanish as ETCs (Evangelizadores de Tiempo Completo—Evangelizers Working Fulltime) and in English as Fulltime Lay Missionaries. Thus the two concepts, evangelization and mission, are neatly captured in the same term, ETC.

ETCs have grown to 1,000 missionaries in a relatively short time. In turn, they have trained 35,000 part-time catechists (also thought of as missionaries). Many of these catechists are indigenous whose first tongue is something other than Spanish, and typically, they are bi- or multilingual. By 2006 the Mexican ETCs were operating as missionaries in five Latin American countries and were about to open a mission in a sixth country, Brazil.

The work done by Catholic World Mission in evangelization showed its organizers that while short-term catechesis (nonformal education) may be the only practical pastoral strategy, schools do a better job in producing long-term effects. Catholic World Mission began building and providing resources for schools in a spin-off project: Mano Amiga (Helping Hands).

This Helping Hands project antedates larger missionary impulses and began in 1963 at Mexico City as a Legionnaire project among the poor. The project evolved from a tiny program to start a kindergarten, and grew with a primary school, then a middle school, a high school, and adult education and job training for teens. Mano Amiga now has 28 schools and was spread largely by Mexican missionaries to Venezuela, Chile, Argentina, El Salvador, Colombia, and Brazil.

In the rapidly mushrooming world of the Legionnaires, mission work spread to the medical field through the creation of Helping Hands Medical Missions in 1996. Within ten years, the group had mounted 53 short-term medical missions: 24 in Mexico, 27 others in Latin America, and 2 missions in the Philippines. The two enterprises, evangelization carried out by ETCs, and charity work represented by Helping Hands Medical Ministry, came together in one funding agency, Altius Foundation. More importantly, ETCs provide local coordination prior to the start of the medical missions through canvassing neighborhoods to identify persons most in need of medical care. The medical mission lasts one week and nine missions are scheduled each year. Again the team is comprised primarily of laypeople, typically 35-45 volunteers, with a priest and a seminarian who are described as spiritual support, not leaders nor directors, of the medical missions.

Short-term Missionaries

Given the various life-obligations of both adults and university students, the role of the short-term missionary has increasingly been employed. This activity flows from acknowledgment of the obligation of grown-ups and the almost-adult Catholics to offer themselves in service and it brings to good use those persons excluded from fulltime service because of life circumstances. However unsatisfactory short-term or part-time missionary service is for long-term effects,[11] the fulfillment of voluntary service, even on a limited scale, is a monumental change in perspective from the times when laypeople thought only religious professionals could serve as missionaries.

The benefits of short-term mission trips for the volunteers and for the church are many: they gain a wider religious-cultural and socioeconomic awareness; they experience spiritual growth; and, above all, they develop a larger sense of vocation as laypeople. In this latter regard, some go on to become long-term missionaries. Some recruit and support new volunteers, often spreading enthusiasm from their student-day missions to parishes where they settle later as adults. Many become committed to the support of missionaries in prayer and financially. In sum, they become more deeply affiliated with the church and with its goals.

Miguel Petty's summer voluntary missionaries to Patagonia had to devote themselves to learning about their faith and the reasons for their faith in order to evangelize Argentines in remote places; thus, they deepened their own beliefs and their commitment to the church. The positive effect of limited voluntary commitments has been shown repeatedly by evangelicals and by Catholics in Canada and the United States but is only now becoming evident in Latin America.

Petty explained his motives for his Patagonia project in careful theological and educational rationales in his *La promoción humana en los medios rurales marginales.*[12] In effect, he says this project is what educated Christians should be doing. He never mentions the evangelical challenge, nor, in an interview with him, did he refer to this challenge. Repeatedly in viewing missionary endeavors at the grassroots, it was clear that the Catholic Church shared actively in the religious revival occurring in Latin America, rather than merely reacting to the evangelical challenge, as is so often asserted by journalists and other observers.

While Maryknoll and the Legionnaires have taken the intellectual and charismatic lead in the missionary movement, a wide sector of other missionary groups exists. One has only to view the website of Mexican missionaries to see a solid phalanx of new and ancient names in mission. In Mexico and other Latin American countries the backbone of the missionary impulse are the religious orders and congregations that began seeding other regions with missionaries. Organizations well known in Italy but not as well known in the United States, such as Comboni and Consolata, have quietly and effectively been recruiting and sending Latin Americans as priests to serve in countries of their main concern in Africa.

As the church in Latin America evolved, new missionary organizations emerged. One of these grew organically from the efforts at evangelization. An Italian Comboni priest, Luis Butera (see Chapter 7), now in his late seventies, had his heart set from an early age on serving in Africa. Instead, he served in Mexico. He drew around him young lay Mexicans who, like many others, were appalled by the religious ignorance of their fellow Mexicans and dedicated themselves to religious instruction (evangelization) of the people around them. Beginning in the early 1980s, the numbers of lay participants and the work both grew to the point that Butera formed two groups: one "would leave everything" and spend a year full-time in evangelization; the second group held full-time jobs and worked part-time as evangelizers. A number of the first group continued as catechists after their initial year's commitment.

The young men and women in the full-time group made a public vow both to commit themselves to evangelization and to live as closely as they could to the spirit of the early Christians. The perseverance in this activity and in the state of life among the full-time members brought the need for greater structuring. Two years of novitiate were required; members made religious vows and they lived a community life (shared living quarters and purse). They had a clear goal: *to evangelize laypeople so that they in turn would evangelize other laypeople.* This, in many ways, was both the novelty of the organization and the clearest evidence of what was happening in an important sector of the church. Laypeople felt they had a hand in saving the church. While the core group of evangelizers became a religious congregation with vows to give them structure and stability, they focused on preparing the laity to evangelize.

In contrast to the hundreds of Mexican religious congregations that were formed over the last century to serve religious needs *in Mexico*, they became legally an Institute of the Consecrated Life *for the Missions* and evolved into the more traditional forms of religious life in 1990s. The men called themselves Missionary Servants of the Word (they are priests for the most part) and the sisters the Missionary Sister Servants of the Lord. They see themselves as going to overseas territories. Wherever they will be, their aim is being at the side of laypeople who will evangelize.

Contributions to Christian Missionary Thinking

From the traditional view of missions as going to non-Christian regions, Latin Americans added the special emphasis of option for the poor. "Non-Christian," after all, could mean persons and groups who are fabulously wealthy in money and resources (oil) and culturally rich. Among the many choices missionaries might make in choosing to spend their lives, preference should be given to target populations that suffer socioeconomically.[13] They believe that this is true because God has special care for the poor and so should they.

Second, inculturation is certainly not the special intellectual possession of Latin American intellectuals and pastoral experts. Asian Catholics have been dealing seriously with this issue for centuries. What Latin America showed the rest of the church was how successful inculturation could be carried out; how a full range of lay talents, especially those of catechists, can be put to use; and how (rather quickly) indigenous theology can be created by the indigenous themselves.

183

Again, Latin American missionaries affirmed that ideas of God are presumed not only to be present but also planted as "seeds of revelation" in non-Christian cultures. These concepts have been discovered and matched with Christian revelation: the Bible and tradition.

Third, the concept of missionary situation that Latin American intellectuals emphasized would imply that persons working in other cultures would devote attention to "special care situations." In the United States this would be the gangs, the homeless, and, of course, the migrants. Church leaders would not just allow Latin gangs to be marginalized concerns or solely the responsibility of local pastors; rather, mission-minded persons and teams would attempt to reach them.[14] Again, the work does not principally have to be done by priests.

A remarkable aspect in this new missionary outreach and in most of the enterprises of the Latin American church is the reliance on theological reflection on virtually everything that is undertaken. It is a "vision thing" and, if the recounting of history herein has been correct, Latin Americans excel in providing a vision for the church and its activities. At the very least, after five hundred years, Latin Americans have internalized responsibility for the global church in ways that are new and promising.

Notes

Introduction

1. Philip Jenkins, *The Next Christendom: The Coming of Global Christianity* (New York: Oxford University Press, 2002).

2. Statistics are made available each year by the Vatican. Many are available through the yearly editions of the *National Catholic Almanac* and at the Religion in Latin America website maintained by the University of Texas, http://lanic.utexas.edu/project/rla/index.htm.

3. *PMV Special Note* (Brussels: Pro Mundi Vita Institute) 15 (October 1970), 3.

4. For Chile, *Datos Estadísticos 1996: Clero Secular, Congregaciones Religiosas, Sacramentación en Chile* (Santiago, Chile: Oficina Sociología Religiosa, 1997).

5. "Liberal Theologians Sway Latin America," *National Catholic Reporter*, November 26, 2007.

6. Brian Froehle and Mary Gauttier, *Global Catholicism* (Maryknoll, NY: Orbis, 2003), 159–271.

7. Reginaldo Prandi, "Religião paga, conversão e servicio," *Novos Estudos Cebrap* 45 (1996), 65–78.

8. Guillermo Cook, interview with author, March 17, 1993, New Haven, CT.

9. Andrew Walls, interview with author, May 28, 1998, Nashville, TN.

10. Thomas J. Reese, "Synod for America," *America*, December 13, 1997; *Tablet* (London), December 20–27, 1997.

11. See Timothy J. Steigenga and Edward L. Cleary, *Conversion of a Continent: Contemporary Religious Change in Latin America* (Piscataway, NJ: Rutgers University Press, 2008), for a "companion" to the present volume.

12. Prandi, "Religão," 65–78.

13. *Veja* (São Paolo, Brazil), April 10, 1991, 41–44.

14. Interviews by author with urban professionals, 1967, 1992, 1994, 1996, Brazil.

15. Thomas C. Bruneau, "The Catholic Church and Development in Latin America," *World Development* 8, nos. 7–8 (July–August, 1980), and panel of social scientists, "Conflict of Loyalty: Political Polarization in the Catholic Church in Latin America," Latin American Studies Association International Congress, 1980.

16. Renato Poblete, "Are Pentecostals Overtaking Catholics in Latin America?" *Doctrine and Life* 48, no. 8 (October 1998): 473.

17. *Origins* 27, no. 43 (April 16, 1998), 717, 719–21.

18. Edward L. Cleary and Juan Sepulveda, "Chilean Pentecostalism: Coming of Age" in Edward L. Cleary and Hannah Stewart-Gambino, eds., *Power, Politics, and Pentecostals in Latin America* (Boulder: Westview, 1997), 97–121.

19. Kenneth Scott Latourette, *Christianity in a Revolutionary Age,* vol. 5 (Grand Rapids, MI: Zondervan, 1969), 214.

20. Everett Wilson, "Guatemalan Pentecostals: Something of Their Own," in Cleary and Stewart-Gambino, eds., *Power, Politics, and Pentecostals*, 148.

21. Virginia Garrard-Burnett, *Protestantism in Guatemala: Living in the New Jerusalem* (Austin, TX: University of Texas Press, 1998), 162. See Timothy Evans, "Percentage of Non-Catholics in a Representative Sample of the Guatemalan Population," paper presented at Latin American Studies Association International Congress, 1991, and his "Religious Conversion in Quetzaltenango, Guatemala," PhD diss., University of Pittsburgh, 1990.

22. Garrard-Burnett, *Protestantism in Guatemala*, 169.

Chapter 1

1. Enrique Dussel, *History and Theology of Liberation* (Maryknoll, NY: Orbis, 1976).

2. Cited by Gustavo Gutiérrez, *Las Casas* (Maryknoll, NY: Orbis, 1993), 46.

3. Ibid.

4. See especially Consejo Episcopal Latinoamericano, *De una pastoral indigenista a una pastoral indígena* (Bogotá: Consejo Episcopal Latinoamericano, 1987).

5. "Maya Catholics in Chiapas, Mexico," in Edward Cleary and Timothy Steigenga, eds., *Resurgent Voices in Latin America* (New Brunswick, NJ: Rutgers University Press, 2004), 196.

6. Ibid.

7. Ibid.

8. Helen Rand Parish started a new phase in scholarship on religion in the Colonial era through her research at the Bancroft Library at the University of California at Berkeley.

9. For a contrary view, see Allan Figueroa Deck, SJ, "The Trashing of the Fifth Centenary," *America*, December 19, 1992. "Black Legend" was coined by Julián Juderías in 1914 to describe a tendency to denigrate Spain. Starting in the sixteenth century, this anti-Spanish literature has exaggerated the negative aspects of the Inquisition, the colonization of the Americas, and other events in more recent times.

10. See, for example, Paul S. Vickery, *Bartolomé de las Casas: Great Prophet of the Americas* (Mahwah/New York: Paulist Press, 2006); Juan Friede and Benjamin Keen, eds., *Bartolomé de las Casas in History: Toward an Understanding of the Man and His Work* (DeKalb, IL: Northern Illinois University Press, 1971, 2008).

11. The text is included in *Vitoria: Political Writings*, ed. Anthony Pagden and Jeremy Lawrance, Cambridge Texts in the History of Political Thought (Cambridge, UK: Cambridge University Press, 1992). It is also available online, in a translation by John Pawley Bate, at http://www.constitu tion.org/victoria/victoria_.htm.

12. Letty Russell, *Human Liberation in a Feminist Perspective—A Theology* (Philadelphia: Westminister Press, 1974); *Inheriting Our Mothers' Gardens: Feminist Theology in Third World Perspective* (Philadelphia: Westminster Press, 1988); María Pilar Aquino, *Our Cry for Life: Feminist Theology from Latin America* (Maryknoll, NY: Orbis, 1993); *Feminist Intercultural Theology: Latina Explorations for a Just World* (Maryknoll, NY: Orbis, 2007); Ivone Gebara, *Longing for Running Water: Ecofeminism and Liberation* (Minneapolis, MN: Fortress, 1999); *Out of the Depths: Women's Experience of Evil and Salvation* (Minneapolis, MN: Fortress, 2002); María Clara Bingemer, *El rostro feminino de la teología feminina* (San Jose, Costa Rica: Editorial DEI, 1986); (with Ivone Gebara), *Mary, Mother of God, Mother of the Poor* (Maryknoll, NY: Orbis, 1989); Elsa Tamez, *Through Her Eyes: Women's Theology from Latin America* (Maryknoll, NY: Orbis, 1989); *Bible of the Oppressed* (Maryknoll, NY: Orbis, 1982).

13. Interviews by author with Letty Russell, November 15, 1993; Margaret Farley, February 16, 1994; Robert Ellsworth (Orbis Books), February 17, 1994.

14. This international congress on the environment, commonly called the Rio Earth Summit, was held at Rio de Janeiro, June 3–14, 1992, and published various documents, including the noteworthy Rio Declaration on Environment and Development.

15. Ivone Gebara, *Longing for Running Water: Ecofeminism and Liberation* (Minneapolis, MN: Fortress, 1999).

16. "Latin America's Emerging Environmental Democracy," *Portal* 2 (2006–2007), 7.

17. Strictly interpreted, Mendes's cause was primarily about the rights of the rubber tappers, but he became a symbol of stopping the devastation of the Amazon. James Brooke, "Why They Killed Chico Mendes," *New York Times*, August 19, 1990, viewed at http://www.nytimes.com (accessed July 16, 2008).

18. Marilyn Berlin Snell, "Bulldozers and Blasphemy," *National Catholic Reporter*, September 21, 2007.

19. Jane Perlez and Lowell Bergman, "Tangled Strands in Fight over Peru Gold Mine," *New York Times*, October 25, 2005, http://www.nytimes.com (accessed September 26, 2007).

20. Statement of Comisión Nacional para Pastoral Ecológica del Episcopado Dominicano, November 4, 2004.

21. Snell, "Bulldozers and Blasphemy."

22. Accessible on the Vatican website at http://www.vatican.va/holy_father/benedict_xvi/messages/urbi/documents/hf_ben-xvi_mes_20071225_urbi_en.html; see also Ian Fisher, "Pope Makes Appeal to Protect Environment," *New York Times*, December 25, 2007, http://www.nytimes.com (accessed August 13, 2008).

Chapter 2

1. See Xavier Rynne, *The Third Session* (New York: Farrar, Straus, and Giroux, 1965), 50.

2. See Thomas C. Bruneau, "The Catholic Church and Development in Latin America," *World Development* 8, nos. 7–8 (July–August, 1980): 537, and the LASA Session on Conflict of Loyalty, Bloomington, IN, 1980.

Notes

3. Thomas Bruneau (scholar of Brazilian religion and professor, Naval Postgraduate School, Monterey, CA) interview with author, March 27, 1989.

4. Yves Congar, *Lay People in the Church* (Westminster, MD: Newman, 1965) and *Priest and Laymen* (London: Chapman, 1966); Karl Rahner, "Notes on the Lay Apostolate," in *Theological Investigations*, vol. 2 (Baltimore: Helicon, 1963), 319–52, and *Christians in the Market Place* (New York: Sheed and Ward, 1966).

5. Puebla Conference Final Document, No. 629.

6. Voluntary organizations in the U.S., such as candy stripers in hospitals or Boy Scouts, are especially adept at attracting participants through symbols and activities such as costumes, titles, and functions that are perceived to be worthwhile.

7. Opening Address at the Puebla Conference, in *Puebla and Beyond*, ed. John Eagleson and Phillip Scharper (Maryknoll, NY: Orbis, 1979), 57–71.

8. See Clodovis Boff, *Comunidade ecclesial, communidade politica* (Petrópolis: Vozes, 1978); P. Demo, *Communidade: Igreja na Base* (São Paulo: Paulinas, 1974); and SEDOC (Petrópolis: Vozes), nos. 81, 95, 115, and 118.

9. See Alvin Lingran and Norman Shawchuck, *Let My People Go: Empowering the Laity* (Nashville: Abingdon, 1980).

10. *National Catholic Reporter*, November 12, 2004.

11. (São Paulo: Loyola, 2004).

12. Quoted by Robert Pelton in the *National Catholic Reporter*.

13. Margo de Theije, "CEBs and Catholic Charismatics in Brazil," in Christian Smith and Joshua Prokopy, eds., *Latin American Religion in Motion* (New York: Routledge, 1999), 111–24.

14. See Gottfried Deelen, "La Iglesia al encuentro del pueblo en America Latina," *Pro Mundi Vita Boletín*, 81 (April/June 1980):18–19, and Bishop Tiago Cloin, "The BEC Will Produce a New Kind of Priest," LADOC, *Base Christian Communities*, 41–44.

15. Kenneth Serbin, *Needs of the Heart: A Social and Cultural History of Brazil's Clergy and Seminaries* (Notre Dame, IN: University of Notre Dame Press, 2006).

16. Medellín Conference, Document on Joint Pastoral Planning, no. 10.

17. Press conference, Puebla, February 8, 1979.

18. Studies on women in Latin America have multiplied rapidly in recent years. Some noteworthy collections of articles or books include: Jane

Jacquette, ed., *The Women's Movement in Latin America: Feminism and the Transition to Democracy* (Winchester, MA: Unwin Hyman, 1989), and Carol Drogus and Hannah Stewart-Gambino, *Activist Faith: Women from the Popular Church and Social Movements in Democratic Brazil and Chile* (University Park, PA: Pennsylvania State University Press, 2005).

19. Cardinal Aloisio Lorscheider, interview, January 29, 1979.

Chapter 3

1. *New Catholic Encyclopedia*, vol. 13, 2nd ed., (Detroit: Thompson and Gale, 2003), 437.

2. For a view of national media attempting to deal with popular religion, see "Sacred Places," special issue, *U.S. News & World Report*, November 26, 2007.

3. Cristián Parker, *Popular Religion and Modernization in Latin America: A Different Logic* (Maryknoll, NY: Orbis, 1996), 128.

4. The description of the full scope of these practices is beyond the space allotted for this work. For a vivid example see "Pilgrim Cowboys," *National Geographic*, August 2007.

5. The *New York Times* (October 19, 2006) carried a large photo of the October 2006 procession without a story, simply to indicate a major annual event in Latin America.

6. See Joseph M. Palacios on the questionable appropriation of the Guadalupe symbols in *The Catholic Social Imagination: Activism and the Just Society in Mexico and the United States* (Chicago: University of Chicago Press, 2007), 109.

7. The history of Catholicism in areas without priests has yet to be written. This history would include Japan, China, Irian Jaya (Indonesia), and other parts of Asia, where the practice of the Catholic faith continued for a long time in spite of the lack of priests due to persecution.

8. See Frei Betto's book-long interview, *Fidel and Religion* (New York: Simon and Schuster, 1987).

9. Manuel Marzal, *Tierra encantada* (Madrid: Editorial Trotta, 2002), 336.

10. Edward L. Cleary and Juan Sepúlveda, "Chilean Pentecostalism," in Cleary and Hannah Stewart-Gambino, eds., *Power, Politics, and Pentecostals in Latin America* (Boulder, CO: Westview, 1997), 110–11.

11. See Fidel Castro's vivid account of his religious upbringing in Frei Betto, *Fidel and Religion* (New York: Simon and Schuster, 1987).

12. The struggle to introduce orthodox Catholicism into Guatemala two generations ago is the centerpiece of a classic anthropological work but framed in difficult language: Kay Warren's *The Symbolism of Subordination: Indian Identity in a Guatemalan Town* (Austin, TX: University of Texas Press, 1978).

13. Consejo Episcopal Latinoamericano, "Pastoral" 6.I.2, in *Medillín* (1968), available online at http://www.celam.org/principal/index.php?module=CELAM&func=conculta_publicaciones.

14. Gregory Stanczak, *Engaged Spirituality: Social Change and American Religion* (New Brunswick, NJ: Rutgers University Press, 2006).

15. Catholic lobbyists in state capitals in the U.S. explicitly stated that accompanying the poor and the vulnerable was their mission. See Edward Cleary and Allen Hertzke, *Representing God at the Statehouse* (Lanham, MD: Rowman and Littlefield, 2005), passim.

16. John Burdick, "The Lost Constituency of Brazil's Black Consciousness Movements," *Latin American Perspectives* 98 (January 1998): 137.

17. David Barrett and Todd Johnson, *World Christian Encyclopedia* 2nd ed. (New York: Oxford University Press, 1980), passim.

18. This chagrins many younger Catholic Pentecostals, who do not know their own history and dislike the association with Protestants. Many theological and social science volumes of the 1970s commonly called Catholic Charismatics Pentecostals.

19. The account here follows Burgess, *The New International Dictionary of Pentecostal and Charismatic Movements* (Grand Rapids, MI: Zondervan, 2003), 955 and passim. However, one should note that many authors cite the pneuma (speaking in tongues, baptism in the spirit) events at Azuza Street Church in Los Angeles from 1906 to 1913 as the beginning of the Pentecostal movement in North America.

20. See Stanley Burgess in *International Dictionary*, 928.

21. Jack Hayford and David Moore, *The Charismatic Century: The Enduring Impact of the Azuza Street Revival* (New York: Warner, 2006).

22. Paul Thigpen, "Catholic Charismatic Renewal," in *The New International Dictionary of Pentecostal nd Charismatic Movements*, Stanley M. Burgess, ed. (Zondervan, 2002).

23. See Gelpi, *Charism and Sacrament* (London: SPCK, 1977), 150–151.

24. Notes from the meeting supplied by Francis MacNutt.

25. Clovodis Boff, "Carismáticos e libertadores na Igreja," *Revista Eclesiástica Brasileira* 60, no. 237 (March 2000): 36–53.

26. English version in Cleary, *The Path from Puebla*, 67–71.

27. The closest counterpart in the United States is John Michael Talbot, a lay Franciscan whose concerts and CDs are widely popular.

28. C. Boff, "Carismáticos," 36–53.

29. National Conference of Brazilian Bishops, *Orientações Pastorais sobre o CCR* (Brasilia: Conferencia Nacional dos Bispos do Brasil, 1994).

30. Note also his profound reservations in Leonardo Boff, *Etica da vida* (Brasilia: Letraviva, 1999), 168–69 and 184–89.

31. Pedro A. Ribeiro de Oliveira, "O Catolicismo: De CEBs à Renovação Carismática," *Revista Brasileira Eclesiática* 59 (December 1999): 823–35.

32. Margo de Theije, "CEBs and Catholic Charismatics in Brazil," in *Latin American Religion in Motion*, Christian Smith and Joshua Prokopy, eds. (New York: Routledge, 1999), 111–24.

33. Despite an overall increase in sisters in 2004, some countries had notable declines.

34. See yearly polls by Latinobarómetro, http://www.latinobaro metro.org/.

35. See John L. Allen, *Opus Dei: An Objective Look behind the Myths and Reality of the Most Controversial Force in the Catholic Church* (New York: Doubleday, 2005).

36. http://www.schoenstatt.cl (accessed September 15, 2006).

37. Sponsored by the National Commission of Laity of the Chilean Bishops Conference, June 12, 2004, Santiago, Chile.

38. http://noticias.iglesia.cl/ (accessed October 20, 2006).

Chapter 4

1. The website, http://www.colorq.org/ (accessed October 14, 2005).

2. José Vasconcelos, *The Cosmic Race / La raza cosmica: A Bilingual Edition*. Translated by Didier T. Jaén (Baltimore, MD: Johns Hopkins University Press, 1997).

3. See the various volumes in the Faith and Cultures Series edited by Robert J. Schreiter and published by Orbis Books, http://www.orbisbooks.com/.

4. José María Arguedas, *Todas las Sangres* (Ediciones Peisa, 1973).

5. Alison Brysk, *From Tribal Village to Global Village* (Stanford, CA: Stanford University Press, 2000), 194.

6. The Catholic Church de-emphasizes to a relatively high degree the foreign character of its clergy in individual countries. Few statistics have been gathered or, having been gathered, are reported about the percentage of missionaries to Latin America. One of the very few attempts to quantify the situation is from Brussels' Pro Mundi Vita Institute, *Special Note: Foreign Priests in Latin America* (1970).

7. P. G. Cabra, "Los religiosos y la evangelización de América Latina," *Iglesia, Pueblo y Culturas* 32 (January–March 1994): 125.

8. Among major creators of liberation theology Jon Sobrino, a Jesuit, was born in Spain.

9. In Brazil and Chile, reforms in the Catholic Church were taking place before Vatican II, and many foreign clergy and women religious reinforced progressive tendencies. In countries where native clergy were notably conservative in the 1970s, such as Nicaragua, foreign clergy tended to take the lead in implementing liberation theology.

10. Xavier Albó, "The Aymara Religious Experience," in Manuel Marzal, ed., *The Indian Face of God in Latin America* (Maryknoll, NY: Orbis, 1996), 153–55.

11. Hans Buechler, *The Masked Media: Aymara Fiestas and Social Interaction in the Bolivian Highlands* (New York: Mouton, 1980).

12. Susan Rosales Nelson, "Bolivia: Continuity and Conflict in Religious Discourse," in Daniel H. Levine, ed., *Religion and Political Conflict in Latin America* (Chapel Hill, NC: University of North Carolina Press, 1986), 222.

13. Edward L. Cleary, *The Struggle for Human Rights in Latin America* (Westport, CT: Praeger, 1997), 93–95. Mark Engler traces an evolution from avoidance to critique to nuanced acceptance of human rights in his "Toward the 'Rights of the Poor'," *Journal of Religious Ethics* 28, no. 3 (September 2000): 339–66.

14. Juan Luis Segundo, *Signs of the Times: Theological Reflections* (Maryknoll, NY: Orbis, 1993), 53–66, passim.

15. See especially, Consejo Episcopal Latinoamericano, *De una pastoral indigenista a una pastoral indígena* (Bogotá: Consejo Episcopal Latinoamericano, 1987) and José Alsina Franch, compiler, *Indianismo e indigenismo en América* (Madrid: Alianza Editorial/Quinto Cententario, 1990).

16. See, for example, Edward L. Cleary, *Crisis and Change: The Church in Latin America Today* (Maryknoll, NY: Orbis, 1985), 5.

17. John Paul II, "Opening Address," Section II; Latin American Bishops' Conference, "Conclusions," passim in Alfred T. Hennelly, *Santo Domingo and Beyond* (Maryknoll, NY: Orbis, 1993).

18. Other expressions of citizens' media include low-cost mimeographed publications and instructional videos.

19. Slow progress is being made at least in Mexico and the Andean region in developing translations of the Bible, especially the New Testament, into indigenous languages.

20. Barry J. Lyons, "Religion, Authority, and Identity: Intergenerational Politics, Ethnic Resurgence, and Respect in Chimborazo, Ecuador," *Latin American Research Review* 36, no. 1 (2001): 7–48.

21. Edward L. Cleary, "Birth of Latin American Indigenous Theology," in Guillermo Cook, ed., *Crosscurrents in Indigenous Spirituality: Interface of Maya, Catholic, and Protestant Worldviews* (New York: E. J. Brill, 1997), 171–88.

22. Instituto de Estudios Aymaras, Chucuito, near Puno, Peru, was founded by Frank McGurn, MM, as part of the Prelature of Juli, under the care of Maryknoll Missioners; Centro de Estudios Regionales Andinos Bartolomé de las Casas, Cuzco, was founded by Dominicans from the Province of Toulouse and has been extended to include Escuela Andina de Postgrado; Instituto Pastoral Andino, Sicuani, originally was situated in Cuzco, and was created by Maryknoll Missioners; Centro de Investigación y Promoción del Campesinado, La Paz, was founded by the Jesuits and maintains ties to Centro de Teología Popular; and Instituto de Desarrollo, Investigación, y Educación Popular Campesino, Oruro, was founded by Canadian Oblates.

23. See for example the works of Manuel Marzal, Xavier Albó, Diego Irarrázaval, Esteban Judd, Miguel Briggs, Hans van den Berg, Luis Jolicoeur, and others. See equally *Pastoral Andina, Allphanchis, Aymar Yatiyawi, Abya Yala News, Revista Andina, Fe y Pueblo, Búsqueda Pastoral,* and publications of CIPCA (Centro de Investigación y Promoción del Campesinado). Some publications extend beyond the Peruvian-Bolivian subregion.

24. María José Caram, "The Shape of Catholic Identity among the Aymara of Pilcuyo," in Thomas Bamat and Jean-Paul Wiest, eds., *Popular Catholicism in a World Church: Seven Case Studies in Inculturation* (Maryknoll, NY: Orbis, 1999), 79.

25. For further background see Brian H. Smith, *The Church and Politics in Chile: Challenges to Modern Catholicism* (Princeton, NJ: Princeton University Press, 1982), 271–72.

26. See, for example, his *Teología en la fe del pueblo* (San José, Costa Rica: DEI, 1999); *Cultura y fe latinoamericanas* (Santiago, Chile: Rehue, 1994); *Rito y pensar cristiano* (Lima: Centro de Estudios y Publicaciones, 1993); and *Tradición y provenir andino* (Chucuito, Peru: Instituto de Estudios Aymaras, 1992).

27. Diego Irarrázaval, *Inculturation: New Dawn of the Church in Latin America* (Maryknoll, NY: Orbis, 2000), 61.

28. Ibid., 68.

29. Ibid., 94.

30. Kevin Healy, *Llamas, Weavings, and Organic Chocolate: Multicultural Grassroots Development in the Andes and Amazon of Bolivia* (Notre Dame, IN: University of Notre Dame Press, 2001), 70.

31. Ibid., 69.

32. Albó repeats St. Augustine's description of religion outside of Christianity as "seeds of revelation," in Albó, "The Aymara," 122.

32. See Irarrázaval, *Inculturation*, on programmatic advances, 50–52.

34. Enrique Jorda, "La cosmovisión aymara en el diólogo de la fe: Teología desde el Titicaca," doctoral dissertation, Faculty of Theology, Pontifical Catholic University, Lima, 1980.

35. See for example comments of Pablo Richard in *Latinamerican Press*, July 11, 1998.

36. Gustavo Gutiérrez, *Las Casas: In Search of the Poor of Jesus Christ* (Maryknoll, NY: Orbis, 1993).

37. Irarrázaval, *Inculturation*, 11.

38. For further explanation of indigenous spirituality see Cleary, "Birth," passim.

39. African-based religions are found in other Latin American countries. The cult of María Lionza, a mixture of indigenous, African, and Catholic beliefs, can be found in many parts of Venezuela and has drawn the attention of both social scientists and the sensationalist press. See, for example: Angelina Pollack-Eltz, *María Lionza: Mito and culto venezolano* 2nd ed.

(Caracas: Universidad Católica Andrés Bello, 1985). The best-known Afro–Latin American religion in the United States is Cuban and Puerto Rican santería.

40. One of the great observers of Latin American society, Ana Guillermoprieto, wrote an engaging account of the white embrace of African religion in "Letter from Rio," *New Yorker*, December 2, 1991.

41. High-level anthropological and religious studies of this region can be found in chapters by Alejandro Frigerio and María Julia Carozzi in Timothy Steigenga and Edward Cleary, eds., *Conversion of a Continent* (New Brunswick, NJ: Rutgers University Press, 2008), 33–51 and 133–52.

42. See: María Isaura Pereira de Queiroz, "Afro-Brazilian Cults and Religious Change in Brazil," in James A. Beckford and Thomas Luckmann, eds., *The Changing Face of Religion* (Newbury Park, CA: Sage, 1989), 95; see also: note 7; this estimate is repeated by Piepke (see note 47 below), 180.

43. Edwin Taylor, ed., *Brazil* (Singapore: APA Publications, 1989), 215.

44. Béhague, "Regional and National Trends in Afro-Brazilian Religious Musics: A Case of Cultural Pluralism," *Competing Gods: Religious Pluralism in Latin America*, Occasional Paper No. 11 (Providence, RI: Watson Institute for International Studies, Brown University, 1992), 13.

45. In regard to sophistication and institutionalization, see especially Diana DeG. Brown, *Umbanda: Religion and Politics in Urban Brazil* (Ann Arbor: UMI Research Press, 1986), David J. Hess, *Spirits and Scientists: Ideology, Spiritism, and Brazilian Culture* (University Park, PA: Pennsylvania State University Press, 1991), and brief remarks made by Roberto Motta in "The Churchifying of Candomblé: Priests, Anthropologists, and the Canonization of African Religious Memory," paper given at Latin American Studies Association International Congress, 1992.

46. Boaventura Kloppenburg, *Umbanda: Orientação pára os Católicos* (Rio de Janeiro: Editora Vozes, 1961).

47. Joachim Piepke, "The Religious Heritage of Africa in Brazil: Investigations about the Religiosity of the Afro-Brazilians Today," *Verbum SVD* 33, no. 2 (1992): 174–75.

48. Some blacks were enslaved by other blacks in Africa. By contrast, free blacks and mulattos have always been in Brazil. These free men and women, often engaged in crafts and trades, were important to African religions, because as Pereira de Queiroz ("Afro-Brazilian," 105, n. 3), says: "Their existence was important for the maintenance of the cults, since

priesthood required a great deal of disposable time. Priests and priestesses were then mostly free men and women."

49. Carlos Aguirre, *Breve historia de la esclavitud en el Perú: Una herida que no deja de sangrar* (Lima: Fondo Editorial del Congreso del Perú, 2007).

50. At the end of the 1980s there were 4 blacks among 339 bishops and 500 blacks among 15,000 priests.

51. Unnoticed except by research university libraries, such as Yale Divinity School Library, which collected its newsletters and other publications.

Chapter 5

1. *The Documents of Vatican II*, Walter M. Abbott, SJ, general editor (New York: The America Press, 1966), 274. In a footnote the editors of this volume anticipated that this paragraph (no. 65) would be interpreted as a criticism of "wealthy persons in some parts of Latin America..." who consign their money to Swiss banks instead of investing it in the development of their own countries.

2. "Modes of moral discourse in the preferential option for the poor," PhD dissertation, Boston College, 2005.

3. Albino Barrera, OP, interview with author, April 2, 2006.

4. http://www.midwestaugustinians.org (accessed August 10, 2007).

5. *The Economist*, August 18, 2007. See Edward Cleary and Allen Hertzke, eds., *Representing God at the Statehouse* (Lanham, MD: Rowman and Littlefield, 2006) and David Yamane, *The Catholic Church and State Politics* (Lanham, MD.: Rowman and Littlefield, 2006).

6. Or, in the case of Virginia, as representatives of individual dioceses.

7. Catholic News from the *Universe*, http://www.totalcatholic.com (accessed September 28, 2007).

8. Pentecostals would later prove that, at least in the 1950s, the poor could in fact support a simplified clergy and rudimentary church buildings, if not first-class schools and hospitals.

9. *Machuca*, a Spanish-language Chilean film available from Netflix.com.

10. See Miguel Petty, *La promoción humana en los medios rurales marginales* (Córdoba, Argentina: Universidad Católica de Córdoba, 1999).

11. The center has evolved into CISOC-Bellarmino (Center for Sociocultural Investigations) and was one of the founding entities incorporated in 1997 into Alberto Hurtado University.

12. (New York: Macmillan, 1962; repr. in paperback by Scribner, 1997).

13. Gustavo Gutiérrez, "Church of the Poor," in Edward L. Cleary, ed., *Born of the Poor: The Latin American Church since Medellín* (Notre Dame, IN: University of Notre Dame Press, 1990), 13.

14. Gutiérrez, "Church of the Poor," 15.

15. Ralph della Cava, "The ten-year crusade toward the Third Christian Millennium: an account of Evangelization 2000 and Lumen 2000," in Douglas Charmers et al., eds., *The Right and Democracy in Latin America* (New York: Columbia University Press, 1990), passim.

16. Congregation for the Doctrine of the Faith, *Instruction on Christian Freedom and Liberation*, March 22, 1986. Available on the Vatican website at http://www.vatican.va/roman_curia/congregations/cfaith/documents/rc_con_cfaith_doc_19860322_freedom-liberation_en.html.

17. John R. Donahue, "The Bible and Catholic Social Teaching: Will This Engagement Lead to Marriage?" in Kenneth R. Himes, ed., *Modern Catholic Social Teaching* (Washington, DC: Georgetown University Press, 2005), 9.

18. *Centesimus annus*, May 1, 1991. Available on the Vatican website at http://www.vatican.va/edocs/ENG0214/_INDEX.HTM.

19. Jeffrey Klaiber, a Chicago Jesuit working in Peru since the 1970s, has been working on a history of the Jesuits in Latin America for some time.

20. A necessary corrective to this viewpoint was supplied by William Foote Whyte in his "Myth of the Passive Peasant," *Estudios Andinos* 1, no. 1 (1969): 1–27.

21. Gustavo Gutiérrez, "La opción preferencial por el pobre de Aparecida," *Páginas* 206 (August 2007): 6–25.

Chapter 6

1. Ivan Petrella, *The Future of Liberation Theology: An Argument and a Manifesto* (Burlington, VT: Ashgate, 2004) and *Latin American Liberation Theology: The Next Generation* (Maryknoll, NY: Orbis, 2005).

2. These dissertations have been completed in the last thirty years and their titles can be found in the widely available World Catalog, a service of OCLC (Online Computer Library Center), http://www.firstsearch. oclc.org (subscription required).

3. Medellín, "Peace," no. 14a (Bogotá: General Secretariat of Latin American Bishops Conference, 1970), 76–77.

4. For a discussion of praxis commonly used by Latin American social scientists and commonly understood by theologians see Edward L. Cleary and Germán Garrido Pinto, "Applied Social Science, Teaching, and Political Action," *Human Organization* 36, no. 3 (Fall 1977): 270.

5. Medellín, "Peace," no. 5.

6. Paulo Friere, *Pedagogy of the Oppressed*, trans. Myra Bergman Ramos (New York: Herder & Herder, 1971).

Chapter 7

1. Some theologians, such as Jon Sobrino, claim that New Evangelization began at the Medellín Conference of Latin American Bishops (1968), which "coined the expression before John Paul II popularized it." See Sobrino, "The Winds in Santo Domingo and the Evangelization of Culture," in Alfred Hennelly, ed., *Santo Domingo and Beyond* (Maryknoll, NY: Orbis, 1993), 181. See also Paul VI, *Evangelii Nuntiandi* http://www.vatican.va/holy_father/paul_vi/apost_exhortations/docu ments/hf_p-vi_exh_19751208_evangelii-nuntiandi_en.html; John Paul II, *Redemptoris Missio* http://www.vatican.va/holy_father/john_paul_ii/ encyclicals/documents/hf_jp-ii_enc_07121990_redemptoris-missio_ en.html, and *Crossing the Threshold of Hope* (New York: Knopf, 1994), 113–14.

2. Gerald Costello, *Mission to Latin America: Successes and Failures of a Twentieth-Century Crusade* (Maryknoll, NY: Orbis, 1979).

3. Despite all the media attention given Brazil's indigenous people, they represent less than one-half of one percent of the population.

4. This political, social, and cultural resurgence and missionary influence is covered in Edward L. Cleary and Timothy J. Steigenga, eds., *Resurgent Voices in Latin America* (New Brunswick, NJ: Rutgers University Press, 2004).

5. For Guatemala, see Mary P. Holleran, *Church and State in Guatemala* (New York: Columbia University Press, 1974); for Mexico, see Albesa Martínez, *La Constitución de 1857: Catolicismo y liberalismo en México* (Mexico City: Porrúa, 2007); and for Argentina, see Arthur Liebscher, "The Catholic Church in Argentine Society: Córdoba. 1883–1928," MST thesis, Jesuit School of Theology at Berkeley, 1986.

6. Estimate supplied by Professor Bruce Calder, Dept. of History, University of Illinois at Chicago.

7. Sheldon Annis, *God and Production in a Guatemalan Town* (Austin: University of Texas Press), 140.

8. Interviews with Maryknoll Missioners, 1981–1991, especially David Kelley, Carroll Quinn, and Bishop Richard Ham.

9. The Catholic Church, as well as the Protestant churches, struggled mightily to reclaim indigenous peoples for Christianity from native practices. That effort deserves separate attention. See, for example, Everett A. Wilson, "Identity, Community, and Status: The Legacy of Central American Pentecostal Pioneers," in Joel A. Carpenter and Wilbert Shenk, eds., *American Evangelicals and Foreign Missions, 1880–1980* (Grand Rapids, MI: Eerdmans, 1990), 131–51.

10. See especially Stephen Judd, MM, "The Indigenous Theology Movement in Latin America," in Edward L. Cleary and Timothy Steigenga, eds., *Resurgent Voices in Latin America* (New Brunswick, NJ: Rutgers University Press, 2004), 210–30.

11. John Gorski, "How the Catholic Church in Latin America Became Missionary," *International Bulletin of Missionary Research* 27, no. 2 (April 2003): 60.

12. Atz appears as a focal point in *Precarious Peace: God and Guatemala*, a documentary film by Rudolph Nelson, Shirley Nelson, et al. (Worcester, PA: Gateway Films, 2003).

13. See, for example, Ricardo Falla, *Massacres in the Jungle: Ixcán, Guatemala, 1975–1982* (Boulder: Westview, 1994).

14. See note 8 above.

15. Native catechists should be included in the comparisons of the numbers of priests versus Pentecostal pastors, since catechists are similarly educated and perform many of the same functions, including preaching.

16. See Vatican II's *Declaration on the Relation of the Church to Non-Christian Religions*, http://www.vatican.va/archive/hist_councils/ii_vatican _council/documents/vat-ii_decl_19651028_nostra-aetate_en.html.

17. The theology of inculturation is treated at length in Cleary and Steigenga, *Resurgent Voices*, 210–30 and passim.

18. Andrew Orta, "From Theologies of Liberation to Theologies of Inculturation," in Sattya Pattnayak, *Organized Religion in the Political Transformation of Latin America* (Lanham, MD: University Press of America, 1995), 97–124.

19. Kay Warren, *The Symbolism of Subordination: Indian Identity in a Guatemalan Town* (Austin, TX: University Press, 1978); Hans Buechler, *The Masked Media: Aymara Fiestas and Social Interaction in the Bolivian Highlands* (New York: Mouton, 1980).

20. For an authoritative account of Mayan resurgence see Bruce J. Calder, "Interwoven Histories: The Catholic Church and the Maya," in Cleary and Steigenga, *Resurgent Voices*, 93–124.

21. For further exploration of ethnic cosmologies see Edward L. Cleary, "Birth of Latin American Indigenous Theology," in Guillermo Cook, ed., *Crosscurrents in Indigenous Spirituality: Interface of Maya, Catholic, and Protestant Worldviews* (New York: E. J. Brill, 1997), 171–88.

22. Legionnaires of Christ website, http://www.legionariesofchrist. org (accessed July 14, 2001).

23. Telephone interview with John Allen, Jr., July 23, 2007.

24. The English translations of the final documents are contained in John Eagleson and Philip Scharper, eds., *Puebla and Beyond* (Maryknoll, NY: Orbis, 1979).

25. Julia Duin, "Evangelization 2000," *Christianity Today*, February 6, 1987, and Thomas Wang, "By the Year 2000," *Mission Frontiers*, May 1987, both at http://www.missionfrontiers.org (accessed April 30, 2008).

26. General conferences are convened about every ten years; ordinary conferences of the Latin American bishops are held yearly.

27. The final document of the Santo Domingo meeting is published in English in Alfred Hennelly, ed., *Santo Domingo and Beyond* (Maryknoll, NY: Orbis, 1993).

28. For the context of the Santo Domingo meeting, see Edward Cleary, "The Journey to Santo Domingo," in Hennelly, *Santo Domingo*, 3–23.

29. Ralph Della Cava, "The Ten-Year Crusade toward the Third Christian Millennium: An Account of Evangelization 2000 and Lumen 2000," in Douglas Chalmers, ed., *The Right and Democracy* (New York: Praeger, 1992), 256–87.

30. A notable exception was Bishop Lugo in Paraguay, who continued to argue a liberationist line, resigned from the episcopate, and was elected president of the country in 2008, partly on his reputation as champion of the poor.

31. An early account of the Brazilian Charismatic Renewal can be found in Brenda Carranza, *Renovação Carismática Católica: Origens, mudanças e tendéncias* (Aparecida: Editora Santuário, 2000).

32. Regina Novaes, a Brazilian expert on Charismatics, believes that Nova Canção is the most effective covenant community in the world. She is quoted in Thaís Oyama and Samarone Lima, "Católicos en transe," *Veja*, August 4, 1998, http://www.veja.abril.co.br (accessed December 29, 2007).

33. Larry Rohter, "Sao Paulo Journal," *New York Times*, June 25, 1999, http://www.nytimes.com (accessed May 4, 2008).

34. For expansion of this church into the United States and the characteristics of its message, see Virginia Garrard Burnett, "Stop Suffering? The Iglesia Universal del Reino de Dios in the United States," in Steigenga and Cleary, *Conversion*, 218–38.

35. IURD also challenges Afro-Brazilian religions and older Pentecostal groups.

36. André Ricardo de Souza, *Igreja in Concert: Padres Cantores, Mídia e Marketing* (São Paulo: Anna Blume Editor, 2005).

37. Susan Rose and Quentin Schultze, "The Evangelical Awakening in Guatemala: Fundamentalist Impact on Education and Media," in Martin Marty and Scott Appleby, eds., *Fundamentalisms and Society* (Chicago: University of Chicago Press, 1993), 415–51.

38. Timothy Steigenga and Edward L. Cleary, eds., *Conversion of a Continent: Religious Change in Latin America* (New Brunswick, NJ: Rutgers University Press, 2007).

39. Cardinal Joseph Ratzinger, "New Evangelization," Address to Catechists and Religion Teachers, December 12, 2000, http://www.ewtn.com (accessed May 4, 2008).

40. The Synthesis document served as the basis of preparation by General Conference participants of the Final Document of Aparecida.

41. CELAM V General Conference Synthesis (Preparatory) Document, 4.3, No. 311 ff.

42. Andrew Downie, "Behind Brazil's Catholic Resurgence," *Time* online http://www.time.com/time/world/article/0,8599,1618439,00.html, posted May 7, 2007 (accessed March 27, 2008).

43. Approximately a two-year lag occurs in reporting statistics in the Catholic Church. These are available in yearly additions of *Statistical Yearbook of the Church*. Selected statistics are also available in yearly editions of *National Catholic Almanac* and on the web through LANIC (http://lanic. utexas.edu/), sponsored by the University of Texas.

44. Interview, New Haven, CT, July 2, 2002.

45. Henri Gooren, "Conversion Careers in Latin America," 52–71, and Timothy J. Steigenga and Edward Cleary, "Understanding Conversion in the Americas," 9 and passim, both in Steigenga and Cleary, eds., *Conversion of a Continent.*

46. Quoted by Downie, "Behind Brazil's Catholic Resurgence."

47. Pew Forum on Religion, Religious Demographic Profile: Brazil, http://www.pewforum.org (accessed March 25, 2008).

48. Figures supplied by the Central Coordinating Office of Brazilian Catholic Charismatic Renewal.

49. See chapters on Brazil in Edward L. Cleary, *The Rise of Catholic Charismatics in Latin America* (Gainesville, FL: University Press of Florida, forthcoming).

Chapter 8

1. Although the first effective human rights organization in Latin America began operating in Brazil a year earlier than in Chile, the impact of the Chilean (and Uruguayan) coups stimulated the great surge of international organizing that announced the beginning of an era.

2. Samuel P. Huntington, *The Third Wave: Democratization in the Late Twentieth Century* (Norman, OK: University of Oklahoma Press, 1992).

3. Other church representatives who were members of the committee are noted in Vicaría de la Solidaridad, *Vicaría de la Solidaridad: Historia de su trabajo social* (Santiago de Chile: Vicaría de la Solidaridad, 1991), 43.

4. In an address to the Inter-American Commission on Human Rights, Washington, DC, on May 27, 1976, Rev. J. Bryan Hehir listed the tasks of the Vicariate of Solidarity as, "among other things: to give juridical assistance to the people detained by the secret police; provide defense for those tried by Military Tribunals; and denounce before the Criminal Courts homicides, illegal detentions, and the disappearance of people." See http://www.usccb.org/sdwp/international/chileiachr.shtml.

5. Cleary, "Struggling for Human Rights in Latin America," *America*, November 5, 1994.

6. In 1981 the Council on Hemispheric Affairs, *Washington Report on the Americas* reported: "With some justice, Mexico can be called the 'Iran Next Door' " (July 14, 1981), 4–5. See also Charles Humana, comp., *World Human Rights Guide*, 3rd ed. (New York: Oxford University Press, 1992), 205–208. See earlier editions of Humana's Guide and Human Rights Watch/Americas, *Human Rights in Mexico: A Policy of Impunity* (New York: Human Rights Watch, 1990); Ellen L. Lutz, "Human Rights in Mexico: Cause for Continuing Concern," *Current History* 92, no. 571 (February 1993): 78–82; Lawyers Committee for Human Rights, Critique Review of the Department of State's Country Report for Human Rights Practices for 1990 (New York: Lawyers Committee for Human Rights, 1991), 155–62; Amnesty International, annual reports, and Minnesota Advocates, various publications.

7. An older comparative view is provided by J. Lloyd Mecham's *Church and State in Latin America: History of Politico-Ecclesiastical Relations*, rev. ed. (Chapel Hill: University of North Carolina Press, 1966). More recent descriptions of church and state relations are: Roberto Blancarte, *El poder salinismo e Iglesia católica, una nueva convivencia* (Mexico City: Grijalbo, 1991); Karl Schmitt, "Church and State in Mexico: A Corporatist Relationship?" *Américas* 40 (January 1984): 349–76; and Claude Pomerlau, "The Changing Church in Mexico and Its Challenge to the State," *Review of Politics* 43 (October 1981): 540–49.

8. Daniel Levy and Gabriel Székeley, *Mexico: Paradoxes of Stability and Change*, 2nd ed. (Boulder: Westview, 1987), 89, characterized the situation: "Churches are organizations and they bring individuals together. The regime would not tolerate the church as a *powerful political organization* (emphasis theirs), capable of influencing national policy and even challenging the regime."

9. Mecham, *Church*, 415.

10. Significant changes were made in January 1992. The changes also affected Protestant churches. See Allan Metz, "Protestantism in Mexico: Contemporary Contextual Developments," *Journal of Church and State* 36, no. 1 (Winter 1994): 77–78. Even under the old restrictions many priests did vote. See also Matt Moffett, "In Catholic Mexico, A Priest's Power Is Limited to Prayer," *Wall Street Journal*, December 6, 1989.

11. For Mexico, see especially Joe Foweraker and Ann Craig, *Popular Movements and Political Change in Mexico* (Boulder: Rienner, 1990) and sources in note 10.

12. Foweraker, "Popular Movements," in Foweraker and Craig, *Popular Movements*, especially 4. See also Alberto Melucci, "Liberation or Meaning? Social Movements, Culture, and Democracy," *Development and Change* 23, no. 3 (1992): 43–77; Joel Wolfe, "Social Movements and the State in Brazil," *Latin American Research Review* 28, no. 1 (Winter 1993): 248–58; and Barry D. Adam, "Post-Marxism and the New Social Movements," *Canadian Review of Sociology and Anthropology* 30, no. 3 (1993): 316–36. A more pessimistic view than many authors is expressed by Diane E, Davis, "Failed Democratic Reform in Contemporary Mexico: From Social Movements to the State and Back Again," *Journal of Latin American Studies* 26, no. 2 (May 1994): 375–408. For Latin America see also: Arturo Escobar and Sonia E. Alvarez, eds., *The Making of Social Movements in Latin America* (Boulder: Westview, 1993).

13. Foweraker, "Popular Movements," 5.

14. "Transitional justice is a response to systematic or widespread violations of human rights. It seeks recognition for the victims and to promote possibilities for peace, reconciliation and democracy. Transitional justice is not a special form of justice but justice adapted to societies transforming themselves after a period of pervasive human rights abuse. In some cases, these transformations happen suddenly; in others, they may take place over many decades." See http://www.ictj.org/en/tj/.

15. See for example Giles Tremlitt, *Ghosts of Spain: Travels through Spain and Its Silent Past* (New York: Walker and Company, 2007), passim. It is noteworthy that Europeans, after military dictatorship and repression, with the exception of the German Nuremberg trials (imposed on, not requested by Germans) did not engage in establishing historical records. The *madre patria*, Spain, elected for a *pacto de silencio* about its Franco past.

16. See Lawrence Weschler, *A Miracle, a Universe: Settling Accounts with Torturers* (New York: Penguin, 1991).

17. In comparison to other Latin American countries, Brazil's record of military violence was lower. Disappearances were estimated at 250 persons and other victims at some 20,000. See Paul Zagorski, *Democracy versus National Security* (Boulder: Rienner, 1992), 99.

18. Weschler, *A Miracle*, 17.

19. Ibid., 10.

20. Conferência Nacional dos Bispos do Brasil, *Rumo ao Novo Milénio: Projeto de Evangelização da Igreja no Brasil em Preparação ao Grande Jubileu do Ano 2000* (São Paulo: Editorial Salesiana Don Bosco, 1996).

21. See, for example, Ralph Della Cava, "The 'People's Church,' the Vatican, and Abertura," in Alfred Stepan, ed., *Democratizing Brazil: Problems of Transition and Consolidation* (New York: Oxford University Press, 1989), 162.

22. His resignation was soon followed by the resignation or removal of presidents Jorge Serrano Elías of Guatemala and Carlos Andrés Pérez of Venezuela.

23. Interview, May 22, 1996, São Paulo.

24. "Getting Away with Murder," *Sixty Minutes*, CBS News, December 1, 1991.

25. One of Brazil's leading newsmagazines, *IstoE*, May 1, 1996, called the sentence "exemplary punishment."

26. As Madeleine Cousineau Adriance says: "Each year there is a Father Josimo pilgrimage, which reinforces the participants' sense of religious legitimacy of their struggle," in her *Promised Land: Base Christian Communities and the Struggle for the Amazon* (Albany: State University of New York Press, 1995), 71–72.

27. For 1996, see *Texto-Base: Justiça e Paz se abraçarão* (Brasília: Conferência Nacional dos Bispos do Brasil, 1996).

28. The foul conditions of Latin American prisons have belatedly received worldwide attention. For an early view of Brazilian prisons see Armida Bergamini Miotto, *A violencia nos prisões* (Goiõnia: Editor Universidade Federal de Goiás, 1983).

29. Interview with Joel Postma, OFM, staff member, National Conference of Brazilian Bishops, May 29, 1996.

30. Kempton, quoted by Fleming Rutledge, *Commonweal*, January 14, 1994.

31. *Brazil: A Mask Called Progress* (Oxford: Oxfam, 1991), 102.

32. Interview, February 15, 1996, Providence, RI.

33. Movimento Nacional dos Direitos Humanos, *Relatorio do VII Encontro Nacional* (Brasília: Servico de Editoracão Rumos, 1992), 11.

34. For a personal account see Ricardo Rizende, *Río María: Song of the Earth* (Maryknoll, NY: Orbis, 1994).

35. *Promised Land*, 112.

36. "Brazil: The Meek Want the Earth Now," *The Bulletin of Atomic Scientists* 52, no. 6 (November–December 1996): 21.

37. Margaret Keck, *The Workers' Party and Democratization in Brazil* (New Haven: Yale University Press, 1992), 47.

38. Interview, November 10, 1996, University of Notre Dame.

39. Alfredo Wagner Berno de Almeida, "Amazonia: Rite of Passage from Massacre to Genocide." Paper presented at symposium on The Rule and the Underprivileged in Latin America, University of Notre Dame, November 9, 1996.

40. See account in *Correio Brasilense*, May 28, 1996.

41. Interview with Pinheiro, November 10, 1996, University of Notre Dame. The extensive program was published as: Fernando Henrique Cardoso, *Programa Nacional de Direitos Humanos* (Brasília: Presidência da República, Secretaria de Comunicacão Social, 1996).

42. *The Workers' Party*, 49.

43. Interviews, Rio de Janeiro, May 20–24, 1994; São Paulo, May 18–24, 1996; and Brasília, 1996.

44. Anthony Dewees and Steven J. Klees, "Social Movements and Transformation of National Policy: Street and Working Children in Brazil," *Comparative Education Review* 39, no. 1 (February 1995): 87ff.

45. Paul Jeffrey, "Targeted for Death," *Christian Century*, January 20, 1993.

46. Diniz and Boschi, "A consolidacão democrática no Brasil: Atores políticos, processos sociais e intermediacãco de interesses," in Diniz, Boschi, and Renato Lessa, *Modernizacão e consolidacão democática no Brasil: Dilemas da Nova República* (São Paulo: Edições Vétice, 1989), 58–59.

47. Dewees and Klees, "Social Movements," 91.

48. A strong sense of this impetus was evident in the twin Workshop and Policy Forum on the Rule of Law and the Underprivileged in Latin America for high-level hemispheric leaders, Kellogg Institute, University of Notre Dame, November 9–11, 1998.

49. See Edward L. Cleary, *Mobilizing for Human Rights in Latin America* (Williamsburg, MA: Kumarian Press, 2007) for a survey of human rights organizations and their activism.

Chapter 9

1. Samuel Huntington, *The Third Wave: Democratization in the Late Twentieth Century* (Norman, OK: University of Oklahoma Press, 1991).

2. After militaries relinquished direct government rule in Latin America, several of them (Argentina, for example) threatened civil war if military abuses during their rule were investigated and punished.

3. Ecumenism in Central America generally was practiced by main-line Protestant churches but not by Pentecostals. See Edward Cleary, "Religion in the Central American Embroglio," in Thomas Walker and Ariel Armony, eds., *Repression, Resistance, and Democratic Transition in Central America* (Wilmington, DE: Scholarly Resources, 2000), 187–209.

4. The multi-volume report of the Comisión de Esclarecimiento Histórico (CEH) is entitled *Guatemala: Memory of Silence* and a summary of the main findings have been made available in English and on the web through the American Academy for the Advancement of Science's Science and Human Rights Center at http://shr.aaas.org/guatemala/ceh/report/english/toc.html.

5. The categories for scholarly analysis of what occurred in Guatemala have also included genocide and disaster. For the argument for the use of ethnocide instead of genocide see Anika Oettler, "Guatemala in the 1980s: A Genocide Turned into Ethnocide?" Working Paper 19 (2006) of the GIGA Institute for Ibero-American Studies, Hamburg, http://www.giga-hamburg.de (accessed May 22, 2008).

6. The historiography of the Cold War, especially in Guatemala, has made major advances with the opening of important archives, especially in the United States. Nonetheless, most historians to date have ignored religious groups or engaged in anticlerical diatribes. For a notable exception see the revealing and careful research of Edward T. Brett, *The U.S. Catholic Press on Central America: From Cold War Anticommunism to Social Justice* (Notre Dame, IN: University of Notre Dame Press, 2003). See endnote 9 for references.

7. Martin Kettle and Jeremy Lennard, "Clinton Apology to Guatemala," *The Guardian* (Manchester) March 12, 1999, http://www.guardian.co.uk/ (accessed May 10, 2008).

8. See Jennifer Schirmer, *The Guatemalan Military Project: A Violence Called Democracy* (Philadelphia: University of Pennsylvania Press, 1998), and Stephen Schlesinger and Stephen Kinzer, *Bitter Fruit: The Story*

of the American Coup in Guatemala. (Cambridge, MA: Harvard University, David Rockefeller Center for Latin American Studies, 1999).

9. Edward L. Cleary, "Examining Guatemalan Processes of Violence and Peace: A Review of Recent Research," *Latin American Research Review* 37, no. 1 (2002): 230–44.

10. The narrative here follows especially Susanne Jonas's *Of Centaurs and Doves: Guatemala's Peace Process* (Boulder: Westview, 2000) and Rachel Sieder's *Guatemala after the Peace Accords* (London: Institute of Latin American Studies, 1998).

11. For a fuller account of the causes of Guatemalan violence, see Cleary, "Examining Guatemalan Processes," *Latin American Research Review* 37, no. 1 (2002): 230–44.

12. For an early and vivid account, see Donna W. Brett and Edward T. Brett, *Murdered in Central America: The Stories of Eleven U.S. Missionaries* (Maryknoll, NY: Orbis, 1988).

13. See Bruce J. Calder, "The Role of the Catholic Church and Other Religious Institutions in the Guatemalan Peace Process." Paper presented at Latin American Studies International Congress, September 1998.

14. An English summary was published in the U.S.: Proyecto Interdiocesano Recuperación de la Memoria Histórica, *Guatemala: Never Again!* (Maryknoll, NY: Orbis, 1999).

15. See *Challenge* 9, no. 1 (Spring 1999), 4–5.

16. Delegates of the Word are laypeople designated to lead small Christian communities, especially in the absence of priests.

17. A third report of human rights abuses in Guatemala was carried out by a nongovernmental human rights group, el Centro Internacional para Investigaciones en Derechos Humanos, a group that collected thousands of testimonies through Mass-based, largely indigenous organizations.

18. In Gerardi's last interview before the presentation of his report, given to Radio Nederland, he stressed the obscurity in which Guatemalans were forced to live. Interview was posted at http://www.c.net.gt (accessed June 15, 1999).

19. Francisco Goldman, *The Art of Political Murder: Who Killed the Bishop?* (New York: Grove Press, 2007), 357.

20. The report in Portuguese was called *Brasil: Nunca Mais.* An English version appeared as Joan Dassin, *Torture in Brazil: A Report* (New York: Vintage Books, 1986).

21. Edward L. Cleary, *Mobilizing for Human Rights in Latin America* (Bloomfield, CT: Kumarian Press, 2007), 72.

22. For further details see Edward L. Cleary, *The Struggle for Human Rights in Latin America* (Westport, CT: Praeger, 1997), 43–60.

23. Mary Ann Glendon, "The Forgotten Crucible: The Latin American Influence on the Human Rights Idea," *Harvard Human Rights Journal* 16 (2003): 27–39; Paolo Carozzo, "From Conquest to Constitutions: Retrieving a Latin American Tradition of the Idea of Human Rights," *Human Rights Quarterly* 25, no. 2 (2003): 281–313.

24. Cleary, *Mobilizing*, 1–14.

25. Private communication, May 10, 2008.

26. Interview, April 9, 2008.

27. Among other histories of their lives see Penny Lernoux et al., *Hearts on Fire* (Maryknoll, NY: Orbis, 1995) and Martin Lange and Reinhold Iblacker, *The Persecution of Christians in Latin America* (Maryknoll, NY: Orbis, 1991).

28. See, for example, Anna Carrigan, *Salvador Witness: The Life and Calling of Jean Donovan* (New York: Ballantine Books, 1986), and *Roses in December*, a widely seen documentary film. For further films, plays, and a musical, see Jean Donovan entry in Wikipedia, http://en.wikipedia.org/.

29. Probably the best-known icon of Romero is by Nancy Oliphant. It can be viewed at http://www.bridgebuilding.com/narr/norom.html.

30. Ismael Moreno, "La subversiva memoria de todos los mártires," *Envío*, December 1999, http://www.envio.org.ni/ (accessed May 21, 2008).

31. Paul Jeffrey, "After 25 Years 'St. Romero of the World' Still Inspires," *National Catholic Reporter*, April 15, 2005, http://www.ncronline.org (accessed May 22, 2008).

32. Stanley Rother, *The Shepherd Cannot Run: Letters of Stanley Rother, Missionary, Martyr* (Oklahoma City: Archdiocese of Oklahoma City, 1984). Readers have found Henri Nouwen's account of Rother in Nouwen's *Love in a Fearful Land* (Maryknoll, NY: Orbis, 2006) especially moving.

33. Anne Burke, "No Greater Love" (1987) and Darrell Barton and Larry Audas, "Death of a Priest" (1982).

34. Stephen Blythe, "Santiago Atitlán—A Human Rights Victory," http://www.travelhealth.com (accessed May 21, 2008).

35. Robert Pelton et al., *Monsignor Romero* (Notre Dame, IN: University of Notre Dame Press, 2004).

36. For further details of the 2004 judgment see http://www.human rightsfirst.org.

37. Saravia was tried under the Alien Tort Claim Act. See details at http://www.humanrightsfirst.org.

38. Quoted in "U.S. Court Decision Sparks Call to Reopen Archbishop Oscar Romero Case in El Salvador," *Goliath Business News*, September 23, 2004, http://goliath.ecnext.com/ (accessed May 21, 2008).

39. Ibid.

40. See Pilar Hogan Closkey and John P. Hogan, eds., *Romero's Legacy: The Call to Peace and Justice* (Lanham, MD: Rowman and Littlefield, 2007).

41. Emelio Betances, "The Catholic Church and Political Mediation in the Dominican Republic: A Comparative Perspective," *Journal of Church and State* 46, no. 2 (Spring 2004): 341–63.

42. Jeffrey Klaiber, "The Catholic Church's Role as Mediator: Bolivia," *Journal of Church and State* 35, no. 2 (Spring 1993): 351–66; Betances, "The Catholic Church," 341–64.

43. The *Tablet* (London), September 28, 2002.

44. Jeffrey Klaiber, "The Catholic Church's Role," 351.

45. Ibid.

46. Guillermo O'Donnell, "Reflections on Contemporary South American Democracies," *Journal of Latin American Studies* 33 (2001): 600.

47. Argentina as a sovereign nation defaulted on its international loans.

48. Emelio Betances, "The Catholic Church and Political Mediation in the Dominican Republic," *Journal of Church and State* 46, no. 2 (Spring 2004): 341–64.

49. Kenneth Serbin, *Secret Dialogues: Church-State Relations, Torture, and Social Justice in Authoritarian Brazil* (Pittsburgh: University of Pittsburgh Press, 2000).

50. This status also accounts for the papal nuncio being considered as the dean of diplomatic corps accredited to Latin American states, unless the church uses the word *pro-nuncio* or chooses a lesser rank than that of ambassador for its representative.

51. At various times in the democratization process Latin Americans expressed lack of confidence in democracy as a system, as shown in various polls. The trend of disapproval diminished to small percentages of those holding negative views of democracy by 2007.

52. Ivan Vallier, *Catholicism, Social Control, and Modernization* (Englewood Cliffs, NJ: Prentice Hall, 1970), passim.

53. Edward Cleary and Allen Hertzke, eds., *Representing God at the Statehouse: Religion and Politics in the American States* (Lanham, MD: Rowman and Littlefield, 2006).

54. Penny Lernoux, *The People of God* (New York: Doubleday, 1980).

55. A married layperson, Lernoux was buried among the Maryknoll Sisters, in an unusual gesture, in their large cemetery near Ossining, NY.

56. They are widely known but consider the choice of their new religious affiliations largely private.

Chapter 10

1. Gerald Costello, *The Missionary Crusade: Successes and Failures* (Maryknoll, NY: Orbis, 1979).

2. *Documento de Puebla* (Bogotá: Conferencia Episcopal Latinoamericana, 1969), No. 368.

3. Bryan T. Froehle and Mary Gautier, *Global Catholicism* (Maryknoll, NY: Orbis, 2003).

4. Private communication July 16, 2007 from Mary Gautier, coeditor of *Global Catholicism* (Maryknoll, NY: Orbis, 2003).

5. Maryknoll missionaries were highly instrumental in the founding and organizational shape of the Guadalupe Missionaries. Bishop Alonso Escalante, Mexican Maryknoll missionary who had worked in China and Bolivia, was the superior at the beginning of the new mission society.

6. Interviews with church officials in Guatemala in the 1980s indicated, however, that they apparently failed due to lack of financial resources.

7. John Gorski, "How the Catholic Church in Latin America Became Missionary," *International Bulletin of Missionary Research* 27, no. 2 (April 2003): 60.

8. See for example, Consejo Episcopal Latinoamericano, *De una pastoral indigenista a una pastoral indígena* (Bogotá: Consejo Episcopal Latinoamericano, 1987).

9. For a theological account of this encounter see Nicanor Sarmiento, *Caminos de la teología india* (Cochabamba: Editorial Verbo Divino, 2000).

10. Josuel dos Santos Boaventura, "Comunidades afro e experiencia cristâo," *Teocomunicacâo* 37, no. 155 (March 2007): 61–87.

11. Short-term missionaries have been widely utilized and studied by evangelical denominations, although few reliable statistics about missions exist. But according to Dwight Baker, a reliable informant from the Overseas Missions Study Center whose knowledge is based on years of discussing the topic with mission leaders, the positive effects on the mission-receiving persons have been found to be problematic and frequently negligible. (Communication from Dwight Baker, July 31, 2007).

12. (Córdoba, Argentina: Editorial Universidad Católica, 2003).

13. This Catholic theological emphasis has influenced Latin American Protestant missiologists. See Andy Crouch, "Liberate My People," *Christianity Today* 51, no. 8 (August 2007): 30–33.

14. Chicago Office on Evangelization website, http://www.going forth.org/ (accessed October 16, 2006).

Index